WHEN HAVE YOU SEEN REVIEWS SUCH AS THESE?

· ·

"Harry Golden writes what he wants to about anything he wants to. He writes about historical events, ancient and modern, with freshness of viewpoint and a vigorous enthusiasm. He loves people and books and America. He tells us things we don't know, he gives a new look to things we do know, and he makes us think about things that we know but have avoided thinking about. It's nice to live in the same country with him."

—MAURICE DOLBIER, *New York Herald Tribune*

"What a writer! Whatever your faith may be, he is writing to you as a human being."

—EMERSON PRICE, *Cleveland Press*

"ONLY IN AMERICA will go a long way toward restoring one's faith in the human race."

—WILLIAM DU BOIS, *The New York Times*

[*Continued on the last page*]

ONLY IN AMERICA was originally published at $4.00 by The World Publishing Company.

HARRY GOLDEN

ONLY
IN
AMERICA

Foreword by
CARL SANDBURG

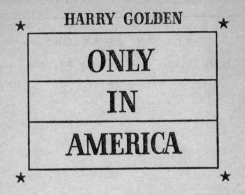

PERMABOOKS • NEW YORK

This Permabook includes every word contained in the original, higher-priced edition. It is printed from brand-new plates made from completely reset, clear, easy-to-read type.

ONLY IN AMERICA

World Publishing edition published July, 1958

Permabook edition published August, 1959
6th printing........................August, 1959

L

Permabook editions are distributed in the U.S. by Affiliated Publishers, Inc., 630 Fifth Avenue, New York 20, N.Y.

 Permabook editions are published in the United States by Pocket Books, Inc. and in Canada by Pocket Books of Canada, Ltd.—the world's largest publishers of low-priced adult books.

To Tiny, Dick, Harry Jr., Bill,
and in memory of Peter

Acknowledgment

I am indebted to Harry Golden, Jr., of the *Detroit Free Press* for the selection of the essays from my writings and for editing the manuscript

Contents

FOREWORD BY *Carl Sandburg*   XV

INTRODUCTION   xvii

1. DEATH AND THE CALL GIRL

Why I never bawl out a waitress   1

A lesson in bread   2

The show must go on!   3

Getting paid for her "favors"   4

Causerie on death   6

How to get a husband   15

I am now kosher   18

Fathers and sons   19

A true short, short story   22

Southern gentlemen   24

Why other planets have not contacted us   25

Wink at some homely girl   26

Sex morals on the Lower East Side   26

It was better when papa was the boss   27

America on a huge breast binge   28

We are not alone   29

Many widows live in college towns 29

The landlord 30

The shame of nakedness 30

Parents work night and day 31

Why do they climb the mountains? 32

First day of school 33

2. WE TOAST THE JOURNEY—FOR TWO CENTS PLAIN

The poets were paid 34

Buying a suit on the East Side 35

For two cents plain 41

My Uncle Koppel and free enterprise 47

Marriages were made in heaven 50

Two-for-a-nickel movies 56

The passion of Morris Kaplan 57

The Fifth Avenue Bus—and America 59

The greenhorns slept on the "lunch" 62

The "suckers" escaped 65

Little girls on the East Side 67

The Triangle fire 68

The scaleman 74

Ess, ess, mein kindt 75

My mother and God 78

You paid fifty cents and kissed the bride 80

The rent 82

2,500 handsome Jewish policemen 83

Customers for the dry-goods store 83

This little sex offender went to market   85

You couldn't beat this fellow   86

Four cents an hour   87

Four dollars a week   87

Raising pigeons   88

Everybody got paid but the doctor   88

3. DOES IT SELL FLOUR?

Why women live longer than men   90

Are things too good?   91

The Methodist "Guardian of Israel"   93

I miss the holy men of the 1930's   95

Wishing you long years   96

Lil ole Tin-Pan Alley   97

Boiled beef flanken comes to Charlotte   98

Does it sell flour?   100

The "Organization Men"   102

You never saw a Yenkee?   104

4. THE VERTICAL NEGRO

The Vertical Negro Plan   105

Carry-the-Books Plan   108

Timothy Mulcahy, Hitler, and Skelley's   109

The fettering of the human spirit   110

A short story of America   112

Who has all the money?   114

Everybody is running away from everybody else   116

Racial segregation by law   117

I felt very close to this man · 118

Public right and private preference · 119

A plan for white citizens · 125

Negro and Jew in Dixie · 126

Negro question is a matter of social status · 135

The fellow who flew to Ireland by mistake · 136

My positive cure for anti-Semitism · 137

The burning of the cross · 137

The Downtown Luncheon Club is more exclusive than heaven · 138

Isaac—Ikey—Ike · 139

The Italian Americans · 139

No one gives you a jar of anything · 140

How to get a note renewed at the bank · 140

Massa's in de cold, cold ground · 141

The boys were tired, too! · 142

Jew music all the time · 142

The history of the Jews in America · 143

The turban is a very big thing · 143

Jewish food · 144

Secondhand pants, sixty cents · 144

The needle industry coming South? · 145

This could happen only in America · 146

Movies for adults only · 146

Countess Mara and I · 147

We'll soon run out of non-Jews · 148

Closed shop versus open shop · 148

What can you tell Texas Guinan?   149

Explaining the Southerner   149

From the Shpitzinitzer to the Rotary   150

I refuse to look it up   151

5. **GALLI-CURCI AND BUBBLE GUM**

Let's take bubble gum out of the schools   152

Teaching Shylock   157

Shylock and William Shakespeare   158

Galli-Curci lingers   165

Need we defend books?   167

You licked the honey   168

Chopped chicken liver and schmaltz   171

No more newspaper extras   174

Caesar the humanist   177

Alexander Hamilton and Mrs. Reynolds   179

The journalism of Joseph Pulitzer   183

Exit the intellectual, enter the leader   187

Belshazzar's Feast—with real cannon   188

Raisins and almonds   189

Is Greta Garbo an artist?   190

Forget victuals   191

Monday at the "Met"   191

The "workshop" is a bore   192

Greatest single moment in music   192

Shakespeare wrote the works of Bacon   193

They never met a payroll   194

6. TAMMANY, TAMMANY

How Tammany Hall did it   195

The death of Senator McCarthy   199

The politician-women   201

Causerie on the death of Mrs. Leo Frank   203

How Pompey lost an empire   208

When adultery was proof of "loyalty"   210

My sermon on informers   211

Should housewives be in politics?   212

The impeachment of Governor Sulzer   213

Bloc voting   218

The Democratic Party and the South   219

When it's raining, have no regrets   221

Crime investigations   222

The lawyers got a break   223

Negroes on the ballot   224

We hate our own   224

Shakespeare knew all about politicians   225

7. MERRY CHRISTMAS, BILLY GRAHAM

Mayor William J. Gaynor   226

A day with Carl Sandburg   232

William Travers Jerome   238

Judge Otto A. Rosalsky   241

Merry Christmas, Billy Graham   245

James Street   247

Walter Hampden   251

Sweet are the uses of adversity 252

A wonderful newspaper interview 253

Albert Schweitzer 253

Where Irving Berlin wrote his first song 254

8. THE FROZEN RABBI

We would be nothing without each other 256

This you call "bringing Christians"? 258

The best sermon—give 'em hell 261

Bigger and better invocations 262

Don't tell them about shrimp 264

The Frozen Rabbi 264

Brotherhood Week 265

The Ten Lost Tribes? They are the Presbyterians 268

Chocolate matzos 270

Rabbi, make it short 270

Unitarians wait for their first Negro 271

Eddie Fisher and Debbie Reynolds 272

Give us a blond rabbi any time 273

Concerning those who go to services once a year 274

9. COMPLAINTS AND FREE ADVICE, OR TWENTY-SIX NOTES IN CLOSING

The saloon and the cocktail lounge 275

How to hire a stenographer 276

Protest for eleven books 277

No more crying at Jewish weddings 281

Our new breed of knuckleheads 283

How to buy cigars 285

The wise guy is the sucker after all 286

Montor and Keyserling on the Stock Exchange 288

It's the spirit that counts 291

Princess Ileana and Archduke Otto were here 293

What makes Mr. and Mrs. Jones run? 294

How to be healthy 297

Cato's cure for a hangover 299

I'll take care of the tip 299

Where is The Carolina Israelite? 300

And what to drink? 301

Are the no-dessert fellows sincere? 302

How to boost temple membership 302

Is it later than you think? 303

A man called—left no message 304

How do you feel? 305

Percentage-wise 305

How to go on the wagon 306

We have lost something 306

Shed a tear for the smoking car 307

America owes it to Christianity 308

FOREWORD

THE LIFE of Harry Golden divides many ways. Born and raised on the East Side of New York City and living for a time there, he moved to Charlotte, N. C. As the editor of *The Carolina Israelite* he has been called to many cities from coast to coast for talks and lectures. He knows the American scene and the American people as very few men do. He has written the most interesting pro-Semitic book that I have ever read—barring possibly the Old Testament. There are pages to give you rollicking laughter, others a pleasant smile, still others that might have you somber over our American scene and its human conditions.

As a Jew who understands ghetto history Harry Golden sees the plight of the Negro north and south. He loves the Irish to the extent that has him marching in processions where the high cry was "Erin Go Bragh." I have never met so sweet a salutation to Scotsmen as we may read herein, "The Ten Lost Tribes? They are the Presbyterians."

Whatever is human interests Harry Golden. Honest men, crooks, knuckleheads, particularly anybody out of the ordinary if even a half-wit, any of them is in his line. He writes about them. He drops the sheets of writing in a barrel. Comes the time of the month to get out his paper, *The Carolina Israelite*, he digs into the barrel and finds copy. As you go along in this book or in copies of his paper you may be saying, "That fellow doesn't miss anything—he has ears to hear and a pencil to write it down." His own statement in round numbers as to his audience: "This could happen only in America. *The Carolina Israelite* reaches some 14,000 of the most influential citizens of our country. These include approximately: 1000 editors, 1500 Christian clergymen and political leaders; 3000 Christian laymen; 500 rabbis and over 4000 Jewish communal leaders, in addition to many of the most famous people of our time."

Golden is against the check-off system of payment for union dues. He favors the oldtime saloon as against the modern cocktail lounge and he has no respect for the Quiz Champion who "represents Madison Avenue's greatest achievement in the philosophy of the 'tie-in'; the association of scholarship with the sale of laxative, lipstick, and lanolin."

From many quarters the outcry has come that there is too much of conformity and complacence particularly among the young. Among the best healthy and wholesome nonconformists is this writer, independent thinker, Friend of Man, Harry Golden. Someone like this Jew was in the mind of the Yankee, Ralph Waldo Emerson, who wrote: "Whoso would be a man must be a nonconformist."

CARL SANDBURG

INTRODUCTION

I LIVE in a high-porched house built before the Great Wars on Elizabeth Avenue in Charlotte, North Carolina. Here, I write and publish *The Carolina Israelite*.

I should explain that *The Carolina Israelite*, five columns, sixteen pages, is published monthly, is printed entirely in English, and that more than half its subscribers are non-Jews. I print no "news," personals, socials, or press releases. And my last "obituary" was on the assassination of Julius Caesar in 44 B.C.

With the exception of a few "letters to the editor," I write the entire paper myself, 15,000 to 25,000 words a month. I arrange my reading matter in the form of editorials, set in 8-point Century, 24½ picas, with 10-point bold-face heads in caps. I put a short rule between the items, which range in length from twenty words ("How Dr. Samuel Johnson Prepared Oysters") to a 3,000-word article ("Sweet Daddy Grace, the Southern Father Divine").

I draw heavily on history, literature, philosophy. I do not run the editorials in chronological or departmental sequence. I merely try to arrange the columns so that a long article is usually followed by two or three short pieces.

Each month I set the ads first, about one hundred "card" advertisements, with no displays and with as little copy as possible. Then I cram my editorials into every other inch of available space. I sort of slither them in and around the ads on each of the sixteen pages, and with only one beginning and one end. Many of my subscribers have tried to pick individual items of special interest to them; all in vain. The only chance they have is to begin at the top left-hand column on page one, and keep going to the end.

Some of my readers make "an evening" with *The Carolina Israelite*. When the paper arrives other events are put aside, and the high school son or daughter reads my paper from cover to cover to the assembled family. I tell them stories of the Lower East Side of New York where I was born. "It's like a personal letter to me," they write, or "It reminds me of my father when he came home from the shop and read the paper to us."

I have found that people are hungry for this "personal touch." They like to read of the great news stories of the past. I tell them about Dorothy Arnold's disappearance; the sinking of the *Titanic;* how "Hell's Kitchen" got its name; about the old gang wars; about the time someone threw missiles on the funeral procession of a famous rabbi; about the Tong Wars of Chinatown; and about the Thalia Theatre where magician Thurston made a woman disappear from a cage suspended over the audience. I tell them about the first half-dollar I ever saw, given to me by "Big Tim" Sullivan, the Tammany Hall Sachem, and many other such tales, stories, anecdotes, and reminiscences.

For the first few years of its existence, my paper was just another one in that vast stack of periodicals which comes to the "exchange" desk of every daily newspaper. These fall into categories: the "labor" press, the "Negro" press, the "Anglo-Jewish" press, the official organs of lodges and fraternal orders, house organs of government departments and big corporations, organizational media, church periodicals, and magazines that have "home," "mother," "religion," "ladies," or "women" in the title.

I made up my mind to do something about it. I decided to turn my paper into a "personal journal," and put to use the results of almost forty-five years of uninterrupted reading. I also suspected that many Southerners were hungry for a word "above the battle."

There were difficulties. Because they are so far from the main concentrations of the Jewish population, the small Jewish communities of the South live in deadly fear that one Jew may say or do something that "will involve the whole Jewish community." The Jews have a point, of course, since so many Gentiles believe that each of us is "spokesman" for the entire community. But I also knew that since this "mass responsibility" idea involves also the credit jeweler, the pawnbroker, and the textile manufacturer, the Jewish communities of the South would survive a personal journalist, too.

In one issue I asked the question, "Am I a Tar Heel?," and immediately some of the mighty daily papers in the State wrote editorials extending this honor to me. Indeed, they said, Harry Golden is a Tar Heel; to which I replied in their Open Forums that I never carried a designation with greater pride.

All of this is a lesson in sociology. I have found that the Southerner (and any other man, for that matter) arches his back at the fellow who throws a brick over the wall and runs away. But when that same fellow becomes *part of the community*, the attitude toward him changes. He may not particularly endear himself, but he does acquire status, and he is not only respected, but actually welcomed as part of the ebb and flow of daily life.

I believe too that *"Let us not stick our necks out"* or *"Let someone else talk on that subject"* are watchwords of the ghetto, and I do not believe in ghettos: white, black, or Puerto Rican.

Trying to reach the general public with a "Jewish" paper presented another serious problem, but it has proved far less "confining" than it might appear. Since we Jews have been contemporaneous with all of recorded history, we can write with the widest latitude on every event in history and on every work of literature. I took my cue from an old ghetto fable. A lion escaped from its cage in a traveling circus. Thousands of men, women, and children were running through the streets. An old gentleman stopped one of the frantic ones and asked the reason for all the excitement. When told that a wild lion was loose, the old man asked quietly, "Is that good for the Jews, or bad for the Jews?" Enough justification for me to write my pieces about the Eastland disaster, the Dorothy Siegal murder, the trial of Harry Kendall Thaw, and the meeting of the two kings on the "Field of the Cloth of Gold."

The letters I receive each month from Jews and Christians have repaid me for my efforts and my faith in the idea and, as I continue to write of the passing parade, I am as happy as a mouse in a cookie jar.

HARRY GOLDEN

Charlotte, N. C.
March 1958

Only in America

~~~~~~~~~~~~~~~~~~~~

PART 1

Death and the
Call Girl

~~~~~~

Why I never bawl out a waitress

I HAVE a rule against registering complaints in a restaurant; because I know that there are at least four billion suns in the Milky Way—which is only one galaxy. Many of these suns are thousands of times larger than our own, and vast millions of them have whole planetary systems, including literally billions of satellites, and all of this revolves at the rate of about a million miles an hour, like a huge oval pinwheel. Our own sun and its planets, which includes the earth, are on the edge of this wheel. This is only our own small corner of the universe, so why do not these billions of revolving and rotating suns and planets collide? The answer is, the space is so unbelievably vast that if we reduced the suns and the planets in correct mathematical proportion with relation to the distances between them, each sun would be a speck of dust, two, three, and four thousand miles away from its nearest neighbor. And, mind you, this is only the Milky Way—our own small corner—our own galaxy. How many galaxies are there? Billions. Billions of galaxies spaced at about one million light-years apart (one light-year is about six trillion miles). Within the range of our biggest telescopes there are at least one hundred million separate galaxies such as our own Milky Way, and that is not all, by any means. The scientists have

found that the further you go out into space with the telescopes the thicker the galaxies become, and there are billions
of billions as yet uncovered to the scientist's camera and the
astrophysicist's calculations.

When you think of all this, it's silly to worry whether the
waitress brought you string beans instead of limas.

A lesson in bread

ON THE Lower East Side of New York there were many
traditions which we associated with the Jewish civilization until some of us began to read the literature of the world. I found
that so many things were not "Jewish" at all, but they were
part of the tradition of all mankind.

For instance, when we dropped a piece of bread on the
floor, our mothers taught us that we must pick it up, that
bread was the sacred symbol of life. We may have finished
eating but it was necessary to eat that particular slice of bread
which had fallen to the floor. In the Jewish tradition we begin
our meal with a blessing over the bread. The father slices off
a piece as he gives thanks. Carl Sandburg in the book of his
early years, *Always the Young Strangers,* writes that his
mother "held bread to be sacred. If one of us dropped bread
or meat we were taught to pick it up, clean it as best we
could, and eat it." Thus the Swedes, far to the north, had the
same tradition as the Jews far to the east. Sandburg does not
say that you first had to kiss the bread that had fallen to the
ground, as we had to do, but essentially the tradition was
the same. And indeed James Joyce refers to the same idea
among the Catholic Irish, and I am sure we would find the
principle in all the cultures of the world.

The show must go on!

I LOVE the theatre and everybody connected with it, from actor to stagehand. I believe however that this business of "the show must go on" has been overdone a bit as it concerns the acting profession. Not that I doubt the truth behind this tradition. I know very well that performers have faced their audiences with deep sorrow in their hearts; with news of some terrible personal disaster, and as in *Pagliacci*, the clown bravely goes on with the show: "Laugh with the sorrow that's breaking your heart." I rise up to applaud. But I do not applaud actors alone. I applaud people. All people. Life itself. Everybody goes out on the "stage" with sorrow in his heart. For everybody, the show must go on. How many workingmen have come home from the cemetery where they had just buried a child and sat right down at their workbenches, machines, and lathes? How many housewives pitch in to get the children ready for school, do the marketing and household chores, with breaking backs, migraine headaches, and perhaps a personal sorrow, too? THE SHOW MUST GO ON. Not only for actors, but for all of us. We dare not stop "the show" for a single moment.

A few days after my mother died I was behind the counter of my brother's hotel and a guest bawled me out because his laundry hadn't come back on time. For a fleeting moment I had foolishly expected the world to stand still and pay homage to my mother. I checked my mounting anger in the nick of time. "Of course," I said, "this man is blameless. He's interested in his laundry—he's interested in now, in living, in life."

I am indebted to Dr. Frank Kingdon for my interest in the poetry of Sir Rabindranath Tagore. The great Hindu poet tells us a story in exquisite poetry. His servant did not come in on time. Like so many philosophers and poets, Tagore was helpless when it came to the less important things in life, his personal wants, his clothes, his breakfast, and tidying up the place. An hour went by and Tagore was getting madder by the minute. He thought of all sorts of punishments for the man. Three hours later Tagore no longer thought of punishment. He'd discharge the man without any further ado, get rid of him, turn him out. Finally the man showed up. It was midday. Without a word the servant proceeded with his duties as though nothing had happened. He picked up his master's clothes, set to making breakfast, and started cleaning up. Tagore watched this performance with mounting rage. Finally he said it: "Drop everything, and get out."

The man, however, continued sweeping and after another few moments, with quiet dignity he said: "My little girl died last night."

The show must go on.

Getting paid for her "favors"

THE recent newspaper stories about call girls emphasized the cost of such "favors." Readers were astonished that men paid between $100 and $500 for an evening's "entertainment."

Now let us go to the year 41 B.C. and look in on Cleopatra, Queen of Egypt. This was a few years after the assassination of Julius Caesar. A civil war followed between Caesar's killers (Brutus and Cassius) and Caesar's avengers (Octavius and Anthony). The few independent kingdoms left in the world were in a bad fix. They were always in a bad fix when civil war broke out in Rome. They weren't interested in either side. In fact, they would have loved to see both sides destroy each other, but they could not remain neutral. They had to pick one side and hope to high heaven that they had guessed right. Now in this civil war after Caesar's assassination, they all guessed wrong. This was understandable. Octavius (who later became Emperor Augustus) was a young boy, hardly more than seventeen years old, and Anthony, the handsomest man in Rome, spent most of his time with dancing girls and having one big time for himself. Therefore, everybody picked Brutus and Cassius, two experienced generals and particularly sober men, temperate in all things except in the study of politics and philosophy. How could they miss? But they did miss! Young Octavius and Mark (wine-women-and-song) Anthony beat their brains out. Now for the payoff. Octavius and Anthony divided the world with a third party who did not count for much.

Anthony took the East, and the first thing he did was start on a collection tour. Collecting fines and taxes from these independent states and kingdoms that had picked the losers. He was doing fine, real fine. Anthony showed an amazing understanding of world politics. He assessed the people over a long term—so much a year, instead of crippling their economy and productivity with a huge lump-sum fine. His next stop was CLEOPATRA. Cleopatra, too, had sent some monies to help Brutus and Cassius, figuring that she was on the winning side, and Anthony pulled up at the city of Tarsus, and sent word to the Queen of Egypt to present herself to him so that he might pass judgment.

Cleopatra came, but in her own time. While Anthony sat on the throne in the Forum of Tarsus waiting for Cleopatra to plead her case and be judged, she was sailing up the River Cydnus, "in a barge with purple sails, gilded stern, and silver oars to beat time to the music of flutes and fifes and harps. Her maids, dressed as sea nymphs, were the crew, while she herself, dressed as Venus, lay under a canopy of cloth of gold." (Will Durant, *Caesar and Christ*.)

When news of this barge reached the people of Tarsus, they all came out in their Sunday best, lined both banks of the river to watch the wondrous sight. Pretty soon Anthony was sitting in the Forum all alone. His own regiment of Roman legionnaires were at the riverbank. There was nothing left for Anthony to do but to follow the crowd, and, as the barge was fastened to the pier, the crowds made way for

Mark Anthony. He began by reproving her for being late, and ordered her to come to the Forum. Cleopatra, in sweet tones, suggested that they could get their business done in more pleasant surroundings on her barge. Anthony's arm being twisted, he went aboard and stayed the night. The next morning, he gave Cleopatra Phoenicia, Syria, the Island of Cyprus, half of Arabia, Cilicia, and all of Judea.

Now that's what I call "a call girl."

Causerie on death

WHEN we hear the sad news that a friend or a relative died suddenly, walking along the street or in his sleep, we usually say, "That's a good way to die," or we say, "When my time comes, that's the way I'd like to go." This, of course, is completely the bunk. There is no such as "a good way to die," and we utter those foolish sentiments because we cannot think of death except in terms of "*him*"—not "me." Life hangs on desperately—in the shadow of the gas chambers at Dachau, in the Black Hole of Calcutta, and in the wheel chair or hospital bed. After all, what is pain, or even the most terrible physical suffering, compared with that one *absolute*—the only thing that is *absolutely irrevocable* —death?

As long as you can see, or feel, or hear, or have consciousness of the fact that there are friends and loved ones somewhere around you, you hang on, and how you hang on!

Even if we were to look upon the "ways" to die objectively, I do not for a single moment believe it is "better" to die in your sleep. That's nonsense. A man goes to bed with plans, hopes, and appointments for the morrow, and then the morrow never comes. I think that's a much greater tragedy than when there has been some "exhaustion" to life. But basically there is no "good way."

I am reminded of that passage by Dostoevski in one of the ten greatest books of the world, *Crime and Punishment:* The student Raskolnikov wanders about the streets of St. Petersburg in a delirious state. He had murdered two old women with an ax. He feels cut off from mankind. As he passes through the red-light district he muses: "If one had to live on some high rock on such a narrow ledge that he had only room enough to stand, and the ocean and the everlasting darkness, everlasting tempest around him, if he had to remain standing on a square yard of space all his life, a thousand years, eternity, it were better to live so than to die at once. Only to live, to live and live. Life, whatever it may be." Amen.

Monday is the best day of the week to die. The folks have a clear field ahead of them, and can give their activities and the "arrangements" the respect of unhurried dignity. Tuesday is not too bad, but Wednesday and Thursday come close to the danger point, and Friday is completely out of the question. The first thing the folks will think of, when death enters their lives on a Friday, is that their week-end has been completely smashed up.

Instead of being able to sleep late, and take it easy on Sunday, they will be confronted with all these terribly sad disturbances. Monday is really the best. The folks can take their time; they can give it everything they've got, and still be able to look forward to a more or less placid week-end. Then, too, your chances for "immortality" are much better if you cash in on a Monday, because it gives you a clear, unbroken stretch of five full days ahead, so that, as late as the following Friday, someone may still say, "You know, I only saw the guy last week, and he looked fine."

It is best that the "vocal" man should die at the moment that physical disability interferes with his ability to remain "vocal." I am sure that many writers have turned that over in their minds, with perhaps a silent prayer that they do not survive their "silence."

There have really been very few "last words" of any great

consequence. The medical men agree that, in most cases of the
dying, particularly after a serious illness, contact with reality
is lost long before the person has any idea of impending death.
And in the case of a sudden accident or seizure, the shock
paralyzes the senses of perception.

It is sad that the night nurse attending Professor Einstein
could not understand German. It would have been interesting
to know what that great man said, although his last few words
in German may have been completely disassociated from
his life as physicist and philosopher. You remember in Orson
Welles' great movie, *Citizen Kane*, the publisher, who had
won vast wealth and had conquered life at every level of
our society, repeated the word "Rosebud" before he closed
his eyes.

This sent reporters and editors scurrying about to discover the significance of "Rosebud." Did it have to do with
some great business enterprise, or maybe the pet name of
another secret mistress? Orson shows the audience (but
not the reporters in the script) that "Rosebud" was the
trade name on the sled Citizen Kane had used as a poor little
boy on the farm. Heinrich Heine, as he lay dying, repeated
the word "write," and when the nurse could not understand
him, he said, "Paper, pencil." My own mother could no
longer speak after the cancer had shot up into the brain,
but before she died she tugged at my shirt sleeves under the
jacket. When I realized what she was after, I pulled them
out for her. She wanted to see if the cuffs were clean.
Napoleon Bonaparte died in broad daylight and four witnesses
agreed that he repeated twice, "*tête d'armée.*" The chief of the
army, which he had been indeed, and for the same reason
that Heine said, "Write, paper, pencil." We dream what we
are, what we have been, and what we hope to be; and so
far, the most that science has been able to find out is that
death is the process of falling asleep. Cardinal Spellman's
dreams or last thoughts would hardly be concerned with the
conduct of Yom Kippur services in the synagogue. H. G.
Wells, the atheist and bitter critic of the Catholic Church,
kept muttering to himself unintelligibly. When a secretary

put his ear to his lips to catch the words, Wells said, "Can't you see I am busy dying?"

Most men fear the pain, the illness, and the possible disability more than they fear death itself. And nature has insulated us against concentrating too hard on its inevitability.

In a way it is like playing the horses. You know positively, beyond any shadow of doubt, that *everybody* loses, but you figure it *won't* happen to you. You'll beat it. You can see what a wonderful situation this is when considered in the light of all human endeavor, and the risks which have given us so much to live for and so much more to hope for in the future. No man has ever yet looked into the mirror and said, "I have the sentence of death hanging over me."

John Adams, the second President of the United States and the most underrated of our Founding Fathers, died on July 4, 1826—on the fiftieth anniversary of the Declaration of Independence over which he had had some controversy with Thomas Jefferson. The last words of Adams were, "Jefferson still lives." He probably meant it as a question, and a most natural one. They had long since corresponded with mutual affection. And the remarkable thing about it is that down in Virginia, Jefferson was dying on the same day.

The death of Voltaire affected France in much the same way that Roosevelt's death was mourned in America. All work ceased. A priest came to hear his last confession. Voltaire said, "From whom do you come, M. l'Abbé?" "From God Himself," was the answer. "Well, sir," said Voltaire, "your credentials?" But Voltaire did leave a written message: "I die adoring God, loving my friends, not hating enemies, and detesting superstition."

My father was a philosopher, and when he was eighty years old he told us that he would like to go to Palestine for his remaining years. This surprised us because my father had never been an active Zionist, but he explained it this way: "I want to avoid the emotional scenes of the death-bed; sons, daughters, daughters-in-law, grandchildren. It is terribly disturbing; especially in our culture. But when you folks receive a cablegram that your father has passed away, four or five thousand miles away, you'll feel sad, of course, but it will come a day or two after it is all over, and you'll all go about your business."

Thus the degree of our grief (like our love) is conditioned by habit, acceptance, "What will everybody say?" and propinquity, most of all. I'll tell you about a friend I had in New Jersey. You know how emotional we Jews can become about our sons—but this fellow went overboard —would have gladly died if it meant only some added comfort for his children. Yet he wasn't even curious about a son he had had out of wedlock. He knew it was his, he acknowledged it, and he was generous toward its support, but do you think he was interested even to watch the boy come out of school some afternoon?

And this is far from unusual. No virtue has been extolled higher in our civilization than "mother love." But if the child has not "arrived" within the pattern of accepted habit and propriety, she, the mother, has been known to leave it under the bed in a room of a motel, hasn't she?

Our religions have really conditioned us to what we call good taste and propriety. I think of that wonderful Jewish legend of the girl who had been sentenced by the Inquisition to be dragged through the streets to the funeral pyre. She was asked if she had a last request, and she pleaded for a few pins, and when they gave them to her, she pinned her skirts carefully between her legs so that her body would not be uncovered as she was being dragged through the streets to her death. As my dear friend, playwright Noel Houston says, "Ah, Harry, if we Christians only had less of the Hebrew and a little more of the Greek." But it is because Christendom has so much of the Hebrew in it that the average Christian lady worries constantly about her underclothing; so that if she were to die suddenly, she would not be "embarrassed."

And regardless of what anyone says, *death* is still a mystery. Hamlet says: "There are more things in heaven and earth, Horatio, than are dreamt of in your philosophy."

Shakespeare meant, of course, philosophy in general and not just Horatio's.

> To be or not to be: that is the question . . .
> But that the dread of something after death,
> The undiscover'd country from whose bourn
> No traveler returns, puzzles the will . . .

An experienced nurse who has been in the hospital room with many a dying man told me that as long as he is still aware, and regardless of his age, he is making a "pass" in some form or another, right down to the last moment of consciousness. It is funny what the stuff will do, but that is because it represents more than anything else in life —the secret of life—affirmation—the sense of living. I remember riding around the block five or six times after two o'clock in the morning just to be looking at the apartment house in which SHE lived. I am merely revealing something that millions of men have done and shall continue to do, in some form or another, forever. Thornton Wilder, in his magnificent novel, *The Ides of March*, quotes that great man of antiquity, Julius Caesar: "Let us welcome old age that frees us from that desire for their embraces—embraces which must be paid for at the cost of all order in our lives and any tranquility in our minds." Caesar was assassinated long before he reached "old age," but would it really have made any difference? Of course not. The day that Caesar hoped for never comes for any man.

W. E. H. Lecky quotes from the writings of St. Gregory the Great. When celibacy was introduced into the priesthood it was not retroactive—those who had wives were permitted to remain married. St. Gregory the Great describes the virtue of a priest who, through motives of piety, had discarded his wife. As he lay dying, she hastened to him to watch the bed which, for forty years previously, she had been allowed to share, and bending over what seemed the inanimate form of her husband, she tried to ascertain whether any breath remained when the dying saint, collecting his last energies, exclaimed, "Woman, be gone, there is fire yet!"

Sophocles, the Greek tragic poet, cried out for joy on his eightieth birthday: *"Thank God it's over."*

But perhaps Sophocles might not have written an *Antigone*, if "it" had indeed ended for him before he was eighty, and perhaps Caesar might not have left his mark on the Western world if his soldiers had not been able to use their old marching song: "Men of Rome, lock up your wives, our General has arrived."

It certainly did not affect the work of Emperor Justinian of Rome whose wife was Theodora, and quite a girl. The story of Theodora's sex life is not well known to us because it is all in Latin, written down by her biographer, Procopius, and unprintable in the English language, even in this age of Elvis Presley.

But the amazing Theodora did not seem to affect the work of Justinian, who gave the Western world its legal code.

Let us go from the sublime Justinian to the far-from-sublime Aaron Burr—American. Aaron actually accomplished that which most men dream about at least once a week throughout their lives, to be convicted of adultery at the age of eighty. Where Aaron Burr had time to fight duels with Hamilton and organize expeditions against President Jefferson is hard to explain. He devoted more than eighty years to what the French call "the love." And our founding-father Gouverneur Morris does not stand in the shade.

Gouverneur lost a leg jumping out of the window when one of our founding-husbands came home unexpectedly, and over in France he refused to put up the bail for Lafayette, who had helped create our nation, because he, Gouverneur, was in love with Lafayette's wife. I am sure it hurt our ambassador to see Lafayette in the Bastille, but he was tired of jumping out of windows. And when Le Marquis finally was released, Gouverneur ran off to London with the mistress of the Prime Minister, Talleyrand.

And all Gouverneur Morris accomplished (along with James

Madison) was to give us—*The Constitution of the United States*.

Throughout all of history man has been concerned with life after death. What has always amazed me is that such men as Flammarion, Lombroso, Arthur Conan Doyle, and Oliver Lodge were believers in such nonsense as spiritualism —or "talking" with the dead. During the 1920's I was on a committee of five or six boys from Columbia University and we looked into this matter. This was during the popularity of the Ouija board and the spiritist medium. I admit that I did not enter into this work with an open mind. My logic revolted against the idea and all I was interested in was to learn how it was done, if possible. We visited at least fifteen "seances" conducted by some of the most famous "mediums" of the day—Mrs. Cook, Mrs. Williams, "Margery," Mr. Montsko, and a fellow by the name of Carthuser.

What was particularly interesting was the calibre of the personalities who were interested in this stuff. I met tycoons, industrialists, Houdini, and Margaret Wilson, daughter of the former President of the United States, among many others of importance. Thinking back on my experiences I recall having "talked" with William James, Le Marquis de Lafayette, Kossuth, the famous Hungarian patriot, and a young Indian girl who had died three or four hundred years before. Why Lafayette should have talked to me and why some old relative from Galicia hadn't made contact puzzled me, naturally, but I suspected the reason for it was that none of these mediums or any of their confederates could speak Yiddish.

As you get older you are more and more concerned with death; the death of others, of course.

"What did he die of?"; "How long was he sick?"; and "How old was he?" This is the most important of all. When a fellow dies who was fifty-five, and you are fifty-six—that's bad. You feel that perhaps they are beginning to call up your class, and the only thing you can do is toy with the idea that maybe the guy was really more than the age given in the obituary.

Before he died, Benjamin Franklin said to his wife, "Debbie, I have only one wish: I'd lik to come back to earth a hundred years from now to see what progress has been made."

This, of course, may be said by every human being of every age, and at every hour. The "next hundred years" will always be momentous, no matter when it is your time to go.

I sit at the dinner table of a friend and he is surrounded by his wife and three small children. He works much too hard; and as if answering the obvious question, he says: "Well, after the children grow up, I'll be able to take it a little easier and then I can really begin to enjoy them."

But actually it will *never again* be "as good" as it is at this very moment. Now. From *now* on, it rushes on and on toward an anticlimax; and soon the children begin to lead their own lives, accumulate their own problems, and have their own musings about how much "better" it will be "later." And this is as it should be.

The most sensible attitude I think is to do your job and finish the thing out with as few complications as possible. Marcus Aurelius (180 B.C.) said:

> Consider that the great universe, of which thou art only a trivial speck, is governed by fixed laws, and be therefore content in all things, and especially to die at any time, and abide God's will of thee, whether of individual future life, or dissolution into universal mind and matter.

How to get a husband

Do YOU want to know where a large proportion of the money earned by young secretaries, stenographers, bookkeepers, schoolteachers goes?

Well, it ends up in the pockets of Mr. Grossingers, Mr. Concords, Mr. Ye Wayward Inn, Mr. Laurel-in-the-Pines, and other lucky people who own vacation resorts in the Catskills, Poconos, Adirondacks.

Every year the average working girl receives "two weeks, with," and what does she do? For weeks before the vacation she pores over vacation brochures of every color, type, and description. This is a serious business, and in the main, it involves decent, hard-working girls, who are looking for the "right man."

Usually two girls enter into this expedition of conquest. The girls go without lunch beginning on February 15. Several outfits must be taken along for morning; lunch; after-lunch, lounging-around period; and, you should pardon the expression, cocktail time; then an evening dress; and an after-evening dress. Nothing must be duplicated. You must not be seen in the same dress, bathing suit, or frock twice.

After clothes are bought, tennis rackets are borrowed, furs are loaned by various other members of the family, luggage is plastered with stickers from Nice, Monte Carlo, and Cannes, and off they go. To arrive by car is of course best, but in the absence of a car, the girls hire a "hack." This usually costs six dollars one way plus a dollar for the driver who always tells you that he just drove ten handsome young men up to the same place.

The girls arrive, and then—strategy. "Now listen, Mabel, you say we're going up together, but if you meet a fella or if I should meet a fella, then let's agree not to bother about the one who hasn't got a fella (it shouldn't happen). Of course always ask if he has a friend, but if he doesn't, remember, we are on our own—agreed?"

Your entrance into the lobby of course is completely unnoticed, except by the bellboys, who say to themselves, here comes another load of dames! A quick rush to sign in, take a sort of nonchalant look around and see a couple of nice guys at the bar, and you whisk yourself up to your room to start the operations. This you told your mother was going to be a rest (it shouldn't happen). The evening meal is the first crack out of the box. You are seated at a table with four other women, of course, plus two fellas whom you wouldn't even date on a desert island. After an hour of craning your neck to see how Mabel is doing, you decide to speak to the headwaiter. You say sweetly you would like to change your table, the service is terrible or something else in the way of an excuse. Couldn't he please give you a seat, over there, you know, the table with the four lonely men. He complies (for two bucks), and you are finally happy. Later you meander down to the La Mamba Room (or the Cockatoo Lounge) and you wait. You see there is a long corridor about ten feet wide (it seems miles in length) through which you have to pass in order to reach your destination (where all the dancing is going on), but you steel yourself, take a deep breath, and you proceed. Unfortunately, you have to traverse this by yourself as your friend has already made her first conquest. What you didn't seem to notice is that each side of this corridor is falling over at the edges with M E N, all ogling, staring, making comments, and by the time you reach the end, your face is flushed. Now that you have passed the slave market, you stand around for what seems an eternity and decide to sit at a table. The entrance to the chairs and tables is blocked by a tall man who says, "Sorry, only escorted ladies allowed." So, you have to wait. At long last you spy the B A R. Your mother and various other members of your family have told you that the B A R is no place for such a sweet girl like you, but, you say, what the hell. You saunter over and order a PINK LADY. You pay for your own drink and wait. Nothing happens and after three drinks you decide to take things into your own hands. You ask the cute blond guy to your left for a light for your cigarette . . . his girl (who was hidden by his broad shoulders) turns a sweet, sickly sneer in your direction and you again crawl back into your shell. This is terrible. You are at the depths of emotion . . . you feel neglected, tipsy, your make-up is ruined after this ordeal, and you decide never again to go to this rat race. I shall go to bed at an early hour, you decide, and tomorrow is always another day. You slip down from your high perch and start toward the door. All of a sudden, you are confronted by a blue serge suit with white tie . . . and as you lift your eyes two beautiful brown ones meet yours and inquire . . . how about a drink? You're set . . . he's gorgeous . . . what a guy. Wait till I tell the girls about him. What a wonderful place this is. Must tell everyone to come here next vacation.

There is a serious side to all of this of course—an ever-present problem—and I feel terribly sorry for the thousands of girls who go to this trouble and expense. The odds against them are almost insurmountable. These "odds" of course are in the shapes of the many other girls and women who are out only for a good time, and are women of "easy virtue." Thus the "opportunities" to which the men are exposed are so numerous—and it is all "so easy"—that the decent girl with her four-hundred-dollar vacation fund is up against a terrible proposition. Another thing of course is that this decent girl must acquire a sixth sense, a method of communicating to the young man at the bar or at her table almost from the first words she speaks, that this conversation will *not* lead to the bedroom, but only to a possible "date" in the city, and maybe to meet the family. This is not easy, as you can well understand. But let us say for these thousands of working girls, honorably looking for a husband, that they have guts—next February 15, they'll start going without lunches and examining brochures. Let us wish them good luck—next time.

I am now kosher

I HAVE now been mentioned in an editorial in the New York *Herald Tribune* (January 21, 1958), which should more than cancel out all those favorable mentions I have had in the "radical" papers of America, to say nothing of a "Labour" publication in England.

And as a bonus, a favorable comment on my writings in the *Textile Bulletin,* which prides itself, editorially, with being far, far to the right of the late William McKinley.

All of which reminds me of the time I sat in on the sessions of the (Congressman) Walter Un-American Activities Committee, when it was investigating the Communists of North Carolina. As Mr. Arens, the committee counsel, kept calling the witnesses, I felt a cold shiver running up and down my spine—"another subscriber." They were all subscribers, the whole eight of them; the three students, the meatcutter, the book salesman, the poet, and the two unemployedniks. What a spot to be in! But I was thinking fast.

During the lunch hour I went back to my office and pulled out the subscription cards of a dozen textile and tobacco tycoons in the State; the officers of the huge Duke industrial and power empire; plus the two White House subscriptions. With these cards in my pocket for protection, I sat through the rest of the sessions completely relaxed. I was as nonchalant as I would have been at a circus.

I've given all of this a lot of thought, this business of both the "radicals" and the "tories" mentioning me "in the dispatches," as it were, and I have come to the conclusion that it may be concerned with my interest in *people,* as individuals.

About eight years ago I moved into a mill-village in this area. Some of my friends said that it was a gesture of snobbery, in reverse. Maybe so, and I suspect that their observation has kept me from writing anything about those two years on "factory hill." I know in my heart that I had not gone there to "examine" them or to "write them up," as they would say; but I will tell you this one story.

I lived in three rooms (with a separate entrance) of a six-room house. Ah, how the millworkers love to say, "We live in a duplex." So sad, and yet so wonderful. One afternoon I heard some noise outside my door. My neighbor was out there with a chair that had collapsed. She was the grandmother who had done her hitch in the mill and was now taking care of home and grandchildren while her daughter and son-in-law were on the "day-shift" looms. She quickly explained: "When you start to play that music I always pull up my chair outside your door, but the chair broke a leg, and I am mighty sorry." She confessed that she had been listening for nearly a year while I was playing my recordings of—Traviata, and Otello, and a Lotte Lehmann album of Brahms lieder. I said to the woman: "I'll leave you my key and when I go to the office you just come on in here and play all this music you want." She thanked me: "You reckon my son-in-law can show me how to work the machine?"

By this time all I could do was turn my face away from her and say: "I reckon."

Fathers and sons

THERE is a quality about the feeling between a father and a son which far transcends all other human relationships. It is imbedded deeply in all the cultures of our civilization.

The other night I walked into the café at midnight with my morning paper and I was invited over to a booth occupied by a friend and two other men. My friend introduced me to his brother from another city and his brother's son, a fine-looking boy whose age I judged to be about twenty. My friend's brother is a traveling salesman with a highly

successful, nationally advertised "line," and during the course
of the conversation I learned that the boy had recently
decided to leave college and become a salesman, too. I saw
at once that this was a wise decision, that the boy would,
indeed, make a successful salesman. During the half-hour
or so that I sat with these people I realized that the reading
of philosophy is not entirely a waste of time and the salesman-father would have benefited by doing some of it in
his spare time.

Apparently this was the first trip "on the road" for the boy
and the father-salesman was relating some of their hilarious
experiences. Most of the stories were about women, and the
father discussed them with pride, as if to say, "See what
a regular fellow I am with my son—just a couple of buddies."
They spoke of the women they had met and how they
"knocked off" this one here, and that one there, and even
though I am myself a sort of Rabelaisian character, I felt
sorry indeed for the father-salesman and for the son, too,
for that matter. ·

This "buddy-buddy" stuff between father and son will
never last. It cannot last. They haven't a chance in the world.

Because there are two things a son will never forgive his
father for and the first and foremost is *infidelity* ("wronging"
the mother). The son himself can be a "regular" fellow . . .
he can even be as loose as all get-out and spend most of his
time in brothels, but none of this makes any difference whatever. He will forgive the father for being a drunk, or a
poor provider. As a matter of fact, if the father is a drunk
and/or a poor provider, the relationship may even be
strengthened because of a natural sympathy that may be
added to the normal devotion through religion, propinquity,
sentiment, and habit. But *nothing*, absolutely nothing (and
that includes buying him a Cadillac convertible), will ever
alter his feeling (hate) if he finds out directly or indirectly
that the father had "betrayed" the mother. I therefore felt
sorry for the salesman-father and the son, despite the
joviality, backslapping, and "regular fellow" camaraderie.

The son cannot help himself, of course. It goes back

thousands of years. It is deeply grounded in our theologies and in our histories. That is the real reason a second marriage must always come as a shock to the children. This is not wholly a matter of being "selfish," as so many people suppose, or that the "children do not understand that a father (or a mother) has a life of his own." Children look upon their mothers as "virgins" no matter how many children fill the household, and they look upon their fathers not as someone who has had sexual intercourse with the mother, but purely as the instrumentality of their own being. Centuries of taboo have conditioned us. We cannot possibly think of them and ourselves otherwise. Thus the introduction of a "stranger" smashes these concepts and it really doesn't make too much difference whether the introduction of this "stranger" is "legal" or "illegal."

And there is nothing anyone can do about it. It goes back to the Egyptian Isis, the Virgin Mother with her son Horus; the Carthaginians had the Great Mother, Queen Dido, and four of their gods were born of Virgin Mothers; the Romans too worshipped virginity. The Shrine of the Vestal Virgins was important even long after the rationalists, such as Julius Caesar, had discredited the major gods. In this shrine the important men closed their big deals, deposited their wills, and made their binding oaths. The vestals were girls who at the age of six had taken an oath of virginity for a period of thirty years. Among the ancient Hebrews, a wife convicted of adultery was stoned to death. The Persian god Mithra was not only born of a Virgin Mother, but all the generations of mothers in Mithra's family tree had been Virgins. The brilliant Greeks claimed that Plato was born of a Virgin Mother and, of course, we have the Christian concept of Mary, the Virgin Mother; and it all adds up to a basic inner consciousness of our hope for our own "purity."

Let no one suppose for a moment that I speak from experience rather than from study. I have three married sons, former paratroopers and artillerymen, and I doubt seriously whether I have ever told them as much as an off-color story in my entire life. One of my sons is a reporter for a big daily paper and naturally newspapermen are newspapermen whether they are twenty-eight or seventy-eight. Thus I often find myself with him and his friends, and the moment the conversation turns to women (as it should and does among young men), that's when I have to leave. I always have some writing to do at the office, or maybe see about something in the kitchen. In other words, I am on my way, which is as it should be.

You will recall that I started out by saying that there are *two* things of tremendous importance in a father-and-son relationship. The second thing is the *impression* the father makes on his son's friends. This is not as devastating as the first, but it is important enough to leave irradicable scars. Take the time the kid is playing in the street with his friends, and let one of the other kids say, "*Johnny, here comes your father.*" Now, you have one of the most important moments in a boy's life. Do you have any idea what goes through his mind during that fleeting moment? Your appearance, your dress, your walk, your manner, what you say to your son in greeting, and what you say to the other kids; these are matters of life and death to the son, whose heart thumps wildly throughout the ordeal. Of course, this is something he will never discuss with you. You'll *never* find out from him. You must discover it yourself. You've got to get it out of an understanding of human behavior, or maybe reading this book.

A true short, short story

THERE was a woman here in Charlotte who once operated a massage parlor, the kind of establishment that caters to traveling salesmen and to a restricted clientele of a few gay spirits around town. Eventually the police closed her place, and while she continued to meet with a few of her customers privately, it was apparent that her days of "activity" were fast approaching the end. A series of illnesses, plus onrushing middle age, and soon all the valuable "contacts" were gone. It was at this moment in her life that I met her, and I may add, for the *first time*. In fact it was precisely because I had not been a "customer" that she felt free to discuss the activities of the past and the hopes for the future. (Most of the marginal and offbeat people come to see me sooner or later.)

I sent the woman down to a retail establishment for a new dress, some underthings, a pair of shoes; and I told her that there might be a chance for her to carve out a little permanent job as a collector of advertising bills.

But this did not work. A fellow would call me up and start laughing, "Harry, I see you've got an old friend working for you, ha, ha, ha, ha." Several other fellows called me "confidentially" to tip me off about my collector. (We men are terrible gossips. In this case it was the "laymen" who knocked her out of her job.) Despite the fact that the woman was determined to do an honorable job, it was no go, and she herself was the first to acknowledge failure. I gave her a week's wages, wished her luck, and that was the end of that.

And then just about a year later I received a letter from her; one of the most interesting letters written by anyone in this generation. Of course I shall change the locale and say that the letter came from a small town in New England. A middle-aged widower with no children had fallen in love with this woman, and had established her as his wife and partner in his highly successful hardware business. In the letter the woman enclosed a cashier's check for one hundred dollars payable to my order, which I was to use to redeem the pledges she had made during her last days in Charlotte. "I was never able to pay the interest and you'll probably find these things gone by now, but you may have some influence with the pawnshop fellow, so please see what you can do." The frayed and half-torn pawn tickets called for a half-length muskrat coat, a portable Corona typewriter, a lady's wrist watch, a pen-and-pencil set, and one wedding ring.

Her letter continued: "My friend wanted us to be married in the church here and this being a small town the society editor of the newspaper wrote up the story very big and used two pictures of the wedding, as you can see from the clippings enclosed. I was afraid that someone else from this section would send you these clippings first and so I ask your forgiveness. I hope you'll not be offended. The society editor caught me completely off guard with some of the questions, and I had to think fast. . . ."

And so I read the clipping, the story of the wedding, and there in the last paragraph, ". . . the bride was graduated from the public schools of South Carolina . . . and for the past fifteen years had been associate editor of *The Carolina Israelite,* of Charlotte, North Carolina."

Indeed I was not offended! I never had a prouder moment!

Southern gentlemen

IN CHARLOTTE we have the ABC system of retail liquor sales—under supervision of the county government. The clerks in the liquor stores have both imagination and good taste. When you buy a bottle, they wrap it in a paper bag, which fits snugly around the pint or fifth, and most men wrap their hooch in newspapers under their coats, or, if a lawyer, judge, or traveling salesman, slip it right into the brief case or traveling bag. However, the clerks use their imagination when a woman customer enters the store.

They put the bottle into the same skintight paper bag. But then, they put it into a second bag, an oversized job, puffed out at the sides. There's no way in the world to tell that there's a bottle of grog in that bag. As the lady walks down the street, it could be that she's just in from the country, with a dozen fresh eggs, or maybe she's carrying knitting, or a pair of overalls to the cleaners. It's an intelligent system.

She can even go directly to a ladies' meeting with that puffed-out bag and no one would be the wiser that some good Old Rocking Chair whiskey is just waiting for the touch of her little hand.

Why other planets have not contacted us

IN ALL our space literature we automatically picture the Martians or the other Visitors From Outer Space trying to wipe us out and grab our women. Big deal. We are always worried about someone carrying off our women. This is chutzpah (arrogance). I believe the reverse is closer to the truth. I think the Martians and other Visitors From Outer Space are afraid they'll get killed the minute they set foot on this nervous, inhibited, frustrated, and trigger-happy little Earth.

Another thing must worry them. The position with respect to the Sun is, of course, different with each planet; the climatic and atmospheric conditions are different. It is unlikely that any visitors from outer space can conform to the necessary physical requirements we have established—narrow hips, tall, clean-shaven, and no "frizzy hair," which Westbrook Pegler recently pointed out was utterly "foreign." And then what about color? That's important. Suppose the color of their skin is, for instance, navy blue, or even magenta, what then? Wouldn't that set us off into a frenzy the minute we saw one of them? They know it. After all we are comparative newcomers. Some of those planets are not four billion years old, but seventy billion years old.

Old hands. They keep watching and keep saying, "Not yet, Charlie." They have decided to wait. Or maybe George Bernard Shaw was right. Maybe they all use Earth as a sort of interplanetary lunatic asylum.

Wink at some homely girl

SOME years before his death, H. L. Mencken asked his friends to "wink your eye at some homely girl" in remembrance of him. What nonsense! Sheer nonsense! Mencken acknowledged, for many years, a reputation as a woman-hater, which is the external sign of adolescence. A woman-hater is no expert on these matters. The idea is presumptuous, this "winking at a homely girl." Some of the finest loving on this earth has been due to the initiative, ingenuity, and kindness of the "homely" girl. And how does one go about deciding who is a "homely" girl?

Is there really a "homely" girl anywhere in the world? By whose standards? Mencken's, the casting director's, or the girl's husband? And they have husbands, you know—by the million.

"Wink at some homely girl." Every newspaper and literary journal in the country fell for this Mencken kid stuff, while hundreds of thousands of wonderful schoolteachers, social workers, YWCA secretaries, telephone operators, and stenographers laughed themselves sick. Some of them laughed so hard at this nonsense that their eyeglasses fell off.

Sex morals on the Lower East Side

WHEN I recall that nearly three-quarters of a million people lived within the radius of some twenty city blocks, on

New York's East Side, it is interesting that the sex morals were of such a comparatively high standard. I do not remember ever hearing the term "rape," although it is possible that some of those things went on under cover. Basically, however, when you saw an unmarried girl walking down the street with a fellow, you immediately thought of them in terms of marriage. In fact it was a terrible disgrace among Jewish people if a daughter "went out" with a young man for several weeks, without a serious result.

They would go out once, maybe twice, and then the girl would invite the boy to her house for dinner, and if he accepted, you could consider the "deal" closed. Then, too, there was the matter of the brothers of the girl. God help the young man who played fast and loose with a girl on the Lower East Side if she had two or three brothers. Perhaps this higher standard of boy-and-girl relationship could be attributed to the more clearly defined separation between "good girls" and "bad girls," and the existence of a definite "line of demarcation" like the red-light district. Even sociologists do not seem to have the answer. Maybe what's going on now is better, who knows?

It was better when papa was the boss

IF ONLY the American world with its political freedom and technological wonders had also adopted the patrism of the Jews of two generations ago. We'd probably all live to one hundred and twenty, like Moses. It was much better when papa was the boss and ruled the family.

We have most of the automobiles, telephones, washing machines, and beauty parlors in the world, but it is all a mad dash from sun-up to sundown, and a growing alienation from life.

Many wives, of course, tell the truth when they say that

they do not apply any extra pressure on their husbands, but this does not diminish his own needs, what he thinks is his obligation to her to continue to stew in this economic pressure-cooker that is the America of 1958. And when she says, "No, I do not want a new coat this year—we cannot afford it"— it is the unkindest cut of all. She is sincere, of course, but "the times are out of joint." She has merely added another ton of pressure to his shoulders and he is more determined than ever to become Top-Man-in-Sales for the ensuing month.

America on a huge breast binge

AMERICA is on a huge breast binge.

You sit in a movie and when the heroine leans over a little, the whole theatre exhales—ah, oh, ah—the same sounds I used to hear from bearded fellows sitting on the top bench of the Turkish baths. Ah, oh, ah. When I was a kid, legs were the big thing—not breasts. Young sports used to stand around the windy corners to catch a glimpse of a skirt suddenly blown above the ankles. It seems that the sounds were different, too. Instead of "ah, oh, ah," now used for breasts, the boys used to laugh loudly, "ha, ha, ha," as the girl was desperately fighting to keep her skirts down. The difference in the sounds may also mean something because, undoubtedly, this whole thing is psycho. In times of peace and more placid living, legs are important, but during times of great stress and uncertainty the instinct to seek the safety and comfort of a "mother" is probably an important factor in this current tremendous interest in the female chest.

We are not alone

Most of us transfer our nationalism, "we are the best," even when it comes to the heavenly bodies. There are more planets in this tiny corner of our universe than there are grains of sand on the beaches of America. Multiply this single corner of our universe with at least two hundred million more such "corners," or galaxies, and you'll have some idea of the staggering vastness of possibilities, probabilities, and certainties. Obviously, it is silly to believe that out of many trillions of "earths," only this tiny dot possesses the conditions that have made life possible. There is no logic in this at all. It is far more logical to assume that these same life-serving conditions are repeated in at least fifty billion planets out of the hundreds of trillions that are revolving in space.

We are not alone.

Many widows live in college towns

Not all the widows flock to Florida to snatch a new husband. Some of the more imaginative widows settle in the quiet little college towns.

And, of course, the naive professors are easy prey. For the widows it's like shooting fish in a barrel. For one thing, the professors have neither the time nor the money to do much cavorting and courting, and they are helpless when up against a charming and sophisticated widow. The college-town widows have their own scale of preferences, of course. A professor of philosophy is the most desirable, followed by the professors of the Romance languages, literature, history, and art. A little lower down the list are the instructors of the professional courses like business administration, journalism, accounting—and, scraping the bottom of the barrel, is the professor of social science. In keeping up with our times, the widows are terribly afraid of social science—sounds too much like a welfare worker, a hospital attendant, or you-know-what.

The landlord

THE landlord has been the most unpopular figure in all history. This is the one guy on whom all classes, races, and creeds unite in a common prejudice. I guess this goes way back to the feudal days and before, when the "landlord" became a fixture in the minds of the people as "the enemy." It still persists. He is the one man in our society who does not win sympathy under any circumstances. If the roof caves in and the tenants are sitting in the debris, they will laugh like hell. They will endure any hardship as long as it means trouble for the landlord.

The shame of nakedness

I READ an interesting piece in *The Humanist* by my favorite American scholar, Professor Horace M. Kallen, on "Theology and Shame." Professor Kallen tells us that the sense of shame, through nakedness, has played an important role in the shaping of our lives and our thoughts. This article reminded me of the books I have been reading on the

Nuremberg trials of the Nazi criminals. It seems that when the Nazis sent groups of Jews to the gas chambers, they undressed them and forced them to march to their deaths—naked. When fathers, mothers, sons, and daughters are marching together, naked, it seems that the intense "desire" to "cover their shame" (in this case, the only way they could do this was to die) becomes very strong. If they had any fight left in them at all, the nakedness destroyed the last bit of the will to resist.

Parents work night and day

ALL my life I have watched parents work day and night to educate their children—to give them a profession and a start in life—and they do all of this in the certain knowledge that the moment the job is done, they positively lose their children.

This has always struck me as the height of the nobility of the human mind. Sometimes it makes one wonder whether it can all be explained as simply as the psychologists say—"self-love," "you're really doing it for yourself." I admit that now sometimes I find myself with wide-open spaces of doubt with respect to these simple answers. I'm not so sure today that there may not be something else! Especially when I think back to the fellow who used to climb up five flights of stairs twenty times a day with bags of coal in the winter, and fifty-pound blocks of ice in the summer, to earn enough to make his son a lawyer. As I think back to him, I just cannot imagine anything about him that suggested "self-love," "self-identification," or any of these other theories.

Why do they climb the mountains?

THE question has been asked a thousand times. Why do they risk their lives to climb Mount Everest? Why do fine men of great talent risk everything on a single mistake in scaling the icy walls of the wildest mountain on earth? The great mountain climbers have written many books, in which they have given many answers. Those answers include: the desire for further exploration; man's eternal struggle against the elements; or just to see what's on "the other side." No one has even hinted what I believe is the basic reason. I think it is God.

We are still living at the very beginning of time. We have but recently passed our earliest beginnings when all the gods lived on mountaintops. The Babylonians regarded mountains as the natural abode of the gods. The Greeks and the Romans, of course, thought of their gods on high Olympus. The mountaintop has always been regarded with awe by mankind, and, of course, it was from Mount Sinai that Moses descended with the Ten Commandments.

The mountain has another great fascination for man. The vegetation of the earth springs from a layer of topsoil, but it is only the mountain that rises right out of the bosom of Mother Earth. Thus in the mind of man is this lingering feeling for both the Great Mother and the mountaintop to which she has given birth. The mountain climber is not only embracing the Great Mother but clings to the hope that when he gets to the top he may see "The Burning Bush."

First day of school

I BELIEVE the most stirring moment in the experience of a parent comes on the day he leaves the child in school for the first time. This can be so sharp an experience that, where there are two or three children, this ritual has to be alternated between parents. I remember leaving one of mine there all starched up with a look of bewilderment on his face such as I never want to witness again. I held his little hand and got him registered. As we walked through the yard and corridors of the school, he never took his eyes off me, and never said a word. Then came the moment to put him in a line and—leave him.

I tried to be nonchalant as I walked away but I quickly hid behind a pillar; he had never taken his eyes off me. He just looked and looked, and I could see that he filled up, but, since I am bigger, I filled up more. What an ordeal! Yet I knew that the final decision could not be delayed for long. There was no law that forced me to keep watching him. I turned my back and started out slowly and then I practically ran out the door. You have to make a break.

PART 2

We Toast the Journey—
For Two Cents Plain

The poets were paid

My EARLY morning impression of the East Side, and I mean six o'clock in the morning, summer and winter, was of young boys streaming out of tenements to go to the synagogue to say kaddish for a departed parent before going to school, and maybe also carrying up a fifty-pound bag of coal before breakfast. Work, work, work.

Everybody worked all the time, and if there was no job, people worked at something; they sorted rags or sewed garments, or fixed flowers and feathers for hat manufacturers. There were dozens and dozens of halls. Lodge halls, society halls, meeting halls. It was the "meetingest" place in the world. Every other building had space for meeting halls.

These fiction-fakers write about gangsters and they miss the Free Loan Society. Where else did this happen? A man needed fifty dollars to go into some business or to tide him over, and he borrowed, without interest.

People scrabbled for a little living. They did anything for the children. They wanted their children to enter the American middle class. My son will be a doctor, they'd say, or a lawyer, maybe a teacher. I never heard anyone express lesser hopes for his child. A man peddled fourteen hours, maybe, and brought home two dollars after he paid off his merchandise and his cart hire, or he brought home eleven dollars a week from the factory for fifty-four hours' work.

Who has ever seen such optimism anywhere on earth? The night before the High Holy Days—everything would become quiet—that whole teeming district of hundreds of thousands of people in tenements would suddenly come to a complete halt. You'd see workingmen with shiny faces coming out of the public baths and walking home and holding hands with their sons, and you've never seen its equal for brightness and happiness.

We had the Marshall Plan down there a half century ago. Where else on earth, among the poorest people, did you see in every home a blue-and-white box where you were supposed to drop your pennies? Once a week an old woman would come around and empty it and off it would go somewhere overseas—the poorest of the poor helping still poorer ones across the Atlantic somewhere. Hundreds of sweatshop employees, men and women who sat at machines for nine and ten hours a day, came home, washed up, had supper, and went to the lodge hall or settlement houses to learn English or to listen to a fellow read poetry to them. *Paid* readers of poetry. I saw it. I saw gangsters and bums, but I also saw poets, settlement workers, welfare workers, scribes, teachers, philosophers, all hoping and striving for one goal—to break away—and they did, too. The second generation came along and soon the sons took the old folks away, out to Brooklyn or up to the Bronx, and thus they made room for new immigrants. America gave them all hope and life, and they repaid America. There has never been a more even trade.

Buying a suit on the East Side

WHEN did you buy a winter suit, or a heavy overcoat? In the middle of the summer, of course. In July. August was even better. In the summer you could get a bargain. You could maybe pick up a good blue serge suit or a heavy woolen overcoat from the stock which the fellow had not sold during the previous winter. And so the hotter the day the better.

Usually it turned out to be the hottest Sunday of the year. It was always Sunday. You wanted to take along as many members of the family as possible. You left nothing to chance. The word went down: "We are buying Hymie a winter suit"; and the matter was prepared carefully.

It had to be on a Sunday because of the "mayvinn." A mayvinn is a connoisseur. Every family had a mayvinn; usually an uncle or a cousin who was a presser in a pants factory and who knew all about cloth and workmanship. Sometimes you had to put off the expedition because the mayvinn couldn't make it on a certain Sunday.

Finally you were all set. In those days the legitimate clothing stores were on Canal Street (still there) and on Stanton Street (no longer there). The "fake" stores were on the Bowery, and they caused many a heartache among immigrants, but that is another story for another time.

In those days the clothing stores had "pullers-in." These pullers-in stood outside the store and enticed the customer to enter the establishment. The valuable pullers-in were those with a wide acquaintance, members of one of the Landsmannshaften (societies of people from the same town or area in Europe); a fellow who by sight could recognize hundreds of people and call them by their first name—"Reb Joseph, in here—we've got the best merchandise." Some of the pullers-in were highly persuasive. If a man stopped to look at the window display of the store he was a dead duck.

The puller-in really went to work on him. He kept up a rapid-fire conversation, extolling the merchandise and telling him of the special bargain he happens to know about— "When you go inside ask for Max and tell him I said to show you that special suit he was hiding away for my very own brother."

The pullers-in were important. They even organized themselves into a collective-bargaining union, the "Pullers-in Association of New York." Often a puller-in would lose his job in one store and work for a competitor within calling distance, and if someone stopped off at his former employer's store, he'd call out all the curses he knew; maybe that the boss over there does not pay his help.

Now let us get back to the family. It is the hottest Sunday in August. Everybody is there, the mother, the father, the oldest brother, the mayvinn, and, of course, the thirteen-year-old son, Hymie, who is to get the first suit bought expressly for him, a blue serge suit which he is to wear for the first time on the High Holy Days the following October. The mayvinn always knew "a place," perhaps where his friend was the puller-in, and the family immediately set out for the establishment, disentangling themselves from a dozen other pullers-in on the way. Occasionally Hymie would be missing and everybody began to look for him. A smart puller-in had sensed that this was "Operation Hymie" and had "kidnapped" the kid. They looked in all the stores.

And when the party found Hymie, he was already standing on a raised platform trying on a blue serge suit. The salesman of the establishment kept saying: "Look how nice it looks; why don't you let us tell you how much it is?" But all he heard was: "Hymie, take it off!" Perhaps even a cuff on the ear. "Hymie, stick close to us," and they were on their way again.

Finally, "the place." The mayvinn led the party in, after a big hello from the puller-in, who escorted them inside to create the impression that they had come in as a result of his efforts.

The mother picked a stool and seated herself at a point where her eyes could sweep the stairway to the basement, the front door, the mirror, the sales force, and the raised platform where the important work was to be done during the next hour or so. Once seated comfortably, she began to cool herself with a big palm-leaf fan and nodded her head for the operations to begin. The salesman started a big spiel, and everyone let the mother do the preliminary talking.

Her attitude was always challenging with overtones of belligerency. This was good tactics as a bargaining point. The mother raised her arm and said: "Never mind the talk; all we want here is a little suit for a bar-mitzvah boy."

The idea was always to minimize the project; use the word "little" as often as possible, and the religious overtones, "bar mitzvah" (confirmation), couldn't hurt even though the salesman had heard it a hundred times that week-end.

The father, older brother, and the mayvinn took their places in receiving-line style to the right of the platform. Hymie, of course, was already standing there with his pants off. The salesman said, "I've got just what you want," and started to go toward the basement steps. He had a thousand suits on the floor, but he always went to the basement. This gave him a good talking point—the suit was special. And now for the battle of wits. A battle between two brilliant adversaries. The father, older brother, and even the mayvinn were under tremendous pressure for fear that a single word spoken out of turn could tip the balance in favor of the clothing salesman, and so they let the mother speak unless they were actually asked a question. The salesman, now walking toward the basement, was executing a very adroit move; but the mother, alert to every situation, came back with a counterblow: "What are you going to bring us, something you are ashamed to keep on the floor?" This was good. It took the edge off the salesman's early advantage.

Now he will have to expend precious talk in merely trying to recover from that blow. Presently he returned carrying a blue serge suit. Now things began to move. The father, the older brother, and the mother instinctively looked toward the mayvinn. They want him to be on the alert. A moment or two of silence. This is IT.

The salesman helps Hymie with the pants, straightens them out, then the coat, smooths it out in the back, and as he's standing behind the boy, the mother lands another good blow: "What are you doing there behind the boy? Let him stand by himself; we'll see what's what." The salesman walks away from Hymie, but recovers quickly, with a solid punch—"I was saving this suit for my own nephew, my own flesh and blood, for his own bar mitzvah in October, but when I saw such a handsome boy come in I couldn't help it, I had to bring up this particular suit." A good counterpunch. Now the mother moves her stool back a few feet to get a better view of Hymie. "Turn around," she commands, and Hymie keeps turning. "Now on the side; turn to the front again."

Now it is squarely up to the mayvinn, who steps forward—"Take off the coat." Hymie takes off the coat. The mayvinn goes out the door, in the light. Everybody is watching the mayvinn now except Hymie, who is sitting on the floor until the mother sees him. "Stand up and don't dirty the pants; we're not buying this suit—yet," and the salesman sighs. Meanwhile the mayvinn is still outside. He holds the coat up to the sun. He feels it. His hands go into the pockets of the coat. His final gesture; he closes his eyes and rubs the cloth between his fingers, with a separate operation for the lining. He opens his eyes and brings the coat in—he says nothing until he enters the circle of the father, the older brother, and the mother; the salesman leans forward. Even Hymie is tense. Everybody looks at the mayvinn. He is slow and deliberate in his decision. He finally says, "Not a bad piece of goods"—the very highest compliment a mayvinn can bestow. The mother looks with contempt. "Also a mayvinn," she says, but she knows the salesman now has the upper hand.

Things are coming to a climax. Everybody knows what's coming. This is important. The slightest inflection of the voice or the flicker of an eyebrow, for that matter, can have serious consequences. The mother tries to be as nonchalant as possible when she asks the big question: "How much for this secondhand suit which you were not able to sell to anybody all winter long?"

The mother has regained the initiative. Now the salesman has to fight back. "What do you mean, secondhand, and we couldn't sell it all winter long?" But the mother senses the kill and does not let him continue. "All right, so why do you still have a winter suit on the hottest day in the summer? Answer me that!" The salesman begins, "Listen, lady . . ." but the mother follows up her advantage, "How much?" The salesman is groggy. Now he becomes belligerent and fairly yells, "Fourteen dollars." A mistake. The mother had goaded him too much. The man wasn't himself. "Fourteen dollars?" the father and the mayvinn say in unison, and then the mother begins to laugh, which is the signal for everybody else to laugh; everybody except the salesman and Hymie, who wants to know, "Where is the toilet?"

When the salesman shows him, the mother delivers another blow—"Watch out for the pants, Hymie, we are going someplace else." Silence. The mother stands up and starts walking out. "Tell Hymie to take off the suit when he comes back," she says to no one in particular. Hymie obeys his father without any fuss, and as he takes off the coat and then the pants, the salesman says, "What did I say that was so bad? I was saving this suit for my own flesh and blood." No one is listening.

They all follow the mother who is already outside the door talking to the puller-in. The salesman catches up with the party on the sidewalk. The mother is annoyed. She shakes her head and in a low, compassionate tone of voice explains, "There's nothing further to talk about. If you said maybe ten dollars, we would think you were crazy." They keep walking. Now the mayvinn is catching hell. "Also a mayvinn—'not a bad piece of goods,' he says; also a mayvinn; who needed you?" They go to two other stores, but this is only a maneuver—a necessary bit of East Side protocol. They would have never forgiven themselves if they had made the purchase in the first store without "looking around." At the second place the mother says, "Fourteen dollars? We just saw a suit for fourteen dollars that's a regular doll-suit and we didn't even take it."

Finally, between four and five o'clock, they come back to the first store.

Only the mother goes in. The salesman tries to act surprised. Actually he expected them to return. She now becomes palsy-walsy with the salesman—"All right, take the ten dollars and let the boy have a nice suit for his bar mitzvah." The salesman whispers, "So help me, I am doing something against my own flesh and blood when I give you this suit for twelve dollars." The deal is closed. Then she calls in the father, the older brother, Hymie, and the may-vinn to make sure that they are getting the same suit, and they go home tired but very, very happy.

The mother takes her place in the kitchen to make some potato latkes for everyone. And she resumes her traditional status within the family circle—"Hymie, did you give your father a big kiss for the suit he bought you today?"

For two cents plain

THE rabbinical student in Europe and in America had a regular schedule of "eating days." Mondays he ate with family A; Tuesdays with B; and so forth. On the Lower East Side this system still lingered to some extent, but it usually involved a young boy who had immigrated without a family. His fellow-townsmen set up his seven eating days. Usually this was a very religious boy who would not take a chance to eat "out" or could not yet afford to buy his meals. Some of the hosts on these eating days used the fellow to check up on the melamed (Hebrew teacher). The melamed came at half past three and taught the children for a half-hour—for a twenty-five-cent fee. Learning the prayers was entirely by rote. There was no explanation or translation of the Hebrew into English or Yiddish. Once in a while the mother would ask the eating-days fellow to come a half-hour earlier. The boy came with his usual appetite, but soon learned the reason for the early appointment. The mother wanted him to test the children to see if the melamed was doing all right. The boy always gave the melamed a clean bill of health.

Sometimes the eating-days boy ate too much and in poor households this was quite a problem. But in most homes the mother saw to it that he kept packing it away, and in addition always had something wrapped up for him to take back to his room—for later. Many households had these strangers at their tables, but only the very religious boys remained, those who expected to continue their religious studies.

The others were soon gone. America was too great and too wonderful; there were too many things to see and do, and even a hot dog at a pushcart was an adventure, to say nothing of the wonderful Max's Busy Bee.

The streets were crowded with vendors with all sorts of delightful and exotic tidbits and nasherei (delicacies).

Across the border (the Bowery) was the Italian hot-dog man. The hot plate (a coal fire) was mounted on his push-cart, and behind the stove was a barrel of lemonade to which he added chunks of ice every few hours. The hot dog, roll, mustard, and relish was three cents; the drink, two cents; and it was all a memorable experience.

A few years ago I saw a fellow with a similar cart near the Battery on Lower Broadway and I made a mad dash for him. The whole operation was now fifteen cents, but it wasn't anywhere near as wonderful as it was when I was twelve years old.

In the late fall and winter came the fellow with the haiseh arbus (hot chick-peas). He started to make his rounds a few minutes before noon as the children were leaving the schools for lunch. You sat in the classroom and everything was quiet and dignified, and all of a sudden you heard those loud blasts—"Haiseh arbus," "Haiseh, haiseh" (hot, hot)—and you knew it was time to go. Sometimes he was a little early and the teacher had to close the window. The price was one penny for a portion which the man served in a rolled-up piece of newspaper, like the English working people buy their fish and chips. There were also fellows with roasted sweet potatoes; two cents each, and three cents for an extra large one. These people used a galvanized tin contraption on wheels which looked exactly like a bedroom dresser with three drawers. In the bottom drawer were the potatoes he was roasting, while in the upper drawers were the two different sizes ready to serve. On the bottom of everything, of course, was the coal-burning fire. He had a small bag of coal attached to the front of the stove and every once in a while he shook up the fire.

My uncle Berger once operated one of those sweet-potato pushcarts with the stove on the bottom, and years later he always said that he began life in America as an engineer. He boasted of this after he had made a million dollars operating the Hotel Normandie on Broadway and 38th Street during World War I.

An interesting fellow was the peddler with a red fez, a "Turk," who sold an exotic sweet drink. He carried a huge bronze water container strapped to his back. This beautiful container had a long curved spout which came over his left shoulder. Attached to his belt, in front, was a small pail of warm water to rinse his two glasses. The drink was one penny. You held the glass, and he leaned toward you as the liquid came forth.

Nuts were very popular. There were pushcarts loaded down with "polly seeds." I have forgotten the authentic name for this nut but the East Side literally bathed in the stuff. "Polly seed" because it was the favorite food of parrots—"Polly want a cracker?"

Indian nuts, little round brown nuts. The father of one of the kids on the block sold Indian nuts, of all things. On his pushcart he had a huge glass bowl the size of an army soup vat, and it was filled with Indian nuts. I had day-dreams of taking my shoes off and jumping up and down in that vat of Indian nuts, like the French girls make champagne.

This was the era when people walked a great deal. Shoe-shine parlors were all over the place. On Sunday mornings you went out to get a shine and did not mind waiting in

line for it either. "We are going for a walk next Saturday
night." Sounds silly today, but it was an event, and make
no mistake. And on every corner there were pushcarts
selling fruit in season. Apples, pears, peaches, and above all,
grapes. A common sight was a boy and girl eating grapes.
The boy held the stem aloft as each of them pulled at the
bunch and walked along the street. The grapes were sold by
weight per bunch; the other fruits were sold individually, of
course. And "in season" there was the man or the woman with
"hot corn." I did not hear the term "corn-on-the-cob" till
quite a few years later. We knew it only as "hot corn."
The vendor had boiled the ears at home and usually carried
the large vat to a convenient street corner, or he put the
vat on a baby carriage and wheeled it around the neighborhood. A lot of women were in this hot-corn business. The
hot corn was a nickel, and there was plenty of bargaining.
"Throw it back, give me that one, the one over there." We
kids waited around until the lady was all sold out, except
the ones which had been thrown back, and often we paid
no more than a penny. There are two moments when it is
best to buy from a peddler, a "first" and the "close-out."

Confections of all sorts were sold, many of them famous in
the Orient and eastern Europe. Fellows sold candy known
as "rah-hott," which sounds Turkish or Arabic. It was beautiful to look at and there were two or three different tastes
with each bite. Halvah, of course, was the real big seller,
and the memory of this has lingered to this day. No delicatessen store today is without halvah, although I shall not do
them the injustice of comparing the East Side halvah and the
stuff they sell today. But at least you are getting a whiff
of it, which is worth anything you pay. I had a Gentile
friend here who had been courting a widow for years without any success and I gave him a box of chocolate-covered
halvah to take to her, and the next time I saw the guy he
was dancing in the streets of Charlotte. We used to eat it
between slices of rye bread, "a halvah sonavich," and it
was out of this world. There was another candy called
"buckser" (St. John's bread), imported from Palestine. It

had a long, hard, curved shell and inside a very black seed with an interesting taste which is hard to describe.

There were pushcarts loaded down with barrels of dill pickles and pickled tomatoes, which we called "sour tomatoes." Working people, men and women on the way home from the needle factories, stopped off to buy a sour tomato as a sort of appetizer for their evening meal, or perhaps to take the edge off the appetite. These tidbits sold for two and three cents each, and you served yourself. You put your hand into the vinegar barrel and pulled one out. Years later a relative of mine asked me to accompany him to a lawyer's office "to talk for him." I met him on the old East Side and we decided to walk out of the district and into Lower Broadway.

Suddenly I noticed that he was no longer at my side. I looked back and there he was biting into one sour tomato and holding a fresh one in the other hand, all ready to go. I had become a fancy guy by then and he was afraid he would embarrass me, but my mouth was watering, Broadway and all.

And then there were the permanent vendors—the soda-water stands. On nearly every corner a soda-water stand. These were the size and shape of the average newsstand you see in most of the big cities today. There was a soda fountain behind a narrow counter, and a rack for factory-made American candy, which was becoming increasingly popular, especially the Hershey bar. The fellow also sold cigarettes. No woman was ever seen smoking a cigarette in those days. The brands were Mecca, Hassan, Helmar, Sweet Caporal (which are still sold), Egyptian Deities, Moguls, Schinasi, Fifth Avenue, and Afternoons.

My father smoked Afternoons. Half the cigarette was a hard mouthpiece, or what the advertising boys today call a filter. I bought many a box of Afternoons and they were seven cents for ten cigarettes. I also bought whiskey. There was no inhibition about it and no sense of guilt. We had no drunks down there, and a kid could buy a bottle of whiskey for his father the same as he could buy a loaf of bread. I read the label many times on the way home, "Pennsylvania

Rye Whiskey; we guarantee that this whiskey has been aged in the wood twenty years before bottling; signed, Park and Tilford." Cost, $1.80 for an imperial quart. No fancy "fifth-shmifth" business.

The fellow with the stand had a small marble counter on which he served his drinks and made change for candy and cigarettes. Along the counter were jars of preserves— cherry, raspberry, mulberry—for his mixed drinks. He also had a machine to make malted milks. How the immigrants took to the malted milk!

Like the other folks, my mother pronounced it "ah molta." But, of course, the big seller was seltzer (carbonated water), either plain or with syrup. A small glass of seltzer cost a penny—"Give me a small plain." That meant no syrup. And for the large glass you said, "Give me for two cents plain." For an extra penny he ladled out a spoonful of one of his syrups and mixed it with the seltzer. Here, too, there was plenty of bargaining. A fellow said, "Give me for two cents plain," and as the man was filling the glass with seltzer the customer said, casual-like, "Put a little on the top." This meant syrup, of course, and yet it did not mean the extra penny. You did not say, "Give me a raspberry soda." It was all in the way you said it, nonchalantly and in a sort of deprecating tone, "Put a little on the top." It meant that you were saving the fellow the trouble of even stirring the glass. Well, the man had already filled the glass with seltzer and what could he do with it unless you paid for it? So he "put a little on the top" but not the next time if he could help it. Often he would take the two cents first and give you a glass of plain. "I know my customers," he'd say. The man who had the stand on our corner was an elderly gent, "Benny," and once when I was playing around his counter, one of his jars fell down and the syrup got all over me. Every time I came near Benny's stand after that he took extra precautions; "Go 'way, hard luck," he always said to me. Benny wore a coat he had brought from Europe and it reached down to his ankles. He would take a handful of that coat, feel it a while, and tell you whether it was going to rain the next day. People came from blocks around to get a weather forecast from Benny and his coat. He rarely missed.

And so you can hardly blame the young boy, the eating-days boy, when he quit the table of those home-cooked meals and went down into this world of pleasures and joys.

My Uncle Koppel and free enterprise

MY UNCLE Koppel (K. Berger) was twenty years old when he came to America. The day after his arrival he opened a small butcher shop on Scammel Street, on New York's Lower East Side. For the next three years he opened up his shop at six o'clock in the morning, worked till after dark, cooked his meals on a stove in the back of the store, and pushed the meat block up against the front door to sleep. What English he learned he picked up from the truck drivers, who delivered the meat and the poultry. There was nothing unusual about this. There were thousands of immigrants who lived, worked, and died within the confines of a few city blocks. But with Koppel Berger it was to be different, because Uncle Koppel had imagination, courage, ability, and, above all, he seemed to know what America was all about.

It was 1904 and all America was singing, "Meet me in St. Louey, Louey, meet me at the Fair . . ." and my immigrant Uncle took the lyrics literally. He arrived in St. Louis, Missouri, with five hundred dollars, a wife, and a vocabulary of about thirty words of broken English. He acquired a lease on a rooming house, which accommodated thirty guests. Again he worked night and day. His wife did the laundry, cleaned the rooms, and made the beds; Uncle Koppel carried the baggage, roomed the guests, kept the accounts, carried the coal, made the hot water, and told his guests that he was an employee so that he could also run all their errands. The St. Louis Fair was a success, and so was Koppel Berger. After two years, he and his wife and infant son returned to New York with a little over eight thousand dollars.

Up on Broadway at 38th Street was the old Hotel Normandie, which was not doing so well under the management of the great prize fighter, the original Kid McCoy (Norman Selby).

With a vocabulary of about seventy-five words of broken English, Uncle Koppel took over the lease on this 250-room hotel in the heart of the theatrical district. Of course, even a genius must have some luck, too, and we must concede that Koppel Berger acquired the Hotel Normandie at exactly the right moment. New York and America were becoming "hotel-minded"; in addition, the theatre was entering upon its greatest era, a "golden age" such as we shall never see again. Between 1907 and 1927, there were literally hundreds and hundreds of road shows and stock companies; burlesque was in all its glory; dozens of opera "extravaganzas" were playing all over the country; vaudeville was at its all-time peak; and on Broadway itself, there were at least one hundred and fifty attractions produced each year.

In those days, "actors" and "actresses" were not particularly welcome at the best hotels. In fact, many New Yorkers will remember the signs on some small hotels and rooming houses, "Actors Accommodated."

In various stages of their careers, Uncle Koppel's Hotel Normandie was "home" to such players as Nat Wills, Wilton Lackaye, Cissie Loftus, Grant Mitchell, Lionel and John Barrymore, Otto Kruger, Doc Rockwell, W. C. Fields, Julian Eltinge, Tully Marshall, Tyrone Power, Sr., Dustin Farnum, Marie Cahill, and, of course, hundreds of lesser-known personalities. They had fun with Koppel Berger. They mimicked his accent; they made jokes of his hotel from the vaudeville stage; and they played tricks on the live fish he had swimming in a bathtub every Friday. Mike Jacobs, too, got started at the Hotel Normandie under Uncle Koppel. The man who later controlled the champion, Joe Louis, as well as the "prize-fight" business itself, started with a small ticket stand at the hotel, and the first time I ever saw Mike, he was sliding down the lobby bannister like a kid, with his brother Jake "catching" him. I used to go to the Normandie once a week after school. My older brother Jack was the night clerk, and my mother insisted that he have a "Jewish" meal every Friday night, so I took the Broadway streetcar to 38th Street, carrying a large carton which included a pot of chicken soup, gefilte fish, horseradish, boiled chicken, and "tsimmiss." My mother had arranged with the chef at old Offer's Restaurant to let me use his stove to get the stuff hot again. It was quite a Friday afternoon, all around.

My brother, who later acquired some hotels of his own, coined the phrase about "sleeping on the sign." A guest came in and was told that the only room available would cost $2.50. The guest said, "You've got $1.50 on the sign," and my brother told him, "Try and sleep on the sign."

Most of the one million dollars Uncle Koppel made in the Hotel Normandie came during World War I, when he put dozens of cots in the lobby and in the upstairs hallways, to take care of the tremendous influx of job-seekers and servicemen. The elevator in the Normandie was the old cable variety, with the operator sitting in a swivel chair and pulling the cable up and down.

One night Uncle Koppel rented the swivel chair to a guest who had to get a few hours' sleep.

During this fabulous era of profits at the Normandie, Uncle Koppel was acquiring other hotels—the old Calvert, the Nassau, the Aberdeen, the Riviera in Newark; and, finally, the famous old Martinique Hotel at the intersection of Broadway and Sixth Avenue.

On the day that Koppel Berger took possession of the Martinique, he stopped talking Yiddish. No one will ever know why he stopped talking Yiddish, or how he expected to get along on a vocabulary of about one hundred and fifty words of broken English; but he saw it through to the bitter end. My mother tried to trap him many times into using a Yiddish word, but he never fell for the bait. Not only did he stop talking Yiddish, but he no longer "understood" it.

My mother would say something to him and he'd look at

her with big innocent eyes and motion to one of us in a help-less sort of way to act as an "interpreter." She would become exasperated, call to him in Yiddish, and when he turned to one of his "interpreters," she would rattle off a string of "klulas" (Yiddish curse words), each of which was a master-piece; but old Koppel Berger did not move a muscle or bat an eye. He simply smiled tolerantly, turned to one of us children and asked, "Vot did she set?"

As you would expect, Uncle Koppel liquidated the Hotel Normandie at the very "top." A year before the crash, he sold the hotel to a fellow (a Mr. Lefcourt), who couldn't wait to put up a forty-story building, but who met the ter-rible depression before he reached the twenty-fifth floor. In his last years, K. Berger retired to California, but he never stopped making money. At the age of eighty-three, he closed a deal for a large and profitable citrus business on the Coast.

With it all, I believe Uncle Koppel was a sentimental man. I remember while I was in high school, he once asked me to do some "writing work" for him. He took me down to the basement of the old Normandie Hotel where there was a mountain of baggage left by guests who had not paid the room rent in years past.

He wanted me to find the last known address of each, for an advertisement, as provided by law, before he could sell the stuff at auction. I looked over the vast number of suit-cases and trunks, and said, "Uncle Koppel, these actors sure took away a lot of money from you."

Koppel Berger gently patted an old battered trunk with a faded "Orpheum Circuit" imprint, and said, "These actors *gave* me a lot of money."

Marriages were made in heaven

THE shadkhan was an important member of the first-generation society which I knew as a boy.

The "outside" people whom the young immigrant met immediately after settling himself with his relatives were first, the fellow who sold him a gold watch and chain "so you'll become a real American," and then the Tammany Hall worker who advised him about night study classes "so you can become a citizen and vote"; and, finally, the shadkhan—the marriage broker.

Usually the shadkhan entered into the preliminary negotiations with the parents of the boy and girl, and in cases of a "single" boy, an orphan, or whose parents were still in Europe, the shadkhan dealt with an aunt or other relatives. After these initial discussions the parents of the girl told her of the negotiations and a formal meeting was arranged. The immediate reaction of the girl was based on an old East Side shadkhan joke: At the age of eighteen, she asks, "What does he look like?" At the age of twenty-five, she asks, "What does he do for a living?" And at the age of thirty, she asks, "Where is he?"

The shadkhan's biggest headache was the amateur competition. Everybody was a part-time shadkhan. The average housewife, with a million things to do for a family of a half-dozen children, always had a few irons in the fire with at least one shidduch (match) on tap for a niece, a nephew, or even a boarder.

But the professionals, too, started out on a part-time basis. This was not a business which offered an immediate return. The remuneration was based on a small fee in the early days of the negotiations, followed by a percentage of the dowry involved, payable on the evening of the wedding. The shadkhan could not depend upon this profession for a livelihood. Often it was a rabbi or a cantor who embarked on this career as a side line, as well as for its purely religious value: a mitzvah (a good deed added to the final reckoning). A part-time shadkhan I knew on my block operated a small cleaning-and-dyeing establishment. Eventually, his many successful matches gave him a good reputation and he branched out as a full-time shadkhan.

Eventually the shadkhan adopted certain symbols of his

office, namely, a beard, a derby hat, and an umbrella. No one
ever saw a shadkhan without an umbrella.

The umbrella was of tremendous importance to the immigrant people of the East Side. Folks bought an umbrella
even before they bought a pair of eyeglasses, for the umbrella was the symbol of urban middle-class life.

The shadkhan had no sense of humor at all. In the milieu
which practiced humor on a grand scale this fellow never
cracked a smile. There were many jokes about the shadkhan
and he was determined to do nothing that would add to the
hilarity. "This is no laughing matter." No matter how two
people are brought together, they will have the usual stormy
courtship: quarrels, breaking off the engagement, making up,
saying "goodbye forever," etc.

The great anxiety in a Jewish household was concerned
with marrying off the daughter, and the anxiety increased a
hundredfold for each additional daughter. And they had to
be married off in proper sequence according to their age, the
eldest first, and so on. The greatest fear of the family was
that the eldest would be "left"—spinsterhood. The idea that
a younger sister's marrying out of turn was bad luck for the
older girl was based on fact rather than superstition. The
word got around that the younger sister could no longer
wait; this meant the family had abandoned hope for the older
girl; therefore, there must be something wrong with her.

The whole operation required great tact. The first meeting
of the couple was usually a Friday evening Sabbath dinner at
the girl's home. Often the shadkhan came along, casual-like,
just an old friend of the family bringing along a young stranger to a Sabbath meal. No one gave the slightest indication
of what it was all about.

The younger children of school age were urged and bribed
to be on their good behavior. But now for the problem. The
younger sister who was PRETTY. The young man could very
well come to see the older sister but fall in love with the
younger one. The mother used tact. She began planning this
the previous Wednesday; "Rachel, this Friday night go to
spend the evening with your friend Naomi. I'll tell her

mother when I see her in the market tomorrow." The younger
sister had raised all kinds of hell for this very privilege many
times, but now she is hesitant; she wants to know *why*. She
knows why, of course, but before she is through, her mother
will have to spell it out to her, every detail. The younger
sister goes off to "hide" from her sister's fellow and she is
very happy about the whole thing. She is very happy about it
because she's a woman who has been told she is pretty.

At the inception of the shadkhan's activities, the mother
went into the details of her daughter's qualifications. She can
cook, sew, take care of children, and play the piano.

There were other virtues. "Mein Sarah is alle drei" (My
Sarah is all three). This meant that the girl had completed a
course in business school and was now—"ah stenographerinn,
ah bookkeeperinn, und a typewriterka." These Yiddish words
need no translation. It was a big thing on the East Side for
the girls to become "all three," and it makes me feel a little
sad when I think of the drive behind it; the saving, the
scrimping, the intensity, and the anxiety. Of course, when a
mother extolled her daughter with all these qualifications, it
meant one thing; that the girl was not what you would call
pretty. But the shadkhan listened politely—all the time waiting for takhlis, a wonderful word which means "goal," "purpose," "essence"—the dowry.

The dowry (nadan) was not a "gift." These are two separate words in Hebrew. Neither should this nadan, in cash
or real estate, be confused with the centuries-old custom in
Eastern lands of the purchase price in money or goods for a
wife. This nadan may or may not have been brought into
Europe by the Jews, but it has long been part of the culture
of the West. In fact, the nadan was a mark of *status;* and a
girl in France, Ireland, Spain, and Italy would tease her
friends if her parents had a larger dowry set aside for her.
Often the dowry was part of the marriage contract, even
when the bridegroom had not requested or expected it, or if
he had independent means of his own. This situation added
another English word to the Yiddish language. The word
was "millionaire," and was used indiscriminately for any boy

or man who made more than sixty dollars a week. "My Yetta is marrying a regular millionaire," said the mother to all her friends and neighbors. The use of this word became so widespread that it was modified eventually to "Jewish millionaire," which meant anyone worth $2,500 and up.

Basically the dowry was for the son-in-law so that he could continue to read or study the *Torah*—the Law—as free from financial care as possible. With the expansion of the commercial world, however, the purpose was extended to help the son-in-law get a start in some business. There is many a vast business enterprise in our country today which was started with a bride's dowry.

Since the negotiations involved many people—the two principals, the four parents, a few aunts, and the shadkhan—there were many areas of misunderstanding, perhaps even a bit of chicanery once in a while. A middle-aged widower calls on a widow. During the six or seven weeks of the courtship he has been her guest at the Friday evening Sabbath supper. On each of these Friday evenings, the widower sees the widow's little boy, a cute, curly-haired, eight-year-old child, and the widower grows very fond of the boy. Now could he suddenly break the spell of a pleasant evening and, out of a clear sky, ask, "Do you happen to have other children?" What kind of a stupid question is that? They are married and the day following, the widow's married sister brings over the other children, three little girls, probably. The widow smiles and says to her new husband: "Can you imagine such a thing, every Friday the three girls yell and holler that they want to visit their aunt, so what could I do?" The new-husband-widower listens to this tale as he watches the charming little boy joined by his three little sisters. If the guy has imagination and a sense of humor, he goes along and makes the best of it like a gentleman. But if he's a grubbe yung (ignoramus), he'll sue.

The philanthropists had set up a Jewish court on the East Side, still doing great work, which has saved the State of New York millions of dollars in court costs over a half century.

A groom may have misunderstood the terms of the dowry. The bride's parents may have promised to pay it in installments; the groom may have expected it all in one sum. There were all sorts of problems before the court. I examined the minutes of one such case tried in 1921. The wedding guests were all assembled and the bride looked lovely. The rabbi was there and so were the musicians and the caterers, but no groom. Finally a message came from the groom. It was addressed to the bride's father and later was read into the court records: "You'll not see me there tonight, you faker. You promised a dowry of two thousand dollars cash and I haven't received it." The poor man was staggered and had to make an embarrassing excuse to his two hundred guests. The proprietor of the hall demanded payment for his outlay for one hundred couples. The jeweler was there. He sold the ring to the bridegroom on credit. He immediately changed his status from guest to jeweler and wanted to know where he stood in the matter. During the hearing before the Jewish court, the bride's father testified that he had never promised a dowry of two thousand dollars. "My daughter," he said, "is known as the belle of Washington Heights, and the bridegroom is a window cleaner. Is it reasonable that I, the father of the belle of Washington Heights, would offer a window cleaner a dowry of two thousand dollars? For two thousand dollars I could get a doctor, a lawyer, or a whatnot." The bride's father was suing the family of the groom for one thousand dollars' damages for the wedding arrangements. The court tried a reconciliation between the two young people and when that failed, it decided against the bride's father, stating that "dowry was ordained by rabbis, and each man *must* give part of his property to his marriageable daughter." The court also ordered the bride to return the ring to the jeweler, because that man was an innocent bystander. The court further publicly reprimanded the shadkhan as incompetent.

Most of the litigation before that court today involves business disputes or domestic-relations complaints by litigants who want a quick decision or who cannot afford the legal expenses to see their matter through the State courts. There are not many dowry arguments today. The kids born in America have acquired great resourcefulness. They eased themselves into the American milieu with dances, proms, parties, socials, clubs, introductions, blind dates; and they bring home their own fellows.

Two-for-a-nickel movies

DURING the early days of the movies, there were the-atres on the Lower East Side where the price of admission was "two for a nickel." I went to two of these theatres regu-larly. One was called "The Gem," located on East Houston (*How*-ston) Street, and the other was "The Odeon," on Nor-folk or Suffolk Street. Once or twice a week, I'd get two cents and take up my stand in front of one of these movie houses. I was never alone. You could always count on at least five or six other kids standing in front of the house, each with two cents, joining in the singsong cry that went on with-out any interruption, "Who's got three? Who's got three?"

Suddenly, a "rich" kid would appear. We could spot him a block away. The kid with three cents always took his time. He was not to be rushed. Occasionally he knew one of the kids with two cents, and that ended everything. On other occasions we just took our chances. He would look us over. My chances were never too good, because I was always a fat kid. Occasionally when the theatre filled up, the ushers would go down the aisle and "double up"; make you sit two to a seat. Naturally it was to the advantage of the kid with three cents to pick a skinny partner in case this emergency arose. On numerous occasions, the owners of the theatre would come out (especially when it was cold), and it looked hopeless as far as the "three-centers" were concerned, and wave us in on a basis of "two for four cents."

When you entered the theatre, an usher gave you a "late check." It was the size of an ordinary 3 x 5 card with the words, "LATE CHECK" and the name of the theatre. This prevented you from seeing the show three and four times. At the end of one complete show, they picked up the late checks. This entitled you to sit through the entire show, until they picked up the late checks again. During the movie, and especially in the summer, a fellow would go up and down the aisle with a sprayer like a flit gun and pour some perfumed antiseptic stuff above the heads of the audience. Those aisles were always loaded with people, especially with the candy butchers selling peanuts, oranges, and crackerjacks. I never saw popcorn on the Lower East Side. That must have been a later innovation.

The movies themselves, of course, were terrific. John Bunny, Louise Fazenda, Mary Pickford, Ford Sterling, Bronco Billy Anderson, Fatty Arbuckle, and Charlie Chaplin. I am getting a little ahead of the story. These great stars came a little later. Before then, at the two-for-a-nickel movies, we had the "cowboys and Indians" feature, with the 7th Regiment "Calvary" always coming to the rescue of the burning fort. In the pit was the piano player, usually a college boy working his way through school. He would try desperately to fit the music to the action, and the music for the cowboys and the 7th Regiment "Calvary" became familiar to us all. Later an enterprising exhibitor experimented with "talking pictures." This was in a big movie house on Second Avenue. He had a man and a woman seated in a box above the floor audience using megaphones to speak the lines they thought were being spoken on the silent screen. It was a scream.

The passion of Morris Kaplan

EVERY Sunday morning Morris Kaplan, nineteen, took the Third Avenue El carrying a long pole and a heavy package, and disappeared from the East Side for the whole day.

He told his family and friends that he was "going fishing." Fishing? Who ever heard of a Jewish boy going fishing? The Jews bought fish for the Sabbath; but to catch fish? That was for the Italians, who were always catching eels, you should pardon the expression. But no one had ever heard of a Jewish boy "going fishing." Finally the rumor spread throughout the block that this long pole Morris carried every Sunday was nothing more than a blind; that he was actually going to church and becoming a convert to Christianity.

I do not know where this rumor started but anyway that was what everybody said; and poor Mrs. Kaplan, Morris' mother. The old woman could not speak or understand a word of English and there was misery in her eyes when her son said, "Mom, I'm going fishing." She used to plead with him, "Moishele, darling, stay home with your books; tell me, any fish you want, I'll buy it; if you like fish every day instead of only on Friday—tell me, please, darling, I'll make it; but give up what you're doing—don't desert your people."

Morris always smiled at this, and off he'd go every Sunday with that long pole and his heavy package. It was sad to see his mother. The other women would pointedly NOT mention anything. That was the standard rule. The most important phase of Jewish life was this Oriental custom of "face-saving." You never called attention to misfortune. If a family had a crippled child, or a boy who had gone bad, etiquette required that you never speak the words, "boy," "son," or "children" in front of the saddened family. Not only that, but the highborn and the well-bred would never mention their own good fortune for fear that the comparison would emphasize the pain of those "afflicted." For instance, if friends were visiting you and those friends had a wayward son or a crippled child, and your own son always stayed home and studied and had just won top honors at school, you might say, under interrogation, "Our son is all right, thank God, getting along—he refuses to do homework, and he stays out half the night, but let us hope that he turns out all right."

This was the condition with Morris and his "fishing." The other women no longer mentioned Morris or their own children to Mrs. Kaplan: just "How do you do, Mrs. Kaplan?" And after she had gone out of the store, all the women shook their heads—"What a pity, the poor, poor woman."

Morris Kaplan? Every Sunday the guy went to a place called Classon Point, and there he spread his lunch and sat all day—FISHING—and committing to memory Plutarch's *Lives*. But like all pioneers, he and his mother paid a price for "heresy."

The Fifth Avenue Bus— and America

I REMEMBER how often some of us walked out of the darkness of the Lower East Side and into the brilliant sunlight of Washington Square with its magnificent arch designed by Stanford White and dedicated to the founder of our country. This was the starting point of the Fifth Avenue Bus, in the days of the "open top," and for a dime you were treated to the best tour in all the history of travel.

Incidentally, this Fifth Avenue Bus business was the IRISH enterprise to end all Irish enterprise. Everybody from the front office down to the fellow who washed the buses was Irish. Colonel Mangin, one of their head men, took most of his men right into the famous "Fighting 69th" of Father Duffy fame, and after World War I, he went back into the front office and his men went back on the buses. It was no coincidence that the buses were painted green; that they literally flew past St. Thomas Episcopal Church and the

Brick Presbyterian Church, but took it very slow and easy
as they passed St. Patrick's Cathedral.

The most interesting sights to see were, of course, the
homes of the famous millionaires. These mansions were already beginning to make room for business establishments,
but the Astor mansion did not disappear until the twenties,
and neither did the Wendell home, which had an alley on
Fifth Avenue. The Wendell sisters kept it for their cats.
The mansions continued along the Avenue one after the
other, up into the nineties, where stood the Scottish castle
of Andrew Carnegie, with its square block of wrought-iron
fence.

Of special interest to boys from the Lower East Side were,
of course, the mansions of the Jewish tycoons. We took a
special pride in them and made it our business to identify
them properly. The first one on the trip was the home of
Joseph Pulitzer, and someone was always certain to whisper:
"He's a Christian now." But there was a feeling of intimacy
between us and the homes of the Strauses, Warburgs, and
Jacob H. Schiff. These men were well-known on the Lower
East Side through their philanthropy and projects to help
the immigrants. I'd look at the Schiff home and often wonder how things went on inside. Today Schiff's granddaughter,
Dorothy Schiff, publishes the New York *Post*, the leading
labor-liberal daily in America. This is further evidence
that America's true national anthem was the tune Cornwallis' fifes played so prophetically at Yorktown, "And the
World Turned Upside Down."

We must not lose sight of the other magnificent structures
on this Fifth Avenue Bus tour. There was Temple Emanu-
El on 43rd Street. It was a Moorish-type synagogue and
lovers of art and architecture from all over the country made
it one of the sights in New York that had to be seen. Before
I knew anything about Temple Emanu-El I was working as
an errand boy, part time, for a classy fur establishment on
Fifth Avenue at 37th Street. One afternoon I had too
many deliveries to make. I had one box left and it was already getting dark. It was the eve of Yom Kippur, the holiest

day in the Jewish calendar. The fur establishment was already closed, and anyway I was too far uptown to make any further stops at all. The only thing I could think to do was take the box home and deliver it after sundown the following day. Later I realized that maybe I should have phoned the customer and explained the situation, but who made telephone calls in those days? A telephone call was only when someone died, God forbid. I had told my superior, Mrs. Ferguson, about the Jewish holiday and I figured she would put two and two together about the last delivery. However, it seems that the customer called early in the morning and wanted to know what had happened to her fur coat.

Mrs. Ferguson was frantic. She wanted that coat delivered as quickly as possible; but she was also a great hacham (philosopher). She figured it all out. Since this was a Jewish holiday, where would a Jew be on a Jewish holiday? In Temple Emanu-El, of course. So Mrs. Ferguson went up Fifth Avenue to Temple Emanu-El and waited for me to come out with Jacob Schiff, Felix Warburg, Oscar Straus, and Herbert Lehman. At this time in my life Temple Emanu-El on Fifth Avenue was legend. We had heard vague rumors on the East Side that there was a big temple somewhere uptown where fancy Jews sat without hats and listened to an organ, but few of us really believed this.

I delivered the fur coat the following night and I hate like the devil to add anything to this story but, so help me, the customer was Mrs. Frank Vanderlip, the wife of the bank president. I remember her beautiful face and kind heart to this very day. It turned out that she had made only one phone call and when Mrs. Ferguson told her that it was a Jewish holiday, Mrs. Vanderlip understood.

I had the pleasure of seeing President Woodrow Wilson on one of my Fifth Avenue Bus trips. It was a Saturday afternoon and, suddenly, there he was. The bus proceeded very slowly, as quite a crowd was beginning to follow the President, and as the men who passed him tipped their hats, Mr. Wilson also lifted his own high silk hat each and every time. Behind him were two, or maybe more, Secret Service men. He went into Scribner's Book Store while the crowd continued to gather outside and the bus went on its way. It's funny how you remember every little detail about an event of that kind. I also remember how we kids from the East Side (where *bread* was a daily problem) would laugh uproariously at the "funny" clothes of the folks coming out of such places as the Savoy or Plaza hotels. The one privilege the poor kept for themselves was the right to laugh at the rich. Once as we passed that magnificent St. Patrick's Cathedral with its wide-open doors I was fascinated and prevailed upon my buddy, Moe Yasser (who is a manufacturer today up on West 29th Street), to go inside with me to see how it all was in there. We sat down and just kept looking at the wonders of the interior. When we returned to the East Side we told about our experience to an older boy—a smart aleck—who, with a look of horror on his face, told us that we were now Christians. Moe and I walked around the block three or four times, nervous, wondering what to do.

Eventually we agreed that I should tell my father and see what would happen. My father stroked his beard in deep thought for a moment, but apparently he couldn't contain himself, and soon burst into laughter.

The greenhorns slept on the "lunch"

It wasn't until I got into the sixth grade that I learned that the correct pronunciation was "lounge." My mother called it a "lunch." Everybody's mother called it a "lunch."

When the immigrants went to buy furniture, and the salesman said "lounge," the closest the immigrants could come to it was "lunch," and "lunch" it remained for one whole generation.

The "lunch" was a very popular piece of furniture. Some

households had two, even three. A wonderful makeshift bed in homes where sleeping space was at such a premium. "Go sleep on the lunch." I heard that many times.

The "lunch" was six feet long and two feet wide and upholstered in black imitation leather. No sides, just an abrupt incline as the headrest. You could park a whole flock of children on the "lunch" when the household was loaded down with guest aunts, uncles, or newly arrived relatives from Europe who needed a few weeks' board till they found places of their own. In such cases four children could sleep on one "lunch" with little fuss and a minimum of bed clothing. The four kids slept tzu kopfinns, that is, the younger kids with their heads toward the foot of the "lunch" and the two older children using the headrest.

The "lunch" was in the front room, or in the dining room, maybe even in the kitchen. I have seen some "lunches" in the hallway. It was used often for boarders. However, only the newly arrived greenhorn boarder slept on the "lunch." As soon as he found a job in the New World, he moved into a room with a regular bed.

The Jews "invented" psychiatry and most of the practitioners today are Jews. It is no coincidence therefore that psychiatry took this East Side "lunch" and made it into the symbol of their profession—the psychiatrist's "couch." Ah, what stories that "lunch" could tell, if it could only talk.

The boarder occupied a unique and important position in the immigrant culture. He had come from a ghetto of Eastern Europe with all its closely knit family ties and he tried desperately to continue living on the only terms he understood—as a member of a Jewish household. After a while he ceased being a stranger. He even had the authority to whip the children of the household for some infraction, without the slightest infringement of the proprieties. Wherever the family went, they took the boarder. He knew all the ins and outs of the family, their problems, their relatives, and he shared all their joys and sorrows. Often when the husband and wife had an argument, the boarder stepped in to settle it, and each member of the household—

husband, wife, and children—felt free to "pour their hearts out" to the boarder. Of course, many families with a marriageable daughter picked their boarder with the idea of making him a son-in-law, and before they gave the guy a room they wanted to know "who" he was, what town in Europe he had come from, what he did for a living, and how much "learning" his father had. The boarder rarely thought of the marriageable girl in the household in terms of sex. Both sides would have lost face. He knew that if he asked the girl to go out with him two or three times, it meant only one thing—marriage. Often a boarder would take the girl out only once—maybe to the free concert in Central Park or a picnic on Sunday in Van Cortlandt Park—and if he decided that he did not care to pursue the relationship for fear it would lead to marriage, he moved out and became a boarder in another home. If he had remained in the household and did not ask the girl to go out a second time, the whole family would have lost face. He understood the importance of this and so he moved, usually with a good excuse to add to the family's face-saving, like, "My uncle in Chicago wants me to come immediately."

This was important because in those days the female world was divided into two clearly defined classifications—"good" girls and "bad" girls. And all the "bad" girls were in the red-light district, and that's all there was to it. The adult males in general thought of premarital (or extramarital) sex *only* in terms of the professionals—in the brothels. Rarely if ever did they associate sex with "good" girls. The relationship between the boarder and the brothel was in terms of a "necessary detail" in his everyday life. It may be correct to say that it was a thoroughly wholesome relationship. He didn't joke about it or discuss it. He did not care to talk with the brothel girls or know anything about them at all. To him it was a necessary biological function, like going to the public baths once a week, and the quicker he got through with it the quicker he'd be able to get to the lecture at the settlement house or to his union meeting. When the preachers finally won their battle and destroyed the legally established brothel, the whole thing was thrown wide open on an "amateur" basis.

It is all a very wonderful study—the boarder in the immigrant culture. In our home we had a succession of boarders, but the ones I remember best were two young female boarders, two handsome apple-cheeked girls, fresh from Galicia. Ah, if I had only been eighteen instead of eight!

The "suckers" escaped

LET me tell you about the Bowery for a minute. There were clothing stores one after the other on a stretch of two or three blocks. They all looked alike. When an immigrant went in to one of these establishments, the first thing they asked him to do was take his pants off, to try on a new suit. The fellow never saw his pants again, unless he made a purchase.

If the new suit was not to his liking as to quality, fit, or price, his pants were nowhere in sight. Everybody looked, but no pants. The favorite hiding place was the empty fire bucket which they kept near the fitting mirror. Sometimes the fire bucket wasn't empty. What to do? The guy couldn't go out of the store without pants, so he made the purchase. After he paid his money and was already wearing the new suit, the stock boy (usually the boss) came running with the pants, "Well, what do you know, they were here under these suits all the time."

Another trick was the "money-in-the-pocket" gimmick. A fellow came in to buy a suit, and they brought one out approximately his size. The salesman said, "A fellow just your size bought this suit yesterday but brought it back because his wife didn't like the color—we can give you a special bargain on this, three dollars off from the regular," and they quoted him an outlandishly high figure. The fellow said, "That's too high for me; show me something cheaper," but the salesman insisted, "Just try it on, that's all."

They had planned this story about a customer having had the suit overnight because in one of the side pockets of the coat they planted a wallet, a thick one, filled with stage money and with one real dollar bill sticking out. The customer felt the wallet in his pocket and immediately the blood rushed to his head. He fingered the treasure, and the salesman turned his back for a moment to give the sucker an opportunity to peek and see that green dollar bill.

The customer then said, "Good—fits me like a glove." The salesman said, "How about the pants?" and the customer said, "I'll take this suit—don't bother about the pants, just wrap up my old coat with the new pants. I want to get used to my new coat." He wanted to get out of there as fast as possible, his heart pounding every second. The customer then paid his twenty-eight dollars for a twelve-dollar suit and ran to the first saloon on the block, to open that wallet with somewhat less than enthusiastic results.

Another trick was to give the customer the suit at "his" price. The salesman said twenty-two dollars, the customer said fifteen, and the salesman said "Sold."

No matter what he offered, they gave him the suit. But, when they wrapped it, they always left out of the package either the pants or the vest. When the fellow got home and saw that a piece of the suit was missing, he ran back to the store, but was told, "Not here; you didn't buy that suit here, but if you need anything like a pair of pants or a vest, we can match any coat." After going to two or three other stores, he finally came back and "matched" his coat to a pair of pants for ten dollars.

These places did not last long, although they caused plenty of damage among the immigrants. Soon the settlement workers began to educate the people and clamor for protection and ordinances and new cops on the beat. Mayor Gaynor moved in on them and made them get a city license, and Jewish philanthropists set up the Legal Aid Society (nonsectarian) where a man, without fee or expense of any kind, could file a complaint and secure relief.

In the end the "suckers" went up and up, and eventually entered the American middle class; while the wise guys who trimmed them died of tuberculosis on Welfare Island, or spent most of their adult years in Sing Sing.

Little girls on the East Side

FROM the time the little girl was eight or nine years old there were few secrets of life which she did not know, but it was a sort of wholesome understanding. She was not "precocious" as we have come to understand the term, and she never expressed her "knowledge" except on rare occasions and only in the most intimate conversations with her mother. She had an amazing balance and sense of values. The little girl would never discuss "those things" with other little girls. Among themselves the little girls played jacks, and jumped rope. It was a wholesome "maturity" which had developed from a wholesome family culture and religion. At the age of nine the Jewish girl became a sort of junior mother. There was always a baby to take care of, and in thousands of homes when the baby cried, the little sister went to the child in the middle of the night. Hundreds of men who grew up on the East Side will recall the little girls playing "potsy" in the street but keeping an eye peeled on "the bundle"— her baby brother or baby sister. She deposited the bundle on the stoop of the tenement or up against the building. But no fear, the baby was not in any danger.

The little girl was not "taught" in the strictest sense of the word. She was told to watch and learn by doing; and after school she spent hours with her mother in the kitchen and they would talk—women's talk, you can be sure, as they went about their duties of preparing supper or preparing for the Sabbath. The little girl even learned how to eat like her

mother, sitting on the very edge of the chair. How many
times in the lifetime of a Jewish mother did she actually lean
back in her chair? I cannot recall more than perhaps once
or twice a year, maybe when she was convalescing from illness, and the family would say, "Sit still, Mama; you sit
still." And this sitting on the edge of the chair was not forced
upon her, not at all. Everyone sensed that it was part of her
life—her pleasure, if you please.

But soon the little girl came into her own. The endless
ceremonies and observances involving her brothers now were
at an end, and she herself reached the age when she came in
for some attention—she was kaleh moyd, a prospective bride.
This came after she reached the age of seventeen or eighteen.
Up to now she had been left out of nearly everything. She
watched the fuss made over her brother when he first entered Hebrew school, and later when he was bar-mitzvahed,
but it only seemed as though she had been left out. She
understood that she was not only a participant but that none
of this could have happened without her.

And to her the boy, no matter how much older he became, was always the "baby brother." And this lasted all
through life. We have all known Jewish women who have
said, "I'd like you to meet my baby brother—we expect him
any minute," and soon a bald-headed guy comes in who has
a potbelly, and the woman who was once "the little girl"
stands there with pride in her eyes and in her heart the
nostalgia of the once "little bundle."

The Triangle fire

THE Lower East Side had been plunged in sorrow.
It was one tragedy after another, and all of them within
a period of four or five years. There was a disastrous fire
on Allen Street. The Second Avenue elevated structure

practically touched the tenement buildings on both sides of Allen Street, and it was known as "the street where the sun never shines." Ten or twelve families—recently arrived in the Golden Land—were burned to death in a fire-trap tenement. There were the *Titanic* disaster with the loss of the great friend of the East Side, Mr. Straus; the terrible Mendel Beilis case in Czarist Russia at about the same time as the Leo M. Frank case in Atlanta, Georgia; and the worst tragedy of all—the Triangle fire.

The Triangle Shirtwaist Factory occupied the sixth, seventh, eighth, and ninth floors of the ten-story Asch Building on Washington Place near Greene Street. As you made the turn from the front entrance of the building you came into full view of the magnificent Washington Square where America's *Champs Elysées*, Fifth Avenue, begins. In those days the foreign consuls lived in those beautiful red-brick Colonial homes on the north side of the Square. I remember how some of us kids, fascinated by the foreign flags flying from the windows of these homes, tried to identify the less familiar standards.

The Triangle factory manufactured shirtwaists. I may be completely off the beam on this, but it seems to me that the shirtwaist was the same thing the girls now call a "blouse," and it was probably in more general use in 1911, or so it seemed anyway. The factory had about six hundred employees—95 per cent of them girls—needleworkers, operators, finishers, buttonhole makers. They worked nine and a half hours a day, six days a week, and their pay, based on a quota of completed operations (piecework) averaged $15.40 a week. For the six hundred girls there were five restrooms, if they could call them that.

With the tolerance that comes with years, I will not say that Mr. Harris and Mr. Blank, the Triangle employers, were evil men. To dehumanize anyone or any group would be the same process which we have fought against for so many centuries. Neither did they "invent" this business of timing the girls when they went to the toilet. It was done in many of the mills of the South, as well as over in England in the factories of Manchester and Leeds. The brutal employer mores of 1911 were the result of stupidity rather than greed. Both Harris and Blank were Jews, and the girls who died were Jews. If it teaches us nothing else at least we know that we must never talk in terms of "class," "racial traits," or "mass guilt."

It was just that Harris and Blank and all the others did not yet know to what uses industrialization could be put for benefit to *themselves*. It took folks like Sam Gompers, Abe Cahan, Lillian Wald, Frances Perkins, Rose Schneiderman, Reverend John Howard Melish, and a few Yiddish-speaking intellectuals and Christian clergymen to teach them. When I see a millworker in North Carolina going to work in an automobile, owning his home and TV set, I think—how much of all this do you owe to those "foreigners," and how lucky you and your children are that there was no McCarran-Walter Immigration Act in the year 1895.

The male sweatshop employees worked on pants, knee pants, and ladies' cloaks and suits. Workingmen bought pants in those days rather than suits, and it was a very big business. Let us not lose sight of the fact that many employers were also living from hand to mouth. The small capitalist was up against a competition which he could not even begin to combat until the trade union did it for him. This was the system of contractors.

A man set up a sewing shop in his tenement home. His mother, father, wife, son, and daughters pitched in. No rent and no payroll. He made a little living for his family, but he helped create an industrial jungle. The social workers, and the others I have mentioned, fought for legislation and finally made it a crime to operate a factory in a home. Eventually the union began to monitor the competition and establish order out of a chaotic condition. Paradoxically they gave the capitalist the only protection he had ever known—and they also made him rich. The six hundred girls in the Triangle factory were, after all, human beings, young girls with ambitions, hopes, vanities, and dreams. Today they spend more for lipstick than they spent on their entire wardrobe in the year 1911; which is a wonderful thing, and may it get better and better forever.

In 1911 the knee-pants operator usually owned his own sewing machine. My mother also worked on a machine at home, and it seems to me that the collector for the Singer Sewing Machine never stopped coming. Did these people ever keep track of how much they paid? The Singer Sewing Machine collector was a contemporary who grew old with the rest of the family. The Yiddish papers carried advertisements, "knee-pants operators wanted, your own machine." It was piecework, of course, as well as seasonal, and the operator carried the machine on his back. The employer supplied the stand for the machine and the cloth. Since his pay was based on his production, it was to his advantage to start early, especially in the winter. He could not turn the frozen wheel on the sewing machine until the loft was warm. Thus often before sunrise you could see a knee-pants operator gathering kindling as he walked along the street with the sewing machine held on his back by two leather straps.

It was March 25, 1911, at 4:45 P.M. The six hundred girls working in the Triangle Shirtwaist Factory still had more than an hour to go, but the few male employees—cutters, foremen, designers—were laying out the cotton and crepe-de-Chine fabrics on huge cutting tables for the Sunday work. This was the busy season. One man on the way to the toilet lit his cigarette before he got there. The match fell on the floor and some cuttings caught fire. It did not appear too serious for the moment. Several of the men ran into the hallway and grabbed the fire hose from the standpipe.

As they ran back to the flame, the hose rotted in their hands at each of the places where it had been folded. In desperation they tried to flood the place from the standpipe but found that they could not turn the valve. One of the long tables had been used for cleaning and was saturated with highly inflammable cleaning fluids and chemicals. In another minute a sheet of flame was pouring out of the eighth-floor window. The girls were now panic-stricken. In those days they wore their hair long and many of the less hysterical girls ran to the wash stand and covered their heads with wet cloths and garments.

A few were able to reach the fire escape and go up the roof to safety across another building, but soon the whole front of the factory was a sheet of flame. The elevator man fled in panic, but a passer-by ran into the elevator and made trip after trip, thirty girls at a time. He brought two hundred girls down to the street until the elevator shaft itself was ablaze. Some of the girls tried to slide down the elevator cables. They found nineteen bodies on top of the elevator cab.

From the ninth floor three girls huddled together and jumped into the firemen's net. They died instantly, pulling the firemen into the shattered net. They said that three girls jumping, arm in arm, from a ninth floor were equivalent to a solid mass of fourteen tons when they hit the net. The girls who could not reach the windows ran toward the rear exit door and they found it locked.

There was testimony later that there had been some pilfering and so an hour before quitting time the employers had usually sealed up the rear exit so the girls could stand inspection as they walked out the front door. The girls pulled at that heavy iron door but they were soon overcome by smoke and flame. Thirty-four bodies were found piled up in front of that tragic "exit."

In all, 146 girls died, and nearly 100,000 East Side inhabitants followed the funeral procession. They were all buried in a single grave provided by the Arbeiter Ring (Workmen's Circle).

The mourning gave way to public outrage. Mr. Harris and Mr. Blank were indicted for manslaughter. The prosecutor felt that his best case rested on that locked exit door and he had several witnesses from among the survivors. The defendants denied that the door was locked and claimed that only the panic of the girls pushing against the door prevented it from being opened.

But their real defense was Max D. Steuer. Mr. Steuer did

not spend much time during his career fighting for causes like Clarence Darrow. He was a man hired to perform the service for which he was trained—and when you hired Steuer to defend you, you had the best in this world. When he addressed a jury the courtroom was filled with fellow lawyers, sociologists, editors, and the judges who were not holding court that day. At every Democratic National Convention someone was sure to call for the polling of the Tammany Hall delegation (New York County), and as the recorder came to the name Max D. Steuer, delegates from all over the country, especially the lawyers, stood up to get a look at this fellow who was five feet four inches tall, thin, and spry as a jockey. His list of clients and their affairs would present us with a valuable study of our times, our mores, our triumphs and foibles—a sociological report running the gamut from stock exchange to boudoir, from art gallery to brothel.

In the Triangle case the leading witness for the prosecution was Katie Schwartz. She had seen her friends trapped in front of the door. She had covered herself with a coat which she had soaked in water and somehow got out. She told her story and there was hardly a dry eye in the courtroom. This was damaging testimony. If Steuer's clients were to be saved, Katie had to be discredited somehow. Steuer walked toward the witness chair and in a soft voice said, "Katie, just tell your story again. Speak right up, girl, so the jury can hear you." Again the girl told her damaging story, and again the jury scowled at Steuer's clients.

Steuer said, "Katie, didn't you leave out two words this time?" Katie thought a moment and said, "Yes, sir, I left out two words." "Well," said Steuer, "tell us the story again and please put back those two words." During the third recital it began to appear to everyone, of course, that the girl had been rehearsed in her testimony and had committed it to memory. Thus, Steuer, without saying an unkind word to Katie, turned a dangerous witness into one whose testimony resulted in the acquittal of Mr. Harris and Mr. Blank.

But it was far from defeat. Not this time. As a matter of fact, the acquittal actually helped to arouse the people

further to the terrible problem, and out of the tragedy of
the Triangle fire and the 146 girls who died came fire-
prevention legislation, factory-building inspections, workmen's
compensation, liability insurance, and the International Ladies'
Garment Workers' Union.

The scaleman

WHEN I weigh myself I do not look at the results. I
just listen to the gears grind and, when everything quiets
down, I simply step off the scales and walk away. By this
system I have won the battle, leaving the machine frustrated,
if not useless. I was always a fat kid and once when I complained about it my mother said, "Nothing at all to worry
about; in America the fat man is always the boss and the
skinny man is always the bookkeeper."

On the Lower East Side many young men made money
weighing people. The machine was a shiny contraption
about five feet high and on wheels, of course. The fee was
two cents and Saturday was a big night. But a lot depended
on the personality of the young man. Only a good-looking
chap could make a go of it. The trick was for him to get
a bunch of girls giggling. Pretty soon they'd all come troop-
ing, one by one, and pay their fee of two cents, with a crowd
of kids forming a circle and having fun. Can you imagine
kids being amused by such goings-on today? Sometimes a
more enterprising scale fellow would charge five cents "if
I guess your weight within three pounds and *free* if I miss."
This fellow did an even bigger business and the circle around
his operation included adults as well as the kids. It was a
spectator's sport and again much depended on the personality
of the scaleman, as we called him. When the customer was
a male, the scaleman would feel the biceps, and then reach
down and have a feel of the fellow's thighs and sort of pat

him all around. He went out of his way in thoroughly feeling the fellow, which heightened the tension when a woman was the next one to step up to the scales. The spectators would oh and ah and maybe even scream for joy; the girls would giggle all over the place as the fellow made various motions as if to go through the same feeling operation. But it was all acting. The spectators "dared" him and shouted encouragement but, of course, in the end the fellow did no such thing. He merely sized up the girl or woman and made his guess. He was amazingly accurate, of course, but it was really not such a trick for a man who had weighed thousands of people. However, the big thing was the byplay, the personality, and the acting of the scaleman. We have a relative who financed himself through law school pushing a scale on the East Side. His fees are much more than two cents today.

It must be remembered that this weight business could operate on such an uninhibited scale only in a society where people boasted of putting on poundage. "We found a wonderful place in the mountains; I put on five pounds in a week," women told each other. Many girls padded themselves to look heavier, and women practiced sitting postures to simulate a double chin. The first question your family and friends asked you when you returned from a vacation was, "How much did you gain?"

Ess, ess, mein kindt

A few weeks ago I listened to an address by a psychiatrist. He said that when a mother pushes a spoonful of food into her baby's mouth, even before the previous spoonful had been swallowed, the mother really hates the child, or did not want the child. However, she is conscious of this sense of guilt and therefore becomes overzealous in her attempt to feed the child.

I cannot see it that way. I think the tremendous concern with food in the Jewish household, even to the overfeeding of the children, has nothing to do with guilt. I think it has had to do with survival—an association of food with strength and growth. Food and the refinements of food in the Jewish home were also the result of centuries of second-class citizenship. No matter how poor, how restricted his opportunities for a livelihood and citizenship, he could look forward to the Sabbath, its solemnity, its dignity; and the special food of the occasion more than compensated him for the unrelieved hostility he met the moment he stepped out of the door.

Essentially, the Jewish religion centered around the home—the family—the table in the dining room.

The first English words most of the Jewish immigrants learned were: "Take something in the mouth," translated literally from the Yiddish. The minute that door opened it did not matter whether it was a guest, relative, child, or stranger, the first word was *"Eat"*—"take something in the mouth." And I remember in my own home there'd be many arguments about it. My mother would bring the platters immediately, "Eat, eat," and maybe the guy said he wasn't hungry and didn't feel like eating. Then my father would become exasperated and say, "Leave him alone, he doesn't want to eat," and then there'd be an argument and the noneating guest had to step in as peacemaker, but there was only one way he could restore order—"All right, all right, I'm eating, look, I'm eating already."

Trying to gain a foothold on America was not easy. Life in the sweatshops, at the pushcarts, and peddling with a pack on your back was hard work, but everybody had to eat. On Sunday mornings the tables literally swayed under the weight of the food.

I receive many sentimental letters from men and women who were raised on the East Side, and I believe it is more than nostalgia. There was a deep sense of security because of two things: (a) You were not exposed to anti-Semitic experience (except when you wandered off to Little Italy or Hell's Kitchen), and (b) the family tie was very strong. All life centered around the dining-room table, where all the decisions were made and all the religious services conducted. You even withheld news of joy or sorrow until the entire family was grouped around the table. That is why there is such strong sentiment for the East Side, even though there was no money and you worked sixty-six hours a week.

Of course, when you speak of the food, you are bound to run into "the higher criticism" (the Egyptians had monotheism, and the Hindus had the Flood, etc.), and the same is true of Jewish food. "There's no 'Jewish' food, it is Slavic, Roumanian, German, etc."—but by the same token there is *nothing*, not even an American Declaration of Independence. I have no doubt at all that Mr. Jefferson knew about the Magna Carta, and John Locke's constitutions, and the writings of Jean Jacques Rousseau. Jefferson merely breathed life into clay just as the Hebrews, from that borderline where fable ceases and history hardly begins, brought to the world its knowledge of the One True and Everliving God. The "higher criticism" fellows like to chop off the head of every creative man they know, and they spend their lives hoping that "someone else" had written the great man's speeches and that "someone else" had written the great man's plays.

The same thing applies to Jewish food, and Arnold Toynbee would be shocked to hear that no one ever heard of Syrian pickles or Syric rye bread, especially with chopped chicken liver.

And after the chopped chicken liver comes a nice bowl of soup with mondlinn, each mondl as crisp and brown as a nut. What a treat it was to watch your mother make the khaleh, the Sabbath twist loaf, painting the "varnish" on it with a feather with the artistry of a Leonardo da Vinci. And when you speak of kreplach you should think only in terms of Mozart and Shakespeare—those neat, thin puffs of dough which she properly wrapped around spiced chopped beef and after boiling, reverently dropped them one by one into the golden chicken soup. And potato latkes, pancakes fit for a king; and those Passover dishes, the fried matzos and all the other wonderful things. Of course, I do not wish to slight the regular workaday meal, like a good piece of boiled flanken with horseradish and rye bread. This is the dish Jupiter and Juno used to enjoy on Mount Olympus during the days of the Roman Gods. They learned the secret from a few Jewish women, perfume-makers, who lived on the left bank of the Tiber in those days.

And this heritage came down to our Jewish mothers who never really lost the touch, because it concerns *food*, which essentially is the symbol of *tomorrow*. For the Jews it was always tomorrow, and that is why they thought and lived in terms of food. And that is why the very first words a Jewish child heard after birth were, "Ess, ess, mein kindt."

My mother and God

MY FATHER was an intellectual and our home was filled with talk. We are a vocal people to begin with, and it was not unusual for intellectuals to spend hours discussing the meaning of a single sentence in the Law, or for that matter, a single word. We are the greatest hairsplitters in the world. A pilpul is what they call these complicated discussions. But my father went far beyond the Biblical text. He was at home with Henry George, and Eugene V. Debs, and Benjamin Franklin, and the rationalists of the past. He conducted a sort of philosophy discussion group every Saturday afternoon. Five or six of the men would be gathered around the table and my mother was busy serving them. She walked on tiptoe not to disturb the great men, as she brought the platters of boiled potatoes or haiseh bubbes (chickpeas), and silently went her way. But there was always a trace of a smile on her face; if not cynical, certainly one of amusement.

My mother, I would say, was a primitive woman. She spoke only Yiddish. She could read the prayers out of the book but that was all. She spent all her time cooking, cleaning, sewing; sewing for the family as well as professionally for the neighbors. I think my intellectual father guessed at my mother's "amusement." I have had the feeling that he knew that she was not overly impressed. My mother, of course, thought all those discussions were nonsense. What does a person need but God? And she had God. Sometimes I smile at all the goings-on over the radio about God. Whose God are they talking about anyway—what do they know about God? My mother talked with God all the time, actual conversations. She would send you on an errand and as you were ready to dart off into the crowded, dangerous streets, she turned her face upward and said: "Now see that he's all right." She smiled at the boy, but was dead serious when she spoke to Him. She gave the impression that this was a matter-of-fact relationship, part of the covenant. "In the home that boy is my obligation but once he is out on the street, that is Your department and be sure to see to it." And she never permitted a single expression involving the future to be uttered without that covering clause, "With God's help." And this had to follow hard upon the original assertion. Thus if you ran down the hallway saying, "I'll go to the library tomorrow," she chased after you to make sure that there was no great lapse between your stated intention and the follow-up, "With God's help."

I do not know of any people *less* chauvinistic than the Jews. Just imagine if another race had produced the Ten Commandments, for instance. Think of the place that event would have held in history. But the Jews have always insisted that they had nothing to do with any of these wonderful things. God merely used them to establish His moral code among the peoples of the world. This idea influenced our entire history and every phase of our lives. If a dish happened to turn out well, do you think my mother would take credit for it? Not at all. She said it was an act of God. God helped her cook and sew and clean. And sometimes you have to wonder about it. I am thinking of Mother's potato latkes (pancakes) and holishkas (chopped beef and spices rolled in cabbage leaves and cooked in a sweet-and-sour raisin sauce) and kreplach (small portions of dough folded around chopped beef, boiled, and then dropped into a steaming hot platter of golden chicken soup), and I will say this, "If God did not really help her prepare those dishes (as she claimed), how is it that I haven't been able to find anything to equal them in all these years?" This is the kind of evidence that would even stand up in a court of law.

You paid fifty cents and
kissed the bride

THE immigrants on the Lower East Side of New York created happiness for themselves. There were parties galore —weddings, engagements, and bar mitzvahs among the Jews; festivals among the Italians; long and happy processions among the Poles; and lots of band music and beer among the Germans.

Everybody was smiling. Even McCarran would have felt good down there. Everybody belonged to societies, vereins, clubs, and fraternities. When a party was arranged, the whole organization was invited, as well as everybody from "the shop." The shop was the factory where some or all of the members of the family worked.

A Jewish woman gave birth to a boy and the celebrations went on and on. There must have been at least one hundred such events every Friday night. The proud father and his friends from the congregation would sing at the top of their voices; they had no reason to fear the police. In fact, most of the Irish cops learned to speak Yiddish and there was always some "rich" member of the party who treated the cop. The saloons in those days had what they called "the cop's bottle," which they kept hidden near the side Family Entrance for the uniformed men.

Elections were great events. Bonfires galore. On that day, the police turned their backs on these huge street bonfires, and crowds of boys roamed the streets for wood, lumber, and discarded furniture. Sometimes they took stuff which was not "discarded." Every saloonkeeper put a barrel of beer out on the sidewalks (if the Democrats won). Many "voters" would wait till the last minute to get the one or two dollars for their ballot. Up in the Uncle Sam Hotel on the Bowery, the bums were rounded up and as the reports came in— such and such a district needs about a hundred votes, etc. —the bums would be taken in a truck to the polling place, with a slip of paper with the name they were to use (invariably the name of someone who had died between registration and election day)—and thus they supplied the necessary majority.

The big social events, of course, were the weddings and the bar mitzvahs on Saturday and Sunday night. The music would blare forth from the halls hired for the occasion. There was always one big headache—the uninvited guests—gate-crashers by the dozens. Young men would gather in a group and say, "Let's go to a wedding," as casually as you now say, "Let's go to a movie." Getting in was not too difficult. You dressed up in your best clothes and picked the wedding or bar mitzvah that suited you best. They usually tried to hold down the vast number of gate-crashers by charging "hat check"; this was a fifty-cent or seventy-five-cent charge as you checked your hat or coat. Naturally, there was little supervision after that because the concessionaire collecting the hat-check fee would have been willing to let in the whole 7th Regiment. Many distraught hosts would keep looking at the entrance as the people kept pouring in, and still they came on. They danced, ate, kissed the bride, and had a good time. This was not too bad when the weddings or bar mitzvahs had what they called a "sweet table," just cakes and cookies; but the gate-crasher became a real problem when a full-course dinner was served as part of the event. It happened many times that seventy people would sit down to eat, while most of the invited guests were left out of it. It was a big problem which was eventually solved by hiring strong bouncers from the local Tammany club or poolroom.

One system the bouncers used was to challenge the guest as he arrived. They asked, "Whom do you know, the bride or the groom?" and when you took a guess and told them, they heaved you out—"Get the hell out of here—this is a bar mitzvah."

The rent

I wish I had a recording of the conversation between my mother and the landlord, Mr. Wallenstein. Mr. Wallenstein was a big broad man with a huge black beard and he had learned two English words: "The Rent." Twice a month he knocked on the door and my mother went to open it. The man never stepped across the threshold. My mother would say, "Hello, Mr. Wallenstein, how are you; how is your family?" Mr. Wallenstein got scared. Mr. Wallenstein always got scared when he got a big hello. A big hello was bad news, maybe an excuse that the rent was not available or something, so all through my mother's effusiveness, Mr. Wallenstein, without waiting for her to complete a sentence, kept repeating over and over again, "The rent, the rent," and when my mother said, "How about some tea, Mr. Wallenstein?" that really scared the daylights out of him, and he raised his voice, "The rent, the rent!" I wish I had a recording of that.

2,500 handsome Jewish policemen

IN 1912 a Jewish policeman in New York was unknown. Every cop was an Irishman. Later, the Germans joined, then the Poles and Italians.

Now, as I discovered upon inquiry during a recent trip to New York, there are twenty-five hundred Jewish policemen on the force.

I asked a high police official another question that has fascinated me for some time: "How come New York policemen are all such handsome men?"

Has anyone ever seen a homely cop in New York? I wanted to know whether this was an accident. My question: "Suppose a man passes all the examinations with flying colors, but he has buck teeth, or bulging eyes, or disfiguring marks on his skin, do you take him?" The officer said that I was the first one to ask that question, but he couldn't help himself; and, regaining his composure, he said, tactfully, that there are "preliminary examinations" to see if the man has an "aptitude" for the profession. So now we know why all the New York cops are such good-looking fellows.

Customers for the dry-goods store

ONE of the best advertising ideas for the dry-goods store was to open the cases of new merchandise on the sidewalk right in front of the main entrance. They say this idea was originated by A. T. Stewart (later John Wanamaker's), but most of the merchants on 14th Street and Broadway used it when I was selling newspapers around there; 1912-17.

The fanciest women would jump at the opportunity to buy a piece of goods right on the sidewalk, out of the packing case, and carry it off proudly without even having it wrapped. I guess curiosity played a part in this; the same instinct that makes men into sidewalk superintendents. The truck would come along with the new merchandise and they made a big to-do out of unpacking it on the street. The crowd of women would gather and watch the procedure like it was a parade, and dozens of them would follow the shipping clerks into the store. This was "fresh" merchandise. Many of these shipping cases were marked PARIS, FRANCE; ABERDEEN, SCOTLAND; etc.; but now I have my doubts about this phase of "operation sidewalk."

Eventually it became a serious traffic problem and the police stopped it.

This was clever merchandising, but later on some of the methods were not clever, just crude, if not actually dishonest. "SELLING AT COST"; "WE MUST HAVE CASH TO PAY FOR NEW SHIPMENTS AND THEREFORE WE MUST SACRIFICE EVERYTHING." Then there were the LEASE HAS EXPIRED sales. So a year later the guy was still there and said indignantly, "Can I help it if I was able to get the lease renewed?"

And, of course, the GOING OUT OF BUSINESS sales, until it was necessary to crack down on this gimmick by law.

Klein's famous dress shop on 14th Street and Fourth Avenue began a trend of mass-selling. They bought out whole factories of manufactured dresses and sold them for a few pennies' profit. Thousands of women stormed the place on the day they had dress sales at one dollar each. However, Klein's used a gimmick, too. They had at least one hundred and fifty employees, mostly girls and women, and they ordered these employees to report *one hour* before the opening of the store at 9 A.M., and "wait" outside the main entrance. Thousands of early-morning shoppers saw this huge crowd of waiting women and naturally thought something big was going on—and, of course, they joined the throng. And they would call up their friends: "You should see the crowd in front of Klein's—only eight o'clock—can you imagine?—they must know something—you better drop everything—let Beverly get the kids off to school—she's eight years old already; it's time she learned; rush right down here quick—before they open. . . ."

This little sex offender
went to market

I STILL remember the face of a guy who figured in one of those rare "incidents" of sexual trespass on the Lower East Side. He had a heavy, black beard but it was obvious, even to a ten-year-old, that the fellow was a fairly young man. He was lying in the vestibule of a tenement building and about thirty women were pelting him over the head with the contents of their market baskets. One woman was socking him with a freshly plucked chicken; and they were all jabbering like mad and cursing him with all the famous bon mots of the ghetto.

The women kept repeating the "charge" against the fellow, and I remember it well to this day, "Varfindick mit da hent." Which, translated, meant that this fellow walked along the sidewalk among the hundreds and hundreds of marketing housewives and "threw with his hands" in all directions so as to "feel" the women; and now the guy was pleading for mercy.

When I told my father about it, he said that it was hardly likely that the women made a mistake. On the contrary, the concerted action indicated that the fellow had made a habit of it, and that the women decided to put a stop to it once and for all.

When the cop on the beat finally arrived to quell the disturbance, the women told the culprit that they would not press charges if he confessed his guilt right then and there, in public. A strange proposal, but it was the greatest humil-

iation the man could possibly experience in his life. He
got up and began his confession, but one woman stopped
him short until he had recovered his hat. They wanted no
confession with an uncovered head. Finally the guy went on
his way, but one woman chased after him and socked him
with a bunch of carrots. Apparently she had not been able
to get her lick in when the guy was on the floor.

You couldn't beat this fellow

IN THE late spring and summer, the chess players took
their boards into the park after work and played until it got
dark. In some sections, an expert set up his table as a
business and played all comers, at so much per game—
I think it was a nickel. Sometimes he played two or three
opponents at once. There was one fellow in Seward Park
who became a tradition as a chess expert.

Chess players flocked to play at his bench because he was
a highly colorful character who kept up a rapid-fire conversation. He joked about every move and sang sonnets of
triumph every time he made a devastating move or trapped
his opponent's queen. He had a long, flowing beard and it
was not until many years later that it was discovered that
he used the beard to unfair advantage. His opponent would
be intense; watching the game, studying every piece on the
board, and thinking out his own next move, and he paid no
attention to the beard opposite him.

Finally, he would make a move, but the old gent would
start singing. He would lift his beard and hidden behind it
was—a castle—which he moved swiftly, and with amazing
results. As the opponent began to complain that he didn't
see the castle hidden behind the beard, the old gent would go
into one of his singsong sonnets of triumph, shouting "Next."

Four cents an hour

WHEN the reservoir was built in New York, the labor was imported from Ireland. Passage to America and return to Ireland was guaranteed, and the pay was four cents (4¢) an hour. Food, work clothes, and lodgings (tents) were also provided. They worked ten hours a day, six days a week. On Sundays, the Irish laborers were taken to famous Ulmer Park on the outskirts of the city where a picnic of free beer was provided. The first strike by the Irish was for an increase in pay to five cents an hour. They lost.

Four dollars a week

IN THE rear of the East Side tenements there were small shanties used for the storing of rags and other factory waste-products. There were Jewish immigrants who worked over those rags swept up from hundreds of factory floors and who received four dollars a week. They worked ten and twelve hours a day, and at night went to sleep right on top of the newly arrived bundles of waste. The first impact with death I had was when they came to take the bodies of two men out of one of those shanties. The men had died during their sleep because of a faulty coal stove.

Raising pigeons

IN MARLON BRANDO'S prize-winning performance, *On the Waterfront,* the first scene shows Marlon, acting for the gangster labor-boss, enticing a recalcitrant to his death. Marlon induces the fellow to come out of the safety of his flat by telling him that he (Brando) had located one of the fellow's lost pigeons.

My hat goes off to the fellows who wrote these scenes into the picture. It was certainly an accurate phase of life in the slums. Raising pigeons on the tenement roofs. All over the East Side fellows were raising pigeons on the tenement roofs. Why? Was it hunger for some identification with rural life? Farm life? It couldn't have been for the money . . . it took lots of time and patience.

Me, I was always an indoors man. My only connection with pigeons came some years later when a waiter brought me a couple under glass, in a heavily carpeted dining room, and with a three-piece orchestra playing chamber music.

Everybody got paid but the doctor

THE doctors of the neighborhood had an alternating pool, each man donating a full day's services to the treating of hundreds of patients who appeared on the line every morning. I think back, and how sad it is when we realize that many of those patients had cancer (based on symptoms which even a layman understands today) and how the word "cancer" was taboo. My own mother died of cancer in 1924 but no one in the family mentioned it to anyone. The word was whispered, and at that only among the members of the immediate family. In this Free Essex Street Clinic the doctor and a nurse would go down the line, which stretched into the corridors, and make a quick diagnosis on the spot, and write the prescriptions. Epsom salts, bathe it in hot water, sleep a little more, all the "prescriptions" that were not costly. The doctors in those days were sociologists as well as scientists. They had to be. What could a doctor tell a man with a tubercular cough? To go to a dry climate? How could the doctor take that man away from his work? What would then happen to his wife and four children at home? The doctors did the best they knew how, and some of them were the most noble men who ever lived. In this free clinic the United Charities paid the nurses, the technicians, the admission clerks, and the janitors. Everybody got paid but the doctor.

Does It Sell Flour?

~~~~~~

Why women live longer than men

I HAVE just come across a delightful little twenty-five-page booklet which business firms are buying by the bushel and distributing to their salesmen. It is called *Clothes and Appearance* by Paul Linden. The theme is in the subtitle: "What a Salesman Should Know About Clothes and Appearance."

There are five chapters: "Are You Well-Packaged?" "Do You Add or Detract?" "Well Shod Means Well Trod," "Hats Off?—God Forbid," and finally, "Dress Well to Sell Well" The author consulted the leading employers and sales managers of the country.

One leading executive stated bluntly, "I insist on every one of my salesmen wearing not only hats, but also garters and suspenders."

In the last chapter the author sums up by matching the clothes to the proficient salesman. For example, "For men with receding chins, avoid high, full crown and deep-snapped brim," and for the salesman with a long nose, "Avoid narrow front brim and high-tapered crown."

But all of this is only the beginning. Now the guy has to go out and sell, and the competition is fierce as he goes forth with the order book in one hand and the latest bulletin from the sales manager: "This is IT, men, D-Day. This is what your customers have been waiting for. Our new model X651 will knock your customers right off their chairs."

All of this adds up to the fact that we now have some three and a half million widows over the age of fifty. A woman born in the 1950's, the statisticians tell us, may expect to live to seventy-four, while the man can look forward to only sixty-seven years, and the gap is getting wider and wider each year. By the year 2025 the United States of America will be a matriarchy ruled over by some forty-five million widows.

They will hold all political offices, from Presidency to coroner, and occasionally a little widow will sit at the edge of the swimming pool in Bermuda and wax sentimental. "This is the third time I've been to Bermuda. The first time was when my husband won Top Man prize for the month of January, 1957. The second time I was in Bermuda was when Jim got the button for the $100,000 Club, and this was only one month before he passed on. . . ."

The sales managers of America are no dopes. They never send the prize-winning salesman to Bermuda. They always send his wife. This gives the salesman a chance to catch up on the new order forms which now require FOUR carbon copies PLUS an extra carbon for the IBM machine.

Are things too good?

THERE is no parallel for this America of the year 1957 in all the history of mankind, including the Xanadu of Kubla Khan:

> Where Alph, the sacred river, ran
> Through caverns measureless to man,
> Down to a sunless sea.

God forbid that there should be even the suggestion of a depression. In the study of world history we have found that people may give up profits if necessary, and even jobs; but it is a different story when they are confronted with the loss of status. In the depression of the 1930's only a very small segment of our people were "declassed."

In fact, many folks actually achieved a status they had never known. The decline had been preceded by a period during which the two-dollar bettors were no longer interested in the results of the sixth race at Havre de Grace. They now waited for the closing prices on the New York Stock Exchange. Stenographers and bootblacks discussed dividends, earnings, car-loadings, and the Federal Reserve rediscount rate. Thus a fellow finally bought fifty shares of Skelly Oil at eight dollars a share in partnership with the short-order cook at the delicatessen store. Then came the crash, and the fellow stood at a bar with a five-cent glass of beer in his hand, and told all about how the stock market had wiped him out. He thus achieved a status he had never dreamed of—identity with J. Pierpont Morgan, who also lost money in the stock market.

Today it is entirely different. The slightest depression would automatically declass 60 per cent of our population.

Six weeks without a pay check to meet the installments, and everything comes out—down to the waffle iron. Millions of our people have entered the middle class during the past twenty years, and they have all the wonderful things this status implies: beauty contests, garden clubs, League of Women Voters, automatic dishwashers, electric refrigerators which open by themselves, a baking oven which turns the roast over automatically, country clubs, swimming pools, and the suburban churches and temples with kitchens, vestments, processionals, book reviews, Mr. and Mrs. Clubs, and brisket, spaghetti, and bingo.

At no time in the history of the world have so many people had so much; and in a way this is frightening. I suppose this comes from something my mother dinned into my head night and day: "It's bad when things are too good."

The Methodist "Guardian of Israel"

In a small town in the Deep South, the Jewish community of about twenty-five families organized a congregation and made plans to build a temple.

The Christians of the town were enthusiastic. In addition the Methodist minister offered the use of his church for Friday-evening Sabbath services until the temple was constructed. The Jewish members were grateful and began to use the beautiful Methodist church for their Sabbath services. One of the laymen, with considerable learning, acted as reader, and, once a month or so, a visiting rabbi occupied the pulpit. The Methodist minister personally appeared every Friday evening to open the church, turn on the lights, and greet each of the Jews with "Good Shabos."

About the third or fourth Friday evening, the Methodist minister took a seat in the rear of the church, picked up a Jewish prayer book, and participated in the service. In a matter of weeks, he became a "regular," and an honored guest. Well, sir, after about five or six weeks of this, the Jewish members began to show a little nervousness. During the week, the Methodist would stick his head in one of the stores and in perfectly good humor call out, "Joe, you weren't at services last Friday." Joe smiled but his heart wasn't in it. Thus under the watchful eye of the Methodist minister, the Jewish congregation achieved 100 per cent attendance, but every single Friday. Even when a fellow was out of town or actually sick in bed he made sure that the reader made the announcement from the pulpit. "Joe Landberg could not attend services tonight—he is in New York on a buying trip. He'll be back Tuesday." And you can bet he'll be there the following Friday night—early. But that is not the end of the story. As I witnessed the next development, I did not know whether to cry or laugh.

Along about April it gets very hot in that town. Most of the folks have cabins at the beach. The wife and children go down early in the week and the husband joins them Friday afternoon. The temperature begins to average 94 degrees in the month of May. On Friday nights it is always five degrees hotter. What to do? Who would tell him? Finally a couple of fellows took the bull by the horns. "Dr. ——, we have imposed on you long enough. We have met in your beautiful church for six months now. Enough is enough. You have been too kind."

"But your temple is not yet finished," said the Methodist; but the Jews would have none of it.

"No, Doctor, until our temple is finished we'll meet in our several homes."

The Methodist appeared to be a bit downcast, but everything seemed all right. On Sunday, the Methodist asked his Board of Stewards to remain after services for a special meeting. He said, "Look, gentlemen, the Jewish temple is only half-finished, but the members feel they have imposed on us too much. Up till now they have been meeting here on my personal invitation. Let us make it official church business. That should make them feel better."

On the following Wednesday the weekly paper carried the good news. The Stewards officially offer the use of the church until such time as the temple is ready for use. The news, of course, came like a bolt out of the blue, and for the next few days the twenty-five Jews kept walking back and forth to see what progress was being made on the new construction. But they weren't even working on the roof yet.

For Rosh Hashanah the temple will be ready, but nowhere else in the country will a congregation match the attendance record during July and August of this small congregation in the Deep South.

I miss the holy men of the 1930's

THE South is no longer the Bible Belt.

The overthrow of agriculture as the dominant way of life has accelerated the process of urbanization of social life, culture, and religion.

The sawdust trail is slowly but surely coming to an end.

There are two reasons for this. First, the tent evangelist could hardly hope to compete with the fellows who spend ten thousand dollars a week for radio and TV programs; second, the area has undergone tremendous development in the last fifteen years.

More and more the Christians are thinking of their church as a great historic force which has to be respected and maintained, and there is less emphasis on dogma, creed, and ritual. This follows the normal pattern. As economic status increases, there is less and less reason for an answer such as a millworker once gave Dr. Liston Pope, dean of the Yale Divinity School, when he asked her why she had changed to one of the more primitive sects: "I needed more of the Holy Ghost than the Baptists could give me."

Today that lady is probably a member of two garden clubs, two book clubs, and in the League of Women Voters. There is nothing like economic *status*. A tremendously expanding middle class is making the tent evangelist a thing of the past.

Now and then old Mordecai Ham pops up, but he sticks to the unpaved country roads mostly. Gone are the days of Cyclone Mack and Gipsy Smith. Even Hyman Appleman, the Hebrew-Christian evangelist, has gone fancy on us and talks of signing pledge cards, while Brother Armstrong over in Gastonia is selling used cars in his spare time. Today, Dr. Norman Vincent Peale attracts as many people for a short, short invocation as old Cyclone Mack used to gather during a whole week's revival with two Saturday nights thrown in, and before he was through in the old days, you could smell the smoke and actually hear the crackling of the fires below.

I remember when the printers held a convention over near Asheville, and Bill, a friend of mine, went out to a Cyclone Mack revival in the vicinity. After listening for ten minutes Bill was so inspired that he stood up, and, shouting a prayer for forgiveness, took the bottle out of his hip pocket and pitched it out of the open window.

This was no grandstand play. The bottle was at least two-thirds full. The delegates slept two to a room and room-mate Fred was sort of responsible for Bill. They went to bed at midnight, but when Fred got up around four o'clock, Bill's bed was empty. Fred dressed quickly and went out to look for his friend, and sure enough there was Bill with a big stick in his hand beating the tall grass around the revival tent—looking for his bottle.

Wishing you long years

I AM still somewhat uneasy when I receive greetings and congratulations on my birthday. Of course I appreciate the kindness and good fellowship they represent, but even to this day there is something strange about the sentiment.

Celebrating birthdays was not a big deal at all in an Orthodox Jewish household.

This goes way back into our culture and folklore. It is part of the legend of the Evil Eye. I have never seen it discussed in these terms but I believe that behind the Evil Eye legend may have been the idea of TIMELESSNESS—SUR-VIVAL. The opposite of "unendingness" would naturally be a specific period of time in years, months, weeks, days, and hours.

Thus, birthdays were rarely mentioned and your elders scrupulously avoided being pinned down on the exact age of a member of the family. There was less care taken in discussing the ages of the very old, but even here there was no actual pinpointing of dates. If someone asked, "How old is Aunt Freda?" your mother would answer, "My sister Freda was thirty-five when we all came to America," and that was all the information you'd get. If my mother had said, "Freda is seventy-four years old," the Angel of Death, always listening, might have been encouraged to "call" her. The whole idea was to ward off the Evil Eye and confuse the Angel of Death. This was particularly important when you mentioned the name of a person who had died. You would never link a living person with the departed. If it was absolutely necessary, however, you could break the spell of the Evil Eye by a protective phrase, "You were a good friend of my (dead) husband; wishing you long years," or "You look like your (dead) mother, may you live to one hundred and twenty years."

I once coached my local insurance agent, Mr. Williamson, on how to sell a policy to a Jew. I told him that he must never say, "In the event of your death, your family will be protected." This would never work. When he was soliciting a Jew I told him to say, "In case, God forbid, something should happen after one hundred and twenty years, your family will not suffer; wishing you long years."

This worked wonders for Mr. Williamson and before his retirement he had built up a very large Jewish clientele.

Lil ole Tin-Pan Alley

THE Southerners arch their backs at the slightest hint of outside interference in the form of criticism or advice.

This has been an understandable attitude since man first organized himself into a family and a clan.

But the Southerners have not given any consideration to the outside influence that has added so much to their pride, prestige, and prosperity.

Just think what fellows like George Gershwin, Irving Berlin, Wolfie Gilbert, Irving Caesar, Gerald Marks, Gus Kahn, and all the others, have done for the South—"Is It True What They Say About Dixie?" and "Down Yonder"; and " . . . How I love you, how I love you, my dear old Swanee"; and the plea of Jack Yellen and Milton Ager, "Take Me to That Swanee Shore" . . . presumably for the "Alabama Jubilee" in that "Dear Old Southland," to hear those "St. Louis Blues" by W. C. Handy; and that other great Negro song man, Andy Razaf, who sums it all up—"That's What I Like About the South."

Why did these boys, most of them the sons of Jewish and Irish immigrants, the Negroes of the slums and ghettos, create this entirely new American culture; putting to words and music this particular region, The South?

Did Benny Davis ever see a "Carolina Moon"?—was Wolfie Gilbert ever ". . . Down on the levee"?

How did Gus Kahn know that "Nothing Could Be Finer Than To Be in Carolina, in the Morning"?

Why were these Tin-Pan Alley boys forever "Alabamy Bound"? And why did they advise the mothers of America to "Rock-A-Bye Your Baby With a Dixie Melody"?

The South should declare a one-day holiday—in honor of Tin-Pan Alley and those outsiders who did more to perpetuate the legends and the romance of the South than all the *Gone With the Winds* put together.

Boiled beef flanken comes to Charlotte

First there were the Catawba Indians who valiantly defended their land against the Tuscarora and the Cherokee.

Then came the English Episcopalians, followed by the Scotch Calvinists, the French Huguenots, and the German Lutherans. And through the years a trickle of Jews with trade goods from Surinam and the Barbados for the pioneer and the native. When the peddler's pack became too heavy in middle age, he picked his favorite spot and laid the foundation for what is known today as the "department store." The first one in Charlotte was an Aaron Cohen, a veteran of Washington's army, who was also a silversmith. His daughter Elizabeth was the first to be interred in the local Hebrew cemetery.

It was here that the woodsmen cut Lord Cornwallis to ribbons, softened him up for the final blow at Yorktown. It was here, too, that the folks drew up a charter of freedom a year before Jefferson's Declaration. From here the Hornets' Nest Rifles and the Charlotte Greys established an artery of distribution for the products of nearly 70 per cent of all the textile looms in America. And it was here, finally, in 1953, that Izzy and Jack opened up the Brass Rail, a "kosher-style" restaurant.

You have no idea about it at all! For the first two weeks you had to stand in line to get a chopped chicken-liver sandwich or a corned beef on rye with a sour tomato. And such happy faces! It was Christmas Eve, erev Rosh Hashanah, and President Monroe's era of good feeling.

The restaurant is below a main cross-town artery called Church Street, and all the business houses and stores are on the other side, and so it happened that this Church Street began to look like the Red Sea with wave after wave of Israelites crossing over every day for stuffed cabbage with raisin sauce, pumpernickel bread, chicken-in-the-pot, and boiled beef flanken. The Tar Heel waitresses pronounce flanken, like left flank, right flank—"Would you all care for the boiled beef flanken today?" What a wonderful country —America!

And so at noon each day as the church chimes in this greatest of all citadels of American Protestantism peal out, "We're Marching to Zion, Beautiful, Beautiful Zion . . ." the Jews (and many Gentiles) keep pouring across Church

Street to Izzy and Jack who are already slicing the hot pastrami.

Does it sell flour?

RECENTLY I moved my office to one of those old-fashioned dwellings built in the days of big families and big dining rooms. The house is only a few blocks from the heart of the city, and the neighborhood is fast becoming a business section. I combined my living quarters with my office, which, in my opinion, is a sensible proposition. No subways, no buses, no pushing. You get up in the morning, step into another room—and go to work.

But I did make a sacrifice in moving. In the building where I formerly worked, my next-door neighbor was the local office of the National Milling Company. Occasionally the Milling door would be open as I passed down the hall, and there on the wall facing the door was a big sign: DOES IT SELL FLOUR? The sign fascinated me and I thought of it every day.

I visited the office once or twice on some pretext to see what would happen. I tried to catch it when someone connected with the business was entering that door.

Does he say "good morning," for instance, before he starts selling flour, and what about the folks in the office? Do they all rise and face the sign when someone does or says something that doesn't sell flour, or do they just point to it in silent admonition? Alas, I had to move before I solved this problem.

The late industrialist-statesman, Thomas J. Watson, was identified in the public mind with another carefully framed placard to be found now in a million business offices—THINK. This banner far outnumbers the other symbols such as, "It

Is Later Than You Think," "God Bless You Real Good," "Excelsior," and "Does It Sell Flour?"

The man who originally brought this public-relations idea into big business was the "Sage of East Aurora," Elbert Hubbard. Mr. Hubbard sat down one day and wrote himself a little essay that swept the business community off its feet. This was the famous *A Message to Garcia*. It was during the Spanish-American War. Inside Cuba was the rebel leader, Mr. Garcia. We wanted to tell Mr. Garcia that the great United States was in the war and that he was no longer fighting alone. But Mr. Garcia was hiding somewhere in the interior of Cuba and so the Americans picked an officer by the name of Lieutenant Rowan to "bring the message to Garcia." Mr. Hubbard came pretty close to enshrining Lieutenant Rowan as America's great hero of that war, and he was just barely nosed out by Theodore Roosevelt and his Rough Riders.

The entire basis for Rowan's immortality, according to Hubbard, was that he did not stop to ask questions: "Where will I find Garcia?" "Who is Garcia?" "Why not let Charlie do this job?" etc.

Mr. Hubbard hit hard at his most important point: "It is not book learning young men need, but a stiffening of the vertebrae which will cause them to be loyal to a trust, to act promptly, concentrate their energies; DO THE THING— Carry the message to Garcia."

The New York Central Railroad ordered a hundred thousand reprints. The insurance companies put *A Message to Garcia* in pay envelopes and premium notices. Millions of copies were distributed and it was still going strong well into the second decade of the new century.

But one of the questions Mr. Hubbard wrote that Lieutenant Rowan had *not* asked seemed to be pertinent after the matter of security was no longer a factor.

"What does the message say?"

This was never revealed officially or unofficially, and no one knows to this day. They made a movie of *Message* once and everything went fine in the portrayal of Rowan's hair-raising experiences in the Cuban jungle, but, at the end, everybody was watching Mr. Garcia as he read "the message" and the rebel did not change his expression at all. Next thing you knew Mr. Garcia was all dressed up arriving at American headquarters, and the only logical conclusion was that the "message" had merely invited him to lunch.

The same problem confronted the movie people with their story of Stanley and Dr. Livingstone. No man suffered as did Spencer Tracy during eight months in darkest Africa looking for Cedric Hardwicke. "Find Livingstone" had been on the lips of all the civilized world in the 1870's. And when Tracy found Hardwicke the good doctor could hardly tear himself away from a group of blacks to whom he was teaching the hymn, "Onward, Christian Soldiers." The story would have been all right if it had ended with, "Dr. Livingstone, I presume?" But every time Tracy whipped out his reporter's notebook, Hardwicke ran off into the big clearing to continue his rehearsals. In the end Stanley pleads with Livingstone to return to civilization, but the doctor shakes his head in resignation and points to his choral group.

Maybe he was breaking in a new baritone.

The "Organization Men"

Up in Philadelphia, Miss Nella Bogart was the star witness in a trial against a couple of lesser officials of a large domestic corporation. She testified that she had been a sort of roving "call girl" at the company's conventions and sales meetings. At each such function, claimed Miss Bogart, she and several associates were hired to "entertain" prospective buyers.

Miss Bogart further swore that in the privacy of her hotel room she was able to prevail upon prospective buyers to increase their orders, but for this she received no extra

commission. She was paid a flat rate, plus any extra honorarium the buyer gave her on his own.

I hesitate to mention the name of the corporation even
though it was used at the trial, because, (a) the directors
swore that they had no knowledge of these goings-on in the
lower echelon of their organization; and (b) it is an old
story; many others do it in one way or another.

It's funny what the stuff will do, which brings me to an
observation about the "Organization Men."

When the out-of-town buyer comes to town they go stark-
raving-mad. They are so frightened they can hardly put the
three carbon papers into the order book. How terrible is this
condition in our commercial world even at the height of
prosperity. What intense struggle and desperation. The
telephone is busy. "Send up more ice"; "More ginger ale";
"What happened to the valet?"; "How about those theatre
tickets?"; and the bellboys are rushing hither and yon; "Her
phone has been disconnected." This is the calculated risk
between conferences, sales meetings, and conventions: "Her
phone has been disconnected"; "Well, get some new ones";
and, "Send up more ice."

All of this costs a fortune and sometimes the guys don't
even get the order.

But let some scholar, clergyman, or college professor come
to town; a lecturer invited to make a speech, and suddenly
the same "Organization Men" become highly conservative
businessmen.

You never in your life saw such dignity; and they sit
around a table, figuring and figuring for the lecturer: "Transportation—one half from this point to that point—taxi, a
dollar thirty-nine—tips, twenty-seven cents—honorarium—let's
look up the correspondence, what does the correspondence
say?"

You never saw a Yenkee?

COMPARING the modern fund-raiser to the old-fashioned meshullach would be like comparing a member of the New York Stock Exchange to an itinerant peddler.

The meshullach (agent or deputy sent by accredited Jewish institutions to collect funds) was a very hard worker and a colorful character. He would walk the streets calling on his old contacts and forever looking for new leads.

He has now practically disappeared from the scene and in some ways it is a pity.

. Invariably he wore the long caftan-type coat, and a broadbrimmed black hat which made a fitting frame for his wide untrimmed beard.

His pockets were always bulging—on one side, his papers, receipts, and notebooks, and in the other, a package with slices of bread and the usual hard-boiled eggs. This was an emergency ration in case he couldn't find the synagogue sexton or if the president of the shul was out of town; then the meshullach could take his lunch without worrying about eating nonkosher food somewhere.

The meshullach was probably the subject of the original story about the time that the man got off at the Southern Railroad station in a small Georgia town and a few kids hanging around were fascinated by his garb, his beard, his bulging pockets, and his umbrella, and they proceeded to follow him down the street. Suddenly the old gent turned around and said to the kids: "What's the matter, you never saw a Yenkee before?"

PART 4

The Vertical Negro

~~~~~~

The Vertical Negro Plan

THOSE who love North Carolina will jump at the chance to share in the great responsibility confronting our Governor and the State Legislature. A special session of the Legislature (July 25-28, 1956) passed a series of amendments to the State Constitution. These proposals submitted by the Governor and his Advisory Education Committee included the following:

(A) The elimination of the compulsory attendance law, "to prevent any child from being forced to attend a school with a child of another race."

(B) The establishment of "Education Expense Grants" for education in a private school, "in the case of a child assigned to a public school attended by a child of another race."

(C) A "uniform system of local option" whereby a majority of the folks in a school district may suspend or close a school if the situation becomes "intolerable."

But suppose a Negro child applies for this "Education Expense Grant" and says he wants to go to the private school too? There are fourteen Supreme Court decisions involving the use of public funds; there are only two "decisions" involving the elimination of racial discrimination in the public schools.

The Governor has said that critics of these proposals have not offered any constructive advice or alternatives. Permit me, therefore, to offer an idea for the consideration of the members of the regular sessions. A careful study of my plan, I believe, will show that it will save millions of dollars in tax funds and eliminate forever the danger to our public education system. Before I outline my plan, I would like to give you a little background.

One of the factors involved in our tremendous industrial growth and economic prosperity is the fact that the South, voluntarily, has all but eliminated VERTICAL SEGREGATION. The tremendous buying power of the twelve million Negroes in the South has been based wholly on the absence of racial segregation. The white and Negro stand at the same grocery and supermarket counters; deposit money at the same bank teller's window; pay phone and light bills to the same clerk; walk through the same dime and department stores, and stand at the same drugstore counters.

It is only when the Negro "sets" that the fur begins to fly.

Now, since we are not even thinking about restoring VERTICAL SEGREGATION, I think my plan would not only comply with the Supreme Court decisions, but would maintain "sitting-down" segregation. Now here is the GOLDEN VERTICAL NEGRO PLAN. Instead of all those complicated proposals, all the next session needs to do is pass one small amendment which would provide *only* desks in all the public schools of our state—*no seats.*

The desks should be those standing-up jobs, like the old-fashioned bookkeeping desk. Since no one in the South pays the slightest attention to a VERTICAL NEGRO, this will completely solve our problem. And it is not such a terrible inconvenience for young people to stand up during their classroom studies. In fact, this may be a blessing in disguise. They are not learning to read sitting down, anyway; maybe standing up will help. This will save more millions of dollars in the cost of our remedial English course when the kids enter college. In whatever direction you look with the GOLDEN VERTICAL NEGRO PLAN, you save millions of dollars, to say nothing of eliminating forever any danger to our public education system upon which rests the destiny, hopes, and happiness of this society.

My WHITE BABY PLAN offers another possible solution to the segregation problem—this time in a field other than education.

Here is an actual case history of the "White Baby Plan to End Racial Segregation":

Some months ago there was a revival of the Laurence Olivier movie, *Hamlet*, and several Negro schoolteachers were eager to see it. One Saturday afternoon they asked some white friends to lend them two of their little children, a three-year-old girl and a six-year-old boy, and, holding these white children by the hands, they obtained tickets from the movie-house cashier without a moment's hesitation. They were in like Flynn.

This would also solve the baby-sitting problem for thousands and thousands of white working mothers. There can be a mutual exchange of references, then the people can sort of pool their children at a central point in each neighborhood, and every time a Negro wants to go to the movies all she need do is pick up a white child—and go.

Eventually the Negro community can set up a factory and manufacture white babies made of plastic, and when they want to go to the opera or to a concert, all they need do is carry that plastic doll in their arms. The dolls, of course, should all have blond curls and blue eyes, which would go even further; it would give the Negro woman and her husband priority over the whites for the very best seats in the house.

While I still have faith in the WHITE BABY PLAN, my final proposal may prove to be the most practical of all.

Only after a successful test was I ready to announce formally the GOLDEN "OUT-OF-ORDER" PLAN.

I tried my plan in a city of North Carolina, where the Negroes represent 39 per cent of the population.

I prevailed upon the manager of a department store to shut the water off in his "white" water fountain and put up a sign, "Out-of-Order." For the first day or two the whites were hesitant, but little by little they began to drink out of the water fountain belonging to the "coloreds"—and by the end of the third week everybody was drinking the "segregated" water; with not a single solitary complaint to date.

I believe the test is of such sociological significance that the Governor should appoint a special committee of two members of the House and two Senators to investigate the GOLDEN "OUT-OF-ORDER" PLAN. We kept daily reports on the use of the unsegregated water fountain which should be of great value to this committee. This may be the answer to the necessary uplifting of the white morale. It is possible that the whites may accept desegregation if they are assured that the facilities are still "separate," albeit "Out-of-Order."

As I see it now, the key to my Plan is to keep the "Out-of-Order" sign up for at least two years. We must do this thing gradually.

Carry-the-Books Plan

HERE is another plan to help solve the "integration" problem of the South.

There is no vertical segregation. But neither is there "45-degree-angle" segregation if the sitting or leaning Negro is a servant, a domestic, or a chore-boy of some kind.

Therefore the Negro parents of the South should make this proposition to their local school boards: that they will allow their children to carry the books for their white classmates. A system can easily be worked out whereby the Negro boy (going to an integrated school) can meet a white classmate at a convenient corner, a block or so away from the school, and carry the white boy's books into the school building. And if there are sixteen Negro students in a school of four hundred whites, an alternating system can be worked out so that by the end of the semester, each white boy will have had his books carried into the school building by a Negro student, at least once.

The Negro girls would not have to participate in this "Carry-the-Books Plan." The girls should wear a sort of miniature apron over their street dresses, and this would settle everything once and for all. Everybody would be satisfied. Eventually, I suspect, the white girls may even adopt those cute little aprons themselves, but they will have served their purpose.

I know I am calling on the Negroes to make a considerable sacrifice, but it is worth it because this would settle the matter even for the most outspoken white supremacists. If it became known throughout the South that the Negro boys were toting books for the whites, and that Negro girls were wearing aprons to school, all the school kids could go on with their work without any further disturbance from seg-regationist mobs, National Guardsmen, or Federal troops.

Timothy Mulcahy, Hitler, and Skelley's

I just happened to think of my friend and side-kick of years ago, Timothy Mulcahy. Timothy was a happy-go-lucky and witty Irishman. On the big daily papers in New York, the advertising men work in pairs, like the Italian gendarmes. Mulcahy and I teamed up and it was a pleasant relationship. After checking in at our sheet in the mornings, we immediately took the subway up to Skelley's saloon on Sixth Avenue near 42nd Street. Certain saloons attract men of the same profession or trade. Skelley's was the hang-out for the advertising men.

In those days Skelley (his real name was Katz) installed a battery of telephones for private use of the advertising men. This made it possible for a man to go the entire week without once setting foot out of Skelley's. Most of the accounts were "repeats," and involved only a change in copy, and Skelley even provided an errand boy for our use. It was in the early 1930's and whiskey was twenty cents for a two-ounce glass. Mulcahy and I had our own booth where we would sit and argue about politics and literature. Hitler had just become Chancellor of Germany and the headlines were already giving us the prelude of the massacre to come. One day it was the removal of all Jewish officeholders; another day, Hitler announced that all German Jews had been deprived of citizenship, etc.

Toward all of this Mulcahy showed a sincere, albeit restrained, sympathy. Then came the Nuremberg Laws which reduced the entire Jewish people to the status of fourth-class citizens, without hope and exposed to utter destruction. Again Mulcahy shook his head sadly.

One day, I saw Mulcahy tear into the saloon with fire in his eyes. I had never seen him so completely upset. He had the early edition of the afternoon paper in his hand; completely out of breath, hardly able to speak, he pointed to a small news item on page 28 which was to the effect that the Nazis had arrested two nuns for alleged hoarding. Mulcahy pointed to the item with growing rage and shouted, "Now the sonofabitch has gone too far."

The fettering of the human spirit

THE road is hard and long, and I do not refer to the "exclusive" country clubs, luncheon clubs, hotels, and summer resorts. Because unless sanctioned by law and by public opinion, these pinpricks do not necessarily prevent a man from achieving everything in life that his character, ambition, and talent will permit him to achieve.

In the first place, *without* law and public opinion, I have found that the "excluder" loses more human dignity than the "excluded." The "excluder" is worried all his life. He must become a student of ethnology, physiology, the origin of names, and the whole science of semantics. He has nightmares; "I wonder if he's one," he keeps saying to himself. "The name is McGonigle but you can't go by names no more," says jerko, adding in despair, "he sure looks like one." In the end he becomes a nervous wreck.

This fellow has never once in my life disturbed me.

What does concern me, however, is what Gunnar Myrdal called "the fettering of the human spirit." It is entirely different when the law tells you that you *cannot* go to a fifty-cent movie house, despite the fact that you have the price, that you are properly dressed, and that you want to see the movie. That the Negroes of the South still have their sense of humor is one of the great stories of the human spirit itself. I am afraid that if I were confronted with a similar situation I would probably give up, sit around and brood for the rest of my life.

Occasionally, of course, an attempt is made at this fettering, and often with the best of intentions.

Like for instance the fact that the only press release I ever get from the Republican National Committee is when the Administration appoints a Jew to some silly old Government bureau in which I am less interested than I am in the appointee himself. I assume, of course, that they send out other press releases which I never see. I am only on that old Fettering List.

And the Democratic National Committee is no better. I checked up on it. The only press releases they send to the editors of the Negro press of America are those which are concerned with "civil rights," as the saying goes. But not a word about NATO, the Middle East, taxes, or even the budget. It is part of the "fettering of the human spirit" whereby the Negro singer is expected to sing only: "Swing

Low, Sweet Chariot"; and the Negro writers and lawyers are expected to write or handle only Negro "subjects" and Negro "problems."

But fortunately we do possess the cure for this fettering of the human spirit. It is the application of the American principle of democracy, and the strict adherence to the American tradition of freedom. Just a few old ideas; we do not need any new ones.

A short story of America

On my visits to New York *I always* manage to spend three or four hours in the main reading room of the New York Public Library on Fifth Avenue and 42nd Street. I went to the New York Public Library nearly every Sunday afternoon for many years and it is like visiting the house where I was born. My advantage is that this "birthplace" is never "torn down."

On the recent trip I applied for my books as usual and then went to the main reading room to watch for the numbers to flash on the indicator that tells you your books are ready for you. After a while I decided to continue watching the numbers long after mine had been flashed. I was watching something interesting. I was watching the whole story of America. A whole course in sociology within a half-hour. I saw boys and girls go up to pick up their books; boys singly, and girls singly, and then boys and girls together. Many of them were Puerto Rican boys and girls, stepping up to the indicator desk and getting their books, and I thought how "bad" news is really "good" news. We read of the delinquency and the crime—but this is the real answer. It is that people are people, and they reflect the environment and the conditions which surround them. In my day it was Jewish boys and girls who stepped up to that indicator counter. Jewish boys and girls, many of them still wearing the clothes their mothers had made for them for the trip across the ocean. And before the Jewish boys, the Irish boys and girls picked up their books, and after the Jewish boys and girls, the Italians did the same thing, and then the Negroes, and now the Puerto Ricans. And what is going on with the Puerto Ricans is exactly what went on with all the others. The Irish "West Side Dusters" and "Hell's Kitchen" gangs, and the Jewish "Lefty Loueys," and "Gyp the Bloods," and the Italian "Dago Franks" and Mafia, and now the Puerto Rican delinquents, and dope peddlers—all these made the headlines, but America was made in that library and these same people helped make it.

This seems to have followed a pattern. The immigrant needed to accelerate the process of integration, of proving his individual worth, of achieving self-esteem as quickly as possible. It was reflected after each of the great waves of immigration. Right after the Irish came, you had an era of Irish "excellence"—in sports, on the stage, in many of the creative arts.

In those days no one heard of a Jewish baseball or football player. Those days belonged to the John L. Sullivans, and the Jim Corbetts, and the George M. Cohans, the John McCormacks, the Chauncey Olcotts, and the Victor Herberts. Then after the Irish came the Jews, and the same process was in full swing. The days of the settlement house and the introduction of basketball as a major American sport by Jewish immigrants. Those were the days of Benny Leonard, and Marshall Goldberg, and Benny Friedman, and Barney Ross, and Benny Bass, and Irving Berlin, and Fanny Brice, and George Gershwin. They in turn were followed by the Italians responding to the same "need"—to the same environment and to the same rewards. It was the day of DiMaggio, and Perry Como, and Yogi Berra, and Frank Sinatra, and Carmine DeSapio; and now we are entering upon the Negro era, responding to the same need, the same ideas and ideals. Your Irishmen on the playing field, and your Jews and Italians in the prize ring and on the concert stage are now making room for the Jackie Robinsons, the Willie Mayses, the Harry Belafontes and the Pearl Baileys; and as sure as this land endures, the day will one day belong to this new wave of poverty-stricken immigrants, the Puerto Ricans.

In the end they will have judges, artists, ballplayers, prize fighters, and political leaders. Not a single one of these groups started with a "good press." And that is what makes it such an amazing story. The true story of America—boys and girls waiting for their books in the library.

Who has all the money?

AT LAST I was able to eke out the one question or statement which all of us hear, all the time, on all sides, with considerable annoyance: "The Jews have all the money." A fellow in Wilmington finally made me happy by asking the question. He put it politely as follows: "To what do you attribute the success of the Jews in making money?"

Now this is essentially a very silly situation. Based on the mores of our civilization, I should have been highly flattered. In every town across the length and breadth of our nation, the "big" man is the man who has made good—who has made money. Newspaper editors cry for the feature story about the fellow who peddled newspapers and rose to tremendous wealth as Coca-Cola distributor or to a position equally exalted and great; but, of course, this is different, and we all know it is different, although it would be hard to find out why it should be different. At any rate, we certainly agree on one thing; that the statement is never made on a basis of admiration, good will, good faith, or with good intentions, and, in the terms in which it is usually uttered, we are correct in regarding it as a libel.

This was my answer:

In the Southern communities in which we live the American

Jew represents a single-class society of small capitalists. There is no "balance" to the population, no "cross section," so to speak. If a Gallup Poll man wanted to get American-Jewish opinion on something, he certainly would not take any samplings in the South, unless he particularly wanted the viewpoint of manufacturers, salesmen, and retail merchants. Since he is completely unemployable, he must have the capital or connections to employ himself as a manufacturer, distributor, or retailer. If he fails in business and lacks the capital to start up again, he moves to the larger metropolitan centers of the North to find employment.

We had the same situation in reverse on New York's Lower East Side. Undisturbed by the changing tides of immigration there remained several huge "Gentile" business establishments, which continued to do their manufacturing and wholesale distributing amidst that teeming population of Jewish needleworkers, peddlers, and storekeepers. One of those establishments was the Vogelin Company, which was the largest theatrical costumer in the world. In those days at least one hundred and fifty plays opened on Broadway every season, with hundreds of others "on the road," and the Vogelin Company did a tremendous business. For years the family continued to live in one of the big private houses surrounded by the cold-water tenement flats. Thus they gave us the false idea that "the Gentiles have all the money."

In New York City where you do have a "balanced" Jewish population, a true "cross section," you will find a correct proportion of taxi drivers, bus-station dispatchers, post-office clerks, bankers, editors, landlords, tenants, two hundred thousand needleworkers, a million other wage earners, policemen, street cleaners, errand boys, shipping clerks, philosophers, engineers, surgeons, scientists, pickpockets, wardens, jailbirds, millionaires, panhandlers, charity patients, old-age-home inmates, secretaries, bookmakers, poets, teachers, Turkish-bath attendants, and to quote Philip Wylie, "some of the kindest people in the world."

Everybody is running away
from everybody else

UP IN New York I sat around the office of a friend in the real-estate business. He has seven or eight telephones answering inquiries in reply to his many daily advertisements, "Apartments for Rent."

My friend knows of my interest in these matters and arranged for me to listen in on at least forty of the calls.

How very sad that in our civilization so many people find it necessary to start a business conversation with a sorrowful declaration, and how hard they try to be nonchalant: "Oh, by the way, I am a Negro, and I would like to know about your ad marked E-25 . . ." Several asked right off, "Do you rent to Negroes?"

"The apartment is already rented," answered the receptionist.

"But the afternoon paper just came out—this very minute," comes the reply; and a softy like me feels the tears coming into his eyes. And then in many instances, when an appointment was made, the caller said, "Before I go look at it, tell me—are there any Puerto Ricans in the neighborhood?" Then there were people who gave their names and followed it up immediately: "I am not Puerto Rican, I am Spanish." Recognizing the need to obliterate a racial origin and an entire history of a people—and for what? A place to live— a four-room apartment in the Bronx. And yet how often has man gone through this process of dehumanization!

I suspect that my friend, a cynical Irishman, was having some fun with me, because he suddenly came over to my desk and said, "I think, Harry, you should also look in on some of the personal interviews"; and so I went into another office and there was a lady who wanted to move from one apartment building to another one under the same firm management. She said, "I have a fourteen-year-old daughter and two Negro families are already living in the apartment house."

I asked her how long had the Negroes lived in the house, and she said, "They've been there six months and I've been trying to get moved all that time." I asked her, "What makes you think your daughter is in danger; has she been annoyed in any way?" The woman was very angry with me and I was afraid my friend would lose a client, but the guy was in another room laughing fit to be tied. I kept pressing her for something specific to back up her fears and she finally gave me the story: They make noise; they leave the baby carriages in the hallway; and they hang the clothes out to dry on the roof. . . . And I thought to myself—"Isn't this exactly what they said about us (including my laughing friend, the real-estate man) only forty years ago?"

Racial segregation by law

In San Francisco I learned that the Negroes call the South "Egypt." Later on I chided the Negro editor. I said how come—over in Oakland I hear the same old story—children of Italian immigrants moving out of neighborhoods as Negroes move in. The editor smiled and said, "We may call the South 'Egypt' but you didn't hear me calling this the Promised Land, did you?"

I think that Negro editor's good humor and good sense hold the key to the problem. Too often the proponents of racial segregation (by law) point to the far-from-normal racial conditions in other States of the Union. But that is not the point. The real point is that a segment of our population is considered "second class" by statute and ordinance. That is the big point. The fact that in other parts of the country the Negro is discriminated against; that with a college degree he could not hope to compete successfully for the same job with a white man of lesser qualifications; that people move out of neighborhoods as he moves in; all of that remains in the hearts of men. The Negro is not the only minority group which has that to face.

All over the country there are "restricted" areas of residence, "exclusive" clubs, and college quotas, but you maintain your dignity as a man and your creative potentialities are not seriously impaired when such discrimination is not "on the books." It merely remains part of the unending struggle to win the hearts of men, something which cannot be legislated, nor would free men ever tolerate such legislation.

Nothing will happen the day after we remove from our books the law which says that twelve million Negroes—American citizens—are "inferior." Nothing will happen to change the pattern of our lives. Nothing will happen except the lifting of a great weight of responsibility from our shoulders.

I felt very close to this man

I WANT to tell you about an Eastern Carolina friend who visited my office. A big, handsome young fellow, now studying engineering, who looks exactly like all his ancestors looked—like Daniel Boone and Davy Crockett.

We talked of many things—Senator Scott, the United Nations, Adlai Stevenson, and finally we got around to racial segregation. He told me that it was out of the question in his part of the country, and that quite frankly he could never reconcile himself to having his children go to school with Negro children. He spoke of "tradition" and also of the kindness he and his parents have always felt for the

Negroes. Then suddenly he told me something that made me feel terribly sad.

He said that for several years he operated a school bus, and that at each new term he spent a few very uncomfortable days. "I don't mind the grown-up Negroes. We understand them and they understand us, but I had a very bad time of it when the Negro mother put her child on the bus for the first time. She would get on the bus holding the kid by the hand and she would show the child how she must go and sit in the back. The kid would look up front toward the empty seats—just look. And then for the next few days that kid would jump on the bus and take the first empty seat, like kids will do, and then the mother would run up and down the length of that bus watching anxiously through the windows, and then she would mount the bus again and again and lead it back to the back again and again, until it understood." I asked my friend what he was doing during this process and he told me, "I just kept my eyes on the floor in front of me until I was ready to start that darn bus again."

I changed the subject immediately. We talked about politics. Somehow I felt very close to that man, but I was anxious to see him go before we both started to bawl.

Public right and private preference

ALL these plans coming out of the several State legislatures in an effort to block the desegregation decision of the Supreme Court remind me of the old story of sorting potatoes in three different piles according to size. The fellow finally said, "These decisions are killing me."

But if we choose to maneuver and manipulate in order to circumvent these duly constituted agencies of law, how will we explain and justify this action to the children in our public schools? Can we on Monday tell the children to obey the law and have respect for the agencies of law and order, and then on Tuesday tell them they don't have to obey the law, that it is right to circumvent the law as long as they don't get caught? Education takes place in many ways, at many levels. Our children can be educated to deceit and chicanery, as well as they can be educated to integrity and loyalty.

Of course on a broader basis we must understand that racial discrimination is not a Southern problem exclusively; it is a problem of every State in the Union. Racial discrimination does not only concern the activities of a Senator Eastland of Mississippi, but also a Mayor Hubbard of Dearborn, Michigan, who won an election on a platform to prevent the Negroes from renting or buying a house in Dearborn. But when the South points to these inequalities in other parts of the country to justify its own attitudes, we are not being entirely frank about the matter. Race relations in the North are far from being ideal; in many instances the relationships lack even the kindness at the personal level which the paternalism of the South has developed; but we must remember that the discrimination in the North is sanctioned neither by law nor public opinion and that is the important thing. It may be unpleasant, but you do not lose human dignity when you are subject to discrimination based on private preference. When it is on the lawbooks, when the discrimination is in violation of a public right, then it becomes part of a process of dehumanization. Take it off the books; permit each man to burgeon out for himself whatever his energies and his talents will allow him to achieve.

Nor does this mean that the Southern white population has decided to devote its entire human energy to the frustration of the Negro people and prevent them from achieving this public right—first-class citizenship. Of course not. We must remember one thing—that every Anglo-Saxon we know or see on the street, be he taxi driver or lawyer, laborer or public official—belongs to the specific civilization, the Anglo-Calvinist, American world which gave us not only trial by jury, *habeas corpus*, and the free public school, but also the very instruments of the law with which we can fight for these basic civil rights on which the Negroes' lawyers are now preparing their writs for the Federal courts.

The bigots are the ones who are making the most noise. There are millions of Southerners today who know that racial segregation can no longer be tolerated on any religious, moral, or legal basis. And on an economic basis segregation is impossible to maintain. There are some men in the South today who at night belong to various white supremacy groups to maintain racial segregation. In the daytime they are doing a noble work in bringing new industry into their respective States. They do not realize that at lunchtime when they are negotiating for these industrial contracts they are doing more to end racial segregation in the South than all the NAACP's put together. This is their own futile attempt to argue with history. They are holding on to the pleasant memory of the plantation in this age of cogwheels, and this dream of millions of people in the South is not necessarily born out of unkindness.

The South was the last section in this country to surrender its agrarian world, and its fight against the Supreme Court decision is really an unconscious revolt against the loss of a society that had roots in the soil. It was a pleasant time. It was a time when a man's place was known, the duties and the burdens attaching to it were known, as were the advantages, and they were in a large measure fixed. A man walked around his land holding his little six-year-old son by the hand and he said to him, "Sonny, when you take over this land I would suggest that you fill in that ditch." Today the father will probably be in Pasadena, California, and the son, before he is thirty, will have been transferred to Flint, Michigan, by way of Mobile, Alabama. We live in a highly mobile industrial civilization.

But the fact that in my own family we were happier in the days when my mother emptied the drip pan under the icebox does not necessarily invalidate the wonders of the refrigerator which defrosts itself. I am glad to have it. What it does mean is that we have not yet permitted the humanities to catch up with the scientific advances of the past forty years. The wonderful progress of science has brought no improvement in the hearts of men. We are too impatient; we find the evolution that is taking place is now too slow, and we wonder whether the empire of man over nature keeps pace with the empire of man over himself.

If racial segregation was an immorality in that placid agrarian world of the South of three quarters of a century ago, you can well imagine what an evil it is in the highly mobile industrial age of today.

But there is more to it than the mere memory of the agrarian world, and we must be fair about it. Because of racial segregation which was established about sixty years ago, and because the South did not receive any substantial numbers of immigrants from Eastern Europe and the Mediterranean, the Southerners constituted themselves into the largest single homogeneous society of Anglo-Saxons in America. They were one large family. Wherever they looked they saw an image of themselves, the same religion essentially, the same culture and traditions, and the same attitudes. They therefore permitted their private lives to overlap into their public institutions. The classroom, the church basement, and the neighborhood political rally became their social centers, and it was very pleasant. We have all done the same thing under similar conditions. I remember on the East Side of New York as a boy we had the same condition among the Jewish people. The school principal spoke Yiddish to our parents when they were summoned to school, and we went up and down the school corridors discussing our most intimate family affairs without any inhibition whatever. Then one day we were in for a shock—a great change. Suddenly we found "strangers" in the classroom. The Italians were beginning to move into the neighborhood, and we found it necessary to separate our private lives from our public institutions. Those public schools were not ours; they were created by law and operated by public funds, and so the principal no longer spoke Yiddish to our parents. He had to go through the ordeal of speaking through an interpreter, because it was a *public school,* and if there was only one Italian in that entire school his rights were as sacred as the rights of the 1,650 boys of the non-Italian majority, and we became a little more reserved in our classroom. It was no longer a social club. That was all over. And may I add that we did not marry Italians, and the Italians were not interested in marrying us.

And this is what will happen in the South. Nothing else will happen except human dignity and a higher standard of education. Recently a committee in Congress came out with a report that the standard has been lowered in Washington, D. C., because of the desegregation of the public school; but to the credit of our country few people above ten years of age took that report seriously. It was a particularly evil report because it would use the results of racial segregation as the excuse to perpetuate it. On the contrary, after the desegregation of the schools and the necessary period of adjustment the standards of our elementary and secondary schools will be raised substantially. When we find that we must separate our private lives from our public institutions, the teacher will not discuss the recipe for cherry pie with the students. There will be "strangers" in the room. All she can say is, "Students, please turn to page forty-four."

And of course in discussing the "commencement" for an entire race, it is well to inject the usual admonition of the hard work ahead. What the white Southerner fears about desegregation will never happen; and what the Negro hopes for in this desegregation also will never happen. Not for a long time. Actually nothing much will "happen" to balance off these long years of struggle and effort. And it may come as a shock to many Negroes who have looked forward to this event with such great hopes. The law will be through with them. The law concerns itself only with a public right. No Federal judge will listen to a writ which is intended to change the hearts of men. This is not within his jurisdiction. And the hearts of men will not change the day after the

Negro becomes a first-class citizen. The law will wash its hands of the problem and the Negro people will be on their own.

There will be fewer friendships between white and Negro than there have been in the past. Many of these associations have been based on a paternalism, a sense of guilt, an attempt to pay homage to liberalism: "I have a few good Negro friends," he says with considerable pride. Most of that will be gone. The white man will no longer put up the bail when his "favorite Negro" gets in trouble. There will be many heartaches. And it will be better that way. Let each man stand up on his own feet and take "potluck," provided the cards are not stacked against him from the very day of his birth.

The Jews were in the ghettos of Europe for nearly fourteen hundred years, and for most of those centuries they fought to break down the ghetto walls. But when the day finally did come for them to enter the main stream of Western civilization, there was very great anguish. They were terribly bewildered. The security of the closely knit society was no more. It took hard work to make your way on your own. And it came about principally through education. There was such a mad dash to the schools and universities that most of the institutions established a quota system against the Jews. This system exists in most of our schools of higher learning to this very day—and in our own country too. But education, like love, will find a way, even if you have to study by the light of the moon. Hundreds of Jewish students unable to get into a French university used to meet in the courtyard of the school every evening to read their books. They felt that being in the shadow of the edifice was the next best thing to actually being admitted.

In our society today self-esteem comes with the acquisition of wealth; but we must remember that economic equality for the Negro race of the South is still a very long way off; so let us bear in mind that self-esteem (individual worth) comes also with education. In fact at this moment in the history of the American Negro there remains only one course of action—the true wisdom—there must be nothing short of a stampede of the Negroes of the South into the classrooms of America. There is no other way.

A plan for white citizens

EVERY time a Negro child is seen in the neighborhood of a white public school a committee of the "White Citizens Council" or "The Patriots" dashes over to the school board to see "what's up."

The memberships of these white organizations have been under a very severe strain. And the public school is not the only reason for their concern. Another worry is that all the religious denominations in the South have officially endorsed the Supreme Court's decisions to eliminate racial segregation.

The early missionaries of the Protestant sects did their work well. Nothing will ever shake the loyalty of the Negroes from the Baptist, Methodist, Presbyterian, and Episcopalian faiths, and there is always the possibility that some of these individual churches may be desegregated.

Then here is the plan to solve this problem for all the members of the "White Citizens Councils" throughout the South.

BECOME JEWS!

There is little likelihood of any appreciable number of Negroes ever going to shul. Every day when the sun goes down you'll have yourself a nice compact community. You'll never have to worry about Negroes again, and you'll even have yourselves your own country clubs, swimming pools, rummage sales, and book reviews.

Negro and Jew in Dixie

THE JEWS of the Deep South are terribly worried over the immediate future. They are concerned not only about the continued prosperity of their enterprise but for their actual physical well-being. And all of this has nothing to do with any national or sectional disaster or tragedy, or with the activities of the Jewish community itself or even with the delinquency of one of its number. Instead, the fear has grown out of a continued resistance, by stratagems of attrition by their Gentile neighbors against the decision of the United States Supreme Court which declared unconstitutional the segregation between the white and Negro races in the public schools.

Thus in the Deep South today, the white man fears the Negro; the Jew fears the Gentile; and the Negro, the focal point of this entire imbroglio, fears no one. And within the Jewish community it is significant that the fear involves those who have always considered themselves the *most* assimilated, the *most* successful, and the *most* integrated; and most scared of all is the fellow who had a Confederate grandfather.

It is necessary to make one point clear at the outset. The Jew in the South does not consider this problem on the simple basis of being either for or against the elimination of racial segregation. In fact the Jew in the South rarely thinks at all in terms of the Negro, as he wrestles with this problem in his communal meetings or in the communications to his national fraternities and religious organizations. Instead, he sees the problem as merely one of certain fixed jeopardies, any one of which is serious enough to threaten his security. If the textile mills were to shut down, for instance, it would mean economic disaster for the entire South, but to the Jew it would mean much more. It would involve his constant fear that those who may deem themselves responsible for such a tragedy would automatically seek to shift the responsibility to the Jew; charge him with their guilt and the punishment otherwise due them.

It is also significant that in several of the regional conferences of national Jewish organizations, Southern Jews have referred time and again to the anti-Semitic explosion during the famous Leo Frank case. The Jews of the South understand, as if by instinct, that the anger arising out of the Supreme Court order to desegregate the public schools is of one piece with the frustration of the thousands of farmers and sharecroppers in the Georgia of 1913 when local banks could no longer finance the cotton crop. It was terrible economic distress that made it possible for a Tom Watson to unloose the most serious anti-Semitic campaign in the history of the South, culminating in the lynching of Leo Frank. Thus in the present controversy the Jew feels that his own dilemma is the result of decisions and of attitudes in which he has had no part, and which were determined by neither his wishes nor his conduct. In fact his personal convictions are not involved at all. Here and there a Jew with a particular longing for "status" may say, "In our home the darkies always use the back door." But these are isolated cases. In the entire South there is no one less convincing than a Jewish white supremacist (as tragi-comical a figure as the Negro anti-Semite). Of all the ethnic groups in America only the Negroes and the Jews are denied the luxury of two of the constants of our society, white supremacy and anti-Semitism. The Jew of course knows this. And what is even more to the point he knows that his opposite number among the white Gentiles knows it too. But it is precisely for this reason that the Gentile in the Deep South has been pressuring the Jew to join in, or contribute to, his prosegregation organizations. The white Gentile interested in this prosegregation resistance values Jewish support highly because he considers it a defection from the ranks of the "enemy." He places the Jewish prosegregationist in the same category as the occasional Negro "leader" who signs a paper stating, "We Negroes will never be happy in white schools."

The Jew is only vaguely conscious of the more serious implications involved in his acquiescence to the prosegregation movement. And for this the leadership of some of his national religious and social-action organizations may have to bear the responsibility for a long time to come. Because for the Jew in the South such acquiescence means the confirmation of the frightening concept that his freedom and safety, even in America, have a frontier—a frontier involving the necessity to conform to the prejudices of the society in which he lives. It should also be remembered that the Jew thinks of this required conformity in terms of actual survival—"What will happen to us here?"—despite the fact that he has never been excluded from the open society of the Gentile world. At this level there is considerable ambivalence in the Jew's feeling toward the Negro. There is a sense of guilt over the fact that the black man, indigenous to the Southern soil for a dozen generations, and a "minority" like him, has been denied his free access to the open society. But there is envy too. The Jew envies the fact that the Negro, even though denied this access, never thinks of himself in terms of actual survival. All the Negro wants is to ride the buses, go to better schools, and get better jobs. No one has yet heard him say "What will happen to us here?"

The racial question has made the Jew conscious of a basic reality in his relation to the open society, that is, the Gentile desire for Jewish separateness ("All the Goldstein boys in our town married *American* girls"). In recent months the professional hatemongers have changed their anti-Semitic literature from "The Zionist-Bolshevik Conspiracy" to "The Jewish Conspiracy To Mongrelize the White Race." In defending the Jews against this nonsense, a Montgomery, Alabama, editor wrote: "*They* contribute to all *our* charities; *they* head all *our* civic drives; *they* help the poor and sick. . . ." The italics are mine, although it was hardly necessary to call attention to them in a city that had a Jewish Mr. Mordecai among its founders. Only in the small agricultural towns is this status of separateness accepted by the one or two Jewish families, since the relationship at this level is so clearly defined there is no opportunity for ambiguity at all. The Gentile neighbors always think of the one or two Jews in town in terms of a *people*, and it is from this that the few Jews draw their strength even though they are cut off from congregation and organized community. It is in this context that the most kindly disposed prosegregationist cannot deliver on his promise that "it will help the Jewish people all around if they join in the fight for the Southern way of life." Indeed, if all the Jews in the South joined the White Citizens Councils or the Patriots, Incorporated, the anti-Semitic pamphleteers would not lose a single "issue." The Jews are smart, they've all joined the Klan in order to make it easier to mongrelize the white race, the argument would then run. And, of course, this is far from fantasy. In Alabama one of the best-known Jewish communal leaders, who has always fought against any "Jewish" expression on the matter of desegregation, was photographed at a meeting of a local charity organization seated beside a Negro clergyman who also attended the meeting. The photo was blown up and used by the hatemonger Asa Carter as evidence of the Jewish interest in mongrelization. In Charlotte, North Carolina, one of the best-known communal leaders had been particularly active over the years in his attempts, first, to prevent a Jewish organization from entering a "friend-of-the-court" petition in the segregation cases, and later, to prevent the national Jewish organizations from issuing a public expression for the desegregation of the public schools. Ironically this is the man who was specifically singled out by the "Patriots, Inc." and Ku Klux Klan elements as the "head of the mongrelizers of the white race."

The "quality" of the prosegregation forces is another factor in the dilemma of the Jew of the South. While the Ku Klux Klan of the 1920's was predominantly a "wool-hat," rural movement, the anti-integration forces of 1958 include a surprisingly large percentage of urban, middle-class Southerners. This phenomenon has come as a severe blow to the Negro. He had every reason to believe that the Southern manufacturer, lawyer, doctor, agent and white-collar worker would be his allies in the drive to implement the decision of the Supreme Court to eliminate racial discrimination in the public schools. For years it had been this segment of the white society which supported every liberal movement in the cultural, educational, and economic betterment of the Negro. When a Negro ran for public office, his only white support would usually come from the best residential sections of the urban community. Yet at this crucial moment these same people threw their support to the prosegregationists.

This is no great mystery if we consider the entire process of the emergence of the social classes after the overthrow of agriculture as the dominant way of life of the South. The Negro was not the only one segregated. In fact, the Negro, using the back door, had far more access to the white Southern middle class than did the Anglo-Saxon millworker, service-station operator, or unskilled laborer. The stratification of the social classes was effected at every level of the Southerner's culture and religion. First he belonged to a "downtown" church, and when his economic status improved, he joined with his social equals and organized a new church in his own exclusive residential district. The millworkers went to separate schools, separate churches, and used separate entertainment facilities. At an early age the "uptown" children were told *not* to play with the children "on the hill" (cotton-mill area). The process of dehumanization had gone so far that when an uptown teen-ager was seen with a girl "from the (factory) hill" his parents' only concern was expressed in terms of "sowing his wild oats" or risking venereal disease; it was unthinkable that anything serious could possibly develop.

Thus for a half century this upper-class white Southerner had been running away from his own people, Anglo-Saxons of six and seven American generations, and now he was being asked to eliminate the segregation of an outsider, the black man, involving for him, the urban, middle-class Southerner, a sense of guilt which will be very difficult to overcome. And these are precisely the people from whom the Jewish storekeeper class of the South has sought acceptance for so long.

So the Jew now fears his loss of identity with the "best" people as much as he fears the more remote possibility of economic reprisal.

What further makes the position of the Jew uncomfortable is that the Negro takes it for granted that he possesses the sympathy of the Jews. Yet the Negro has not made the slightest move toward enlisting the active support of the Southern Jew in his fight for desegregation. His leadership has stated in no uncertain terms that it would hurt Negroes if another minority were to be in the forefront of their struggle. Thus the Jew is "solicited" only by the prosegregationists, which adds to his deep sense of guilt toward the Negro. This is concerned primarily with a belief which the Jew in the South has expressed hundreds of times that the Negro serves as his shock absorber, his *kapporeh* (sacrificial substitute), and that if the Southerners were to lose their Negro *kapporeh* they would look around for the all-time favorite. Furthermore it was not until quite recently that the Jew fully understood the pressure from the Negro that is as great as the pressure from the white supremacist. He almost overlooked the fact that a very large portion of his business comes from Negro customers. This is particularly true of the credit-jewelry stores, the pawnshops and small-loan companies, and the retail (mostly dry-goods) establishments clustered near "the underpass" of a thousand Southern cities and towns.

The Jew is also well aware of the fact that the Negro, with all his troubles, does not suffer from the terrible ambivalence that the Jew knows in his day-to-day relations with the general community. With a few notable exceptions the Jew has shied away from participation in public or political affairs because the Gentile insists upon this Jewish separateness—"We ought to have a Jew on the City Council." In this drive for full acceptance in the American middle class the Jew steadfastly refuses to participate on these terms. He therefore retires to his temple and country club where he piles one "Jewish" activity upon another and secures for himself the little honors and the self-expression which he feels are being denied to him in the open society. A Jewish manufacturer I knew had fought long and hard to get on the board of directors of his local community chest. He came away from his first meeting with a heavy heart: "They gave me all the Jewish cards."

The Negro, on the other hand, seeks public participation on precisely the terms which the Jew declines: "They should have *a Negro* on the City Council"; "*We* ought to be represented on the Park Commission"; and "What has the Democratic Party of the South ever done for *us?*" Again, with few exceptions, both the Negro and the Jew feel themselves alienated from the local community. One, because he refuses to participate *as a Jew*, and the other, because he insists upon participation *as a Negro*. The white Protestant of the South loves "the Jewish people," but is highly suspicious of the individual Jew. His emotions are in reverse with respect to the Negro. He loves the individual Negro, but hates the "people."

This alienation from the local community has had important sociological consequences for Jew and Negro. The Negro whose ancestors may have lived in a community for over two hundred years will speak only of "The Negroes of the South," or just "The Negroes." He will rarely mention "The Negroes of Kenilworth, South Carolina." He thinks of himself in terms of an entire racial and cultural civilization. The Jew also thinks of himself as apart from the local community. The name of the community on the masthead of his morning newspaper is purely coincidental. It could read "Tallahassee, Florida" or "Greenville, South Carolina" and arouse the same lack of emotion. When he is on a buying trip to New York and meets with an old friend he will reply: "Yes, I have a store in *the South.*" Or he may actually say, "I have a store in Virginia." Neither the Negro nor the Jew is likely to think in the specific terms of the local Chamber of Commerce slogan, "Watch Kenilworth Grow."

As part of his unwillingness to accept the Gentile's terms of Jewish separateness, the Jew of the South has fought hard

against being "committed" by another Jew, or by a national
Jewish organization. He prides himself on being well-inte-
grated in the Gentile society of his community, yet he will
argue for hours against the publication of a resolution passed
by some organization far away in New York. And he does
not see any inconsistency in this. He raises his hands in horror at the mere mention of a kehilla, or "organic" community,
yet he spends many valuable hours worrying about some
Jewish newcomer to the community who is addicted to writing letters to the editor. "We have someone else to worry
about now," he will say. In fact, he makes determined efforts
to control such "Jewish" expressions when it is within his
power to do so. This is really at the bottom of the continued
activity of the few small anti-Zionist groups in Richmond,
Atlanta, Memphis, Birmingham, and Houston. They create
the illusion that they are concerned with the sovereignty of
Israel and its effect upon American foreign policy, but basically their real worry is that somewhere in the country some
Zionist or Zionist group may issue a statement that will "com-
mit" them in the eyes of the Gentile community.

What about the Southern white Protestant who does not
join the "White Citizens Council" or a Ku Klux group? We
must not forget that it was the Southerner himself who,
through the slow and often cruel decades, consciously or
unconsciously laid the foundations for the universality of
ideas embodied in the Supreme Court's decision to eliminate
racial segregation. Today a very large body of these Southerners are convinced that enforced segregation of the races
can no longer be justified on any basis, but the actual problem of integrating the races in the public schools is unprec-
edented for the two generations that have lived with the
laws of Jim Crow.

The situation is intensified by the Southerner's very deep
sense of guilt which affects his daily life. He has been willing
to send the Negro children to elementary school and junior
high school, to provide dental care, lunches, transportation,
and even college training. And after all that trouble and
cost, on the day the Negro receives his college diploma he

also buys a railroad ticket to Camden, New Jersey, or Philadelphia, Pennsylvania. "Ah," says the white supremacist,
"we're getting rid of our Nigras." But it is not that simple,
because this college-trained boy, whom the Southerner denies
the right to use the skills which he himself has taught him,
leaves behind his unskilled father and his illiterate brother.
So the Southerner's welfare and hospital costs keep abreast
of his almost insurmountable cost of a double education
system. He consoles himself now and again with the statement that the Negro is not able to cope with the skills or the
requirements of the upgrading jobs which he denies him,
but he also knows that the Negroes in the South lose over
one half their school graduates each year. Out of 72 graduates
of a Negro college in North Carolina in 1956, 29 were no
longer in the State one year later; and of the others, 4 were
working as waiters and janitors, while the rest were in government service, in the teaching profession, and in the clergy.
But the Southerner's sense of guilt goes even deeper than the
attempt to maintain racial segregation. He knows that in the
South 15 Negroes out of every 1,000 die of tuberculosis, as
against a white death rate of 4 in 1,000; and this at the
height of the greatest prosperity we have ever known. Almost without exception, the condition of the communities
in which the Negroes live favors the spread of tuberculosis
and venereal disease. The Southerner knows too that the second biggest killer in the South is pregnancy, Negro pregnancy. Five times as many Negro women die in childbirth
as do white mothers and part of this story may be explained
by the fact that there are approximately eight hundred and
fifty hospital beds serving the white population (per 100,000
in 1954) as against one hundred and two hospital beds for
Negroes.

The Southerner is fully aware of the fact that education
takes place in many ways and at many levels, and that there
is great danger at the moment that his children may be educated in an atmosphere of evasion. If he continues to maneuver and manipulate in order to circumvent the duly
constituted agency of the law, how will he explain this ac-

tion to his children? The tragedy of the moment is not that the end of racial segregation is being delayed. The Supreme Court will prevail. The greater tragedy by far is that large groups of Southerners are being deluded; they are being served huge doses of self-delusion and false hopes. Politicians and wishful thinkers have been telling the people that the decree of the Supreme Court can be defeated. But the Supreme Court will not be defeated.

Lastly the Southerner's sense of guilt is heightened by the realization that for the first time he finds himself arrayed against his religious leaders and organizations. The Supreme Court's ruling was followed by immediate declarations by the great religious denominations in the South overwhelmingly supporting the decision as an expression of their own commitments to the brotherhood of all people. And while it is true that the main body of Southern Protestantism has not yet followed up on its initial commitment, it is equally true that the real contending forces in the South today are the Protestant churches and the forces of hatred and bigotry. So far the latter are making the most noise; now it is time, and past time, for the Protestant churches to be heard and seen.

Negro question is a matter of social status

Let us consider the huge cotton mill at Danville, Virginia. For many years the Negro has worked there as a "lap-hauler." This is the fellow who opens the bales and cases of raw materials and feeds them to the white workers on the machines. This involves constant association and close contact with the (white) spinners. But there was a labor shortage, and management decided to pick thirty of the experienced Negro workers and make *spinners* out of them; and the white spinners went out on strike in protest. And now they used all the arguments, including the legend about "body odor," a complaint which they had never raised about the Negro when he was a "lap-hauler." This is interesting because as a "segregated" spinner, the Negro would have had *no* contact at all with the white spinners; but one of the ladies, in arguing against this Negro promotion, told the story truthfully, and I quote her: "I am head of the Pythian Sisterhood, and I am a spinner, and now when I walk along the street, this fat colored woman comes along and she is also a spinner, and how do you think that makes me feel?"

This is the old story about race relations. In the North, the white man says to the Negro: "Go as high as you can, but don't come close," and in the South the white man says: "Negro, you can come as close as you can, but don't go 'up'!"

The fellow who flew to Ireland
by mistake

CORRIGAN, an engine mechanic, was preparing for a non-stop flight across the continent, but instead, flew across the Atlantic to Ireland. The incident had tremendous glamour. A young boy, all alone, making this expert flight "the wrong way." On top of all of that, he was Irish and his name was Corrigan. The Irish of New York went wild, and prepared a great reception for him. When he landed back in New York who should be the first to meet him as he got out of his plane but an uncle who was a Baptist preacher.

What a terrible letdown for the Irish Catholics of New York! They dropped him like a hot potato.

My positive cure for anti-Semitism

I HAVE a positive cure for this mental aberration known as anti-Semitism. I think we've been doing it all wrong. I believe that if we gave each anti-Semite an onion roll with lox and cream cheese, some chopped chicken liver with a nice radish, and a good piece of brisket of beef with a few potato pancakes, he'd soon give up all this nonsense. It is worth a try. If the Jews of America make me the chairman of this project, the first thing I will do is institute National Cheese Blintzes Week, with sour cream.

The burning of the cross

RECENTLY there have been a dozen or more cross-burnings in the Carolinas and Georgia. Now let us analyze this for a moment. Here are five or six men who hold various positions in the community—clerk, salesman, truck driver. Average guys. Nice fellows. If you met any one of them in the smoking car, you would discuss the usual things—politics, your home town, your grandchildren. Then at night these same five or six men put on white robes, go into some field, or to the street where a Negro lives, or to the lawn of a high school principal, and they light up a cross and run away.

Now, what is it all about? The principle, of course, is intimidation. You'd better watch your step on that Supreme Court decision, the burning cross seems to say to the white school principal, or you'd better stop your agitating, it seems to say to the Negro on whose street the cross has been fired. But why the cross? Why the burning cross?

This goes back thousands of years, long before the dawn of Christianity. The burning of the wheel or an effigy before Christianity was an attempt to express hate, and is known to historians as "fire-hate." Usually the fire was lit up during a plague or some disaster. The burning of an effigy was in effect the burning of the witch, the evil spirits. The burning of the cross in our times has been known as the "needfire."

The use of a religious symbol for a burning was roundly condemned by all Christian authorities, since it was recognized that the burning of the cross was the same "needfire" of pre-Christian days. The burning of the cross is really a symbol of the burning of Jesus. Jesus spoke for brotherhood and the revolt against this idea would be to burn Him. Thus the clerk or the white-collar worker sitting in the smoking car and who will burn a cross later that night is motivated by instincts which go far back into his origins—the "needfire," the burning of God. The man has become ill at ease under the moral restraints imposed upon him by the Father, and so—he burns Him.

The Downtown Luncheon Club
is more exclusive than heaven

I AM puzzled by the letters and pamphlets I receive from Christian and Christian-Hebrew mission groups urging me to become a convert. I am also puzzled by the vast sums of money appropriated by many church organizations for the purpose of carrying on this mission work. The Downtown Luncheon Club I cannot join.

If they don't want me for one hour at the Luncheon Club, why should they seek my companionship in heaven through all eternity?

Isaac—Ikey—Ike

Now that the name of Ike is sweeping the country, at least two generations of Jewish men whose names are Irving, Erwin, Irvin, Larry, Gary, Barry, Wilton, Dick, and Elbert can change it right back to good old Isaac—or Ike.

I remember in class 8B in P.S. 20, there was an old Irish teacher, Mr. Ryan, who had taught school for fifty years. The day before graduation he put a paper in front of each of us and said, "Now all you Isaacs will want to become Irvings and all those who are called Morris will probably want to change it to Maurice. This is your last chance." He did not say this with any sarcasm. I remember that he said it rather sadly and with a heavy heart.

Our first contact with the Gentile world was not very pleasant. The Irish firemen sitting in the firehouse with the doors open would yell to us indiscriminately, "Hey, Ikey . . ." and send us on errands for cigarettes or fruit. They always laughed loudly every time they yelled, "Hey, Ikey," and I remember that they made sure to repeat it when you returned, "All right, here's a penny for you, Ikey, ha, ha, ha, ha."

So, the wheel does turn—and, if any of those fellows are still around, it is no more than poetic justice that their cry is now, "I like Ike."

The Italian Americans

I WAS reading an article about Carmine DeSapio, the boss of Tammany Hall, a highly favorable piece in *Harper's*.

I thought of something when I read of this Italian politician. Has any group in this country, since the very beginning, had a worse press than the Italians? I doubt it. Their bootleggers and mobsters (no more and no less in number than others) have been spread across the front pages for years and years. In crime books and in radio and TV dramas the Italian has become a stereotype for the gangster and the mobster. This, of course, is not only unfair, but untrue. Yet what makes it remarkable is that the Italians do nothing about it. They have no organized "press relations" or "defense" groups. They just go along eating good spaghetti, singing "O Sole Mio," and becoming leaders of Tammany Hall.

No one gives you a jar of anything

IN THE old days when you visited someone they usually gave you a jar of something to take home—preserves of some kind. My friends down here tell me it was also a custom all over the South. On the East Side, quince preserves was a big favorite. Down here, they tell me, watermelon rind was a *pièce de résistance*. This fine custom is a thing of the past. No one gives you a jar of anything anymore. They are too busy playing with the push buttons in the mechanized kitchens.

How to get a note renewed at the bank

THE American Trust Company of Charlotte is the largest bank in these parts, handling much of the vast tobacco and textile wealth that flows through this State. The other day I went there to get a note renewed for another ninety days. Naturally, I was worried about it. As I entered the institution, who do you suppose was sitting with "my" banker, but Mr. Moses Richter, of Mount Gilead, one of the State's wealthy men. Mr. Richter left his seat, put his arm around me, and gave me the most terrific "hello" it has ever been my pleasure to receive. After that it was easy. When my turn came, I leaned back in my chair with the confidence of a tycoon. There was nothing to it. Who says a bank has no soul? This one has the soul of a Lord Byron.

Massa's in de cold, cold ground

NOVELIST James Street was telling me about the visit to Chapel Hill of a big New York publisher. The publisher, who usually eats either at the Stork Club or at Sardi's, had never been outside the big city. On his first day in de land "where the corn and 'taters grow," he and Jimmie went to visit a mutual friend, another writer in Chapel Hill. This friend was having some extensive landscaping done by a firm of Negro contractors.

As the "Stork Club" publisher approached the house, the Negroes began to hum softly that plaintive tune, "Massa's in de cold, cold ground"; then suddenly they began to shout, "Heave, ho!" "Heave, ho!" "Throw that line!" "Tow that barge!" "Lift that bale!" All the time the New Yorker was standing there with uplifted face of dedication, thinking of John Brown's body a-moldering in his grave. As they went into the house, the host, to keep it in the mood, began to prepare mint juleps; all the time worrying like hell about that dollar and a half an hour he was paying those landscapers out there. The prank was overtime—time and a half.

The boys were tired, too!

A BIG railroad water tank that was an old Charlotte landmark has been toppled over to make way for progress. I have memories about that tank.

Some years ago I knew a very fine old printer who was a pioneer trade-unionist in the South. He established the first typographical unit in Charlotte. He was working at the time on one of the local papers and one night he and a fellow printer were going home around midnight. They decided to have just one more drink—for the road, so to speak. They stopped off under that water tank and hoisted a few in the best printers' tradition. While they were under the tank, the water began to overflow on all sides, and one of the printers said, "Look at that rain!" and the other one said, "Boy, it's sure coming down; can't go home in this"; and with that, they both spread some newspapers on the ground and went to sleep.

Jew music all the time

ONE of my favorites is Rossini's *Stabat Mater*, his great requiem to the Virgin Mary. The "Inflammatus" part was always a great favorite with the cornet soloists in the old days of the free concerts on the Central Park Mall and the melody has stuck with me through the years. I hadn't heard it in a long time, and when I bought a recording of it I played it quite a few times on my record player at the office.

The next-door stenographer met my secretary and said to her, "What's your boss playing that Jew music for all the time?"

The history of the Jews in America

I REMEMBER a folk song on the East Side, "Sha sha der rebbe gayt" ("Quiet, quiet, the rabbi is coming") . . .

> Sha sha der rebbe gayt
> Sha sha der rebbe gayt

And sometime ago I watched the folks dance the "cha cha" in a Jewish country club in a Southern city, and I heard them keeping time with the music, "Cha cha, do-se-do, cha cha."

The history of the Jews in America: "from Sha sha to Cha cha."

The turban is a very big thing

HATS play an important part in the emotions of man. The shako, the fez, the turban, the high hat, and hundreds of other types of head covering have had a great influence on our civilization. Booker T. Washington, in his autobiography, tells us that the first thing the freed slave thought about was a NAME and the second thing was a HAT.

A few years ago a Negro newsman from Pittsburgh made a tour of the South wearing a turban and he was welcomed with open arms in the most exclusive hotels, and in one city of the Deep South a women's society sent him flowers and an invitation to make a speech.

Jewish food

I HAD a couple of friends in from the country where I used to live, ten miles out of Charlotte. I prepared some refreshments—some anchovies, good Liederkranz cheese, a piece of Stilton aged in port wine, and some black olives. With crackers and beer it made a respectable snack. The folks dipped into this and that, and finally the lady, showing great surprise, said, "You all don't eat like we do, do you?"

Secondhand pants, sixty cents

TODAY the secondhand clothing business is organized along the lines of General Motors.

The heart of the old-clothes business is on Elizabeth Street on New York's West Side. It is an old-clothes exchange that operates like an international bank. Hundreds of peddlers bring their purchases and collections for sale to bigger dealers, wholesalers, and exporters. Several million dollars' worth of secondhand clothing is shipped every year to Southern Rhodesia, Hong Kong, Bombay, and the Belgian Congo. The biggest market for secondhand silk hats or opera hats is on the African west coast; they take all they can get. There is a regular exchange, prices determined by supply and demand as well as by quality and condition.

But these fluctuating prices concern only coats and hats; the price for secondhand pants is fixed. If there are no rips and tears in the pants, it doesn't make any difference whether the suit had originally cost $150 or $22.50—all pants are sixty cents. Not a penny more.

The needle industry coming South?

WILL the garment district in midtown Manhattan become the "Fall River" of the needle trade? About forty years ago, the textile plants of Fall River, Massachusetts, and other New England cities began to move South. Today nearly 90 per cent of America's spindles are within a 150-mile radius of Charlotte.

It looks like the needle trades may be following the textile pattern. There is plenty of evidence already. From Orlando, Florida, working northward to the North Carolina-Virginia border, at least three thousand machines have been installed, with 75 per cent of them in South Carolina. Some of them are new plants, but the majority are transplanted establishments from New York.

I think the next ten years will see some great changes. This whole South is still in the pioneer stage as far as industry is concerned. Its climate is probably the best in the country, its natural resources are as yet untapped, and it has an unused labor pool amounting to one third its entire population.

At the present time the median income of this Negro population is a little less than one half of that of the white population. In the next ten years the gap will be closing and you'll have twelve million new customers—for everything, starting from scratch.

Yes, I believe the manufacturers of finished products will continue to move South. They are moving for the wrong reason, of course, but like so many others before them, they'll discover that they had planned much better than they knew. Eventually they'll find to their amazement something they hadn't even remotely counted on—outside their factory door, they'll come upon a brand-new market for all the goods they can make.

This could happen only in America

I NEED a book; a book that may be found only in the Library of Congress, or maybe in the Library of Harvard University. And so I call up the Charlotte Public Library, and ask for either Mr. Galvin or Mr. Brockman. I tell him what I want and where I think it may be found and within a week or ten days the book or the document is delivered to me on a two-week loan. I can renew it if I give them a few days' prior notice, and thus the facilities provided by my city in the South are expanded through cooperation with the facilities and treasures of the whole of America, and merely for the asking. They all combine to make available to me the sum total of all of human thought and experience; at no cost whatever.

Movies for adults only

I HAD a long talk with the operator of an art theatre. He plays the Alec Guinness pictures, and most of the good English, Italian, French, and Swedish films. For most of these pictures he draws an audience of "regulars," but when he adds the phrase "For Adults Only" to an advertisement, he attracts many whom he sees only once in a great while. And they come out of the show mad—hopping mad—angry as all get-out! Their indignation knows no bounds! "What do you mean, 'Adults Only'? There was nothing in that there picture!"

In one film particularly, a Swedish movie, there was one of these Hedy Lamarr sequences where a nude girl runs through the woods, but it all happens very quickly, and anyway the shot was taken at a considerable distance from the subject. Many of the audience came out immediately after this frustrating sequence and demanded their money back. "Why, that was just a flash, there was nothing to that!" What they wanted, of course, was a close-up—or at least for the gal not to run so darn fast. But they keep a-coming. They probably figure that someday that gal may go sprawling over a stump and they want to be in on it.

Meanwhile, the art-theatre operator has adopted a new system. As soon as the "adult" film begins, he puts his hat on and goes home.

Countess Mara and I

ONE of my readers is a gentleman by the name of Al Bierman. Mr. Bierman is a sales manager for a national manufacturer and maintains a suite of rooms in four or five cities of the South. He represents a bit of Broadway and Las Vegas in Charlotte.

A few months ago Mr. Bierman sent me a box of six neckties. Very nice. I sent him a thank-you note. Normally my necktie bill ranges between $4.50 and $6.00 per annum. So I began to wear Mr. Bierman's neckties. When I got to San Diego, California, where the streets are paved with gold, my host leaned over to me during the banquet and said, "My, my, the editing business must be good to wear Countess Mara neckties." I wanted to know who was Countess Mara, and my host showed me something I hadn't noticed before. The initials *C M* were worked into the design. The Countess Mara necktie I was wearing, said my San Diego host, cost fifteen dollars. Fifteen dollars for a necktie? That's nearly six pints of whiskey. Late that night I took the necktie off and replaced it with one of my own dollar-fifty jobs. How can you tie knots in a necktie that costs fifteen dollars? I am saving them for special occasions.

We'll soon run out of non-Jews

WE'LL soon run out of non-Jews to dedicate our temples, synagogues, community centers, yeshivas, and all other ground-breaking ceremonies. Which reminds me of a true story. Some years ago a non-Jewish political leader was invited to dedicate a new synagogue in one of our Southern cities. He called me up and said, "Harry, your people want me to dedicate their new church. Write me up something like a good fellow."

My people? I hadn't even been invited, but the guy did make a wonderful speech, even if I do say so myself.

Closed shop versus open shop

IN the adult study group of a Southern temple, the program chairman decided to have a debate. The question?— the old high school reliable, "Open Shop vs. Closed Shop." Two of the members agreed to take opposite sides.

The fellow with the "Closed Shop" put a notice in the morning paper (a usual practice) to attract a larger audience. The fellow with the "Open Shop" objected to the notice because he did not feel that he should be identified with such a "controversial" subject outside of the discussion room; and there was considerable merit to his objection considering his business connections.

However, this is not the end. The evening paper, innocently picking up the "social" item from the morning paper, made an error and switched "sides," making it appear as though the effervescent "Closed Shop" fellow was taking the

"Open Shop" while our conservative friend, originally billed for the "Open Shop," was speaking for the "Closed Shop."

The conservative member was beside himself with rage— "not enough, a notice is put in the paper, but my employees by the morning paper see that I'm for the 'Open Shop,' while my employees by the evening paper see that I'm for the 'Closed Shop.' "

It was really terrible. The rabbi delivered his usual talk on "Jewish Customs of the Past."

What can you tell Texas Guinan?

I REMEMBER a fellow who owned a tremendous men's clothing business in New York. It was during the big bull market in Wall Street. In those days Calvin Coolidge and Arthur Brisbane wrote a daily market letter, which in effect urged everybody to keep buying stocks—the sky was the limit.

Well, this clothing tycoon, like so many others, brought his business down to Wall Street and proceeded to plunge deeply and over his head. When his friends and relatives pointed out to him that he was risking a steady, high-income business, he said, "How can I tell Texas Guinan that I'm in the clothing business?" He wanted to go to Guinan's night club and be introduced as a stock-market manipulator. Today he's back in the clothing business—a salesman on the road with 6 per cent commission.

Explaining the Southerner

THE late Bill Polk in his charming book, *Southern Accent*, tells the story of a homesick Southerner living up North who wrote to his folks: "I wish I had been born in the South before the Civil War and been killed at Gettysburg."

I came across one that would have warmed Bill Polk's generous heart. It is an excellent (and serious) letter to the editor of the *Christian Century* (May 30, 1956), from a Georgian who takes issue with William Faulkner's recent statements on the desegregation issue. The letter opens as follows: "To begin with, my credentials: I grew up in Alabama, neighbor to Mr. Faulkner's Mississippi. My grandfather was a captain in the 46th Alabama regiment in the army of the Confederate States, and was in the army under Joseph E. Johnston that opposed Sherman's March to the Sea. He lost a leg in the Battle of Atlanta . . . and died of a weakened heart when he rose from a sickbed to give the 'rebel yell' when a train bearing Jefferson Davis blew for a stop at Eufaula, Alabama."

From the Shpitzinitzer to the Rotary

AH, what a wonderful country. This could happen only in America. I am not talking about *three hundred years* of history. I am talking about *forty-five years* of history.

Forty-five years ago the rabbi used to walk along the street on the East Side with a red handkerchief sticking out of his back pocket. And the people on the block used to say, "That's the rabbi," and the toughest kids would stop their wrestling and horseplay to "let the rabbi pass." The rabbi would be on his way to his shul.

The shul always had a tremendous name like "The Ohab Sholom Ansche Ungarn Congregation"—and usually it was a single room above a candy store, and the rabbi would go there to wait for the boys and men to come in to say kaddish (the mourners' prayer after the death of a parent).

And now, only forty-five years later, the rabbi is at the Rotary Club singing "I Was Seeing Nellie Home."

What a country!

I refuse to look it up

THIS is the word: *dichotomy*. Every fancy article you read now uses the word "dichotomy." I can just see the writers smiling to themselves with satisfaction and confidence as they repeat the word two or three times before putting it down on paper. This dichotomy deal started in the *Partisan Review* and has been spreading like a prairie fire to *Harper's, Saturday Review, Atlantic Monthly, Commentary*, and so help me the other day I saw it in an editorial in a daily paper.

Big Chief Dic-Cot-Oh-Me. Oh, me is right. I have written some five million words during these past ten years, all of them printed, and most of them read, and I have not found it necessary to use this dic-cot-oh-me; not once; and I refuse even to look it up.

With five million unemployed we have trouble enough.

PART 5

Galli-Curci and Bubble Gum

Let's take bubble gum
out of the schools

A CLEAR and present danger to our society lurks in the corridors of our new ranch-type schools.

Bubble gum comes with the terrazzo tile.

The magnificent buildings and elaborate facilities have far outstripped the actual processes of education. It's like moving into a fifty-thousand-dollar home with holes in your shoes and no desire or resources to get them half-soled.

In the end, the beautiful new high school building stands as a mockery to the boys and girls who can barely read and write.

In this elaborate construction we are, of course, trying to keep abreast of our business community—bigger and better facilities all the time. This works very well in private enterprise, but in education it is something else. For one thing, we do not "follow" it to its logical conclusion. When a large corporation puts up a magnificent building, it does not turn the edifice over to executives making thirty-two hundred dollars a year. The janitor gets that. For another thing, there is a direct connection between "bigger and better facilities" and expanded production and distribution of goods and services.

There is no connection in education. In education all you

need is a few benches, a desk, a pointer, a blackboard, some chalk, and A TEACHER; everything else is "the fixins."

The big problem which faces us today in education is fairly simple. No one reads books any more.

This may sound like oversimplification, but I don't think so. The high school boys and girls no longer read any books. It is appalling. Today you can stand before a group of high school seniors and tell them the basic tales of our literature: the stories out of Dickens, Verne, Hardy, Conrad, Hugo, Dumas, and Bulwer-Lytton, and they stare at you as if you had just dropped down from the planet Mars.

The students (sic) are required to read one book a semester, but they can usually catch something on TV, and that's that. They are also required to read one thousand lines of poetry—which wraps up their lil ole credits—and away they go; bubble gum and all.

This is not the fault of the teachers. The teachers are *not* permitted to do their job. Our entire system of education needs an overhauling. A magnificent building is all right, but it will never produce educated men and women. Only *teachers* can do that, and they can do it (and they have done it) by candlelight if need be.

Once the parents were afraid of teachers. Now, alas, the teachers are afraid of parents.

Every few months the teachers around the country are annoyed with organized visits by all sorts of groups of "parents" and "civic leaders." On such occasions teachers are brought together and told what to wear and how to conduct themselves in front of the guests. This is part of the story of our present-day education—the four-year high school course which qualifies the kid to enter the State college where he promptly starts on a new two-year course of what they call "remedial English"—learning to read and write. It is part of the system of "letting them do what they want."

I cannot reconcile these high school courses in "cherry pie-making" with the principles of John Dewey, the education philosopher. In a fine pamphlet by Lois Meredith French of Newark State Teachers College, *Where We Went Wrong in*

Mental Hygiene, Dr. French says, "John Dewey, himself, in the later years of his life made various attempts to explain that he never meant his progressive education to turn out undisciplined children."

I think it would be better if we went back to the old system when the teacher sent for a parent and he stood in the hallway with his hat in his hand waiting to be interviewed, and maybe a little scared about the whole thing, too.

This is all of one piece with the fact that the teachers are so badly underpaid. The people of the commercial society are no fools. They understand perfectly well that there are a few people who, because of their careers, have no frontiers in the social structure. These are the teachers, of course, and the creative people.

The first thing our commercial friend does when he makes a lot of money is to sponsor something which has in its title the word, "Education," "Institute," or "Cultural." He feels that no matter how little the teacher gets, the teacher has acquired a special status. Why give him financial security, too? Since the teacher is paid out of tax funds, there is no way this can be resisted, except to be on good behavior when the groups come a-visiting. Luckily we still have *Free Enterprise* so that many creative people can remain privately employed or self-employed, and keep the doors closed to intruders. If all creative people were paid out of taxes you would have a "Parents-Writers Association," a "Parents-Composers Association," and a "Parents-Artists Association."

It is not only that teachers are underpaid, but also that they are interfered with by the "outside," that forces them to become quasi politicians. The academy is gone, even though the British remain encouraging. We had it once, but lost it.

And so at long last we have run smack into something (education) that we just cannot buy—or phony up in any way —frustrating, isn't it?

Is it presumptuous of me to challenge the entire idea of progressive education? I believe that some day the educational system will wake up to this danger of letting them do what they want. What nonsense! Did they really believe that they can replace the schoolteacher with the authority to tell them what to do? Today it is a huge joke. You watch them running from classroom to classroom, and it's all a fake. They know nothing. Nothing at all. If you doubt my word, I dare you to go into a classroom of high school seniors in your own town and ask them five questions:

1. Who was the Marquis de Lafayette?
2. Who was Jean Valjean?
3. Name four members of the United States Supreme Court.
4. Who was the first man to circumnavigate the globe?
5. What do we call the series of letters written by Alexander Hamilton, John Jay, and James Madison which helped bring about these United States of America?

If you get more than *three* per cent correct answers, let me know, and I promise to push a peanut with my nose from Charlotte, North Carolina, to Atlanta, Georgia.

They know nothing. No one reads books any more, and the teachers are helpless. The teachers are paid *twice* as much as they are worth as baby sitters, which they are; and they are paid *half* as much as they are worth as teachers, which the system does not allow them to be.

There are no short cuts! In economics you start with the land. In education you start with the books. Nothing else can do it for you—not even TV, movies, Hopalong Cassidy, ninety million comic books a year, slopping around with paintbrushes, or letting them do what they want. Letting them do what they want belongs in the insane asylum. Half of them can't even tell you the name of the governor of their State, let alone letting them do what they want!

It is a great tragedy. A tragedy for the students, a tragedy for the teachers, and a tragedy for those of us who have read a book. It is most certainly part and parcel of the current drive against intellectualism. When all of these uneducated boys and girls come out of school, they somehow carry with them a vague suspicion of all those who have read a book.

That's how simple it is. It is part of our state of affairs today, and you cannot separate one from the other. It is part of the current fear of "learning." Among the uneducated, "book learning" breeds resentment, fear, suspicion, and hatred; and soon, as it has happened so often, they'll join the first demagogue who comes along and says, "Let's go get them as has read a book." It is difficult for uneducated and unread people to adjust themselves to a tolerant viewpoint. It cannot be done.

This is the grave danger. An uneducated man gets indigestion and has a bad dream. In the dream someone is chasing him around the edge of a mountain with a long spear. He gets up in the morning, puts a revolver in his pocket, and goes out looking for the guy who has been chasing him around the edge of a mountain with a long spear; and pretty soon he recognizes his "tormentor"—by an amazing coincidence it is usually someone who is not a member of his own clan, race, or church. Sometimes the fellow with the spear even turns out to be a business competitor. Then the uneducated "dream boy" lets him have it; or, more often, he just bides his time in anger, fear, suspicion, and hatred. A man's creed, a man's whole life, is in harmony with his intellect.

The crying need at this moment in our history is, first, to qualify our teachers; second, to give them a living wage; third, to divest the little darlings of their bubble gum, comic books, and zip guns; and, fourth, to turn them over to the teachers without any interference. Never mind the beautiful buildings—leave those to Du Pont. What we need in the classroom is a revival of the art of reading books, a revival of homework, and a revival of the complete authority of the teacher.

Teaching Shylock

I KNOW that if anyone suggested the censorship of *The Merchant of Venice* either as a book or as a play, I would fight the attempt with everything I have. But having said that, I will also say that, if it were up to me, I wouldn't teach *The Merchant of Venice* in secondary schools.

I would use *Julius Caesar* and *A Midsummer Night's Dream, Macbeth,* and *As You Like It.* When the student enters college, *The Merchant,* of course, must be read and studied. My view of the secondary schools comes from experience. On several occasions an English teacher in one of the local high schools has asked me to lecture her pupils on the historical background of *The Merchant of Venice.* This, of course, is wonderful. But the mere fact that a humanitarian schoolteacher felt the need for some background "explanation" is evidence enough that the play should be left to the colleges. On each of these occasions I said to myself, how can I stand up before fifty or sixty boys and girls—Presbyterians, Methodists, and Baptists—and tell them that the Shylock play is a satire on the Gentile middle class of Venice? If I even attempted such a course there would be a danger that my words might be interpreted as lack of respect for the Christian faiths.

So all I could really do with the background was recite a bit of history of the Middle Ages, and explain the legal processes by which the Jews were forcibly urbanized and driven to dealing with money. I also traced the development of Shylock; how almost from the very beginning the English actors recognized Shakespeare's purpose and as early as the year 1741 Shylock was portrayed on the English stage as the sympathetic figure in the play. On one of these occasions a boy in the class asked me a question: "Mr. Golden, why the Jews?

Why have the Jews been picked out for all these terrible things?"

It was a good question, a pertinent question. I looked at the clock and saw that I had two minutes to go. I told the boy I'd sit down and answer his question in my paper and send him a copy. And I'll do it soon, of course.

Shylock and William Shakespeare

THE presentation of Shakespeare's *The Merchant of Venice* at Stratford, Ontario, has resulted in a wave of comment in the English-Jewish press. There are Jews who dread to see the play produced and protest its presentation. Others feel that Shylock has been drawn with great imaginative penetration and have no objection to its production. Still others are not interested either way but are against censorship of any kind under any circumstances. This is natural and during each of my lectures on Shakespeare I could always count on the controversy when we came to the lecture on Shylock.

The German Nazis understood Shakespeare very well, and they did not use Shakespeare's Shylock in all their gigantic propaganda campaigns. They spent plenty of money in distributing Budd Schulberg's *What Makes Sammy Run?* but not a single copy of *The Merchant of Venice* reached those shores as part of the defamation campaign. The Germans knew. They knew their Shakespeare. German was the first language into which Shakespeare was translated. Now let us go back a little.

You must remember that the Jews had been expelled from England in the year 1290, and they were not readmitted until Oliver Cromwell's time in 1655. Legally, that is. Actually, the authorities did not enforce the law too rigidly after the ascension of Elizabeth I, a century earlier. Elizabeth sensed that her reign would usher in the age of Gloriana. Trade was the thing. She wanted peace, exploration, and trade and commerce. That meant, let up on the discrimination against the guys who knew all about peace, trade, and commerce. But Elizabeth had a Jewish doctor, Roderigo Lopez, and this Dr. Lopez was arrested and convicted on the charge of attempting to poison Elizabeth. Let us not go into that at the moment. We have enough to worry about. Let us leave Lopez hanging outside the East Gate of London in the winter of 1594. Very likely it was a plot to reactivate the law against the Jews, which Elizabeth was trying to minimize at the moment. We are not sure. If it was a plot, it worked. A wave of anti-Semitism spread over England. The people who love to have their prejudices confirmed were again reminded of the stereotype of the Jew which had persisted in literature and folklore all through the Middle Ages. Now to ride the crest of the wave, the balladeers, poets, playwrights, and journalists jumped into the act to cash in on the revived anti-Semitism. Even the two greatest dramatists of the day, already legends in their own time, could not resist this audience interest. Christopher Marlowe wrote *The Jew of Malta*, and on July 22, 1598, James Roberts entered in the Stationers' Register "The Marchaunt of Venyce, or otherwise called the Jewe of Venyce," by William Shakespeare.

Now let us start all over again.

All through the Middle Ages thousands of anti-Jew plays were produced all over Europe. These plays are lost to us. They were really nothing. No art. No value at all. In the main they were poorly improvised or poorly written. "Passion" plays. They were the standard drama-form of the Middle Ages. Their hostility to Jews was based on a simple formula: "this is evil—because it's evil." And no questions asked. All of these cut-and-dried anti-Jew plays continued for four hundred years, culminating in the work of a literary giant—Geoffrey Chaucer—in *The Prioress's Tale*. Chaucer was a genius, and he was read and how! From the year 1385 right down to this day in every college you must know Chaucer. Well, Chaucer did us more harm with his few lines about ritual murder than all the four hundred years of junk "Passion" plays put together. The myth of the Wandering Jew also flourished through these centuries; a myth of hate, libel, and murder. But Chaucer was not the only immortal to have accepted the stereotype of "evil because it is evil." Christopher Marlowe, one of the giants, also played it straight without a single editorial comment, and Marlowe's hostility could not have been "Wandering Jew" stuff; he was an outspoken atheist. And let us not brood too much over the Middle Ages. Let us come right down to modern times and we find Edward Gibbon, the greatest of all historians, in his *Decline and Fall of the Roman Empire*, speak of ritual murder like he was reporting an automobile accident, also without any editorial comment, and even Winwood Reade, in his *Martyrdom of Man*, who checked every detail of his writings (he even made a special trip to the African coast just to double-check his chapter on Negro slavery). Yet this wonderful man tells how the Jews stole all of Pharaoh's silverware when they left Egypt. *This*, he knew. He had footnotes for everything, but for this he didn't need any footnotes. He was sure. An outspoken atheist, Mr. Reade held up to scorn and ridicule everything in the Bible except those passages which he could interpret as being unfavorable to the Jews. How can you figure it?

Now let us get started on William Shakespeare and *The Merchant of Venice*. Mr. Shakespeare was first and foremost Mr. Theatre. He was a craftsman interested in filling his theatre; earning dividends for his colleagues and partner-producers and providing a livelihood for his fellow actors. He also wrote a "Jew play." BUT THIS WAS SHAKESPEARE. This was not Marlowe, nor Chaucer, nor Gibbon, nor Reade. We are dealing here with the jewel of mankind, the greatest brain ever encased in a human skull.

Shakespeare gave his audience a play in which they could confirm their prejudices—but he did much more. Shakespeare was the first writer in seven hundred years who gave the Jew a "motive." Why did he need to give the Jew a motive? Certainly his audience did not expect it. For centuries they had been brought up on the stereotype, "this is evil because it's evil," and here Shakespeare comes along and goes to so much "unnecessary" trouble giving Shylock a motive. At last—*a motive*.

> Fair sir, you spit on me on Wednesday last;
> You spurn'd me such a day; another time
> You call'd me dog.

Fighting words. Many a Southerner of ante-bellum days did not bother about getting a "pound of flesh." He finished his traducer on the spot. But Shakespeare gives us no rest. He is actually writing a satire on the Gentile middle class and the pseudo-Christians, and he wastes no time. What does Antonio, this paragon of Christian virtue, say to this charge of Shylock's? Does he turn the other cheek? Does he follow the teaching of Jesus to "love thine enemies"? Not by a long shot. This "noble" man replies to Shylock's charge:

> I am as like to call thee so again,
> To spit on thee again, to spurn thee too.

But Shakespeare has hardly begun. Mr. Poet-Philosopher is playing a little game with Mr. Theatre. Shylock loans Antonio three thousand ducats for three months and demands a pound of flesh as security. This is good. This is right up the Middle Ages alley, according to the seven-hundred-year-old pattern—"evil because it's evil," that's all. But Shakespeare does not let his audience off so easily. He makes them reach for it. In the first place, Shylock loans the money to Antonio without interest. But that's only the beginning. Since anti-Semitism is the renunciation of logic, Shakespeare says if that's what you want to believe, I'll not make it easy for you. You must renounce *all* logic. You must also believe that Shylock loaned money to the richest man in Venice and that somehow he knew that this rich man would lose all his money in ninety days and couldn't pay off a debt which was really peanuts to him. How could he possibly know that? A pound of flesh, yes, but how could Shylock figure that within ninety days a storm in the Persian Gulf and in the Mediterranean, and in the Indian Ocean would suddenly destroy all of Antonio's ships, all within the same ninety days?

And, look here, why does this noble Antonio, the Christian merchant, want the three thousand ducats to begin with? Why did Shakespeare go out of his way to show that Antonio's request for a loan was based on cheapness and chicanery? He did not have to do that. Certainly not for an anti-Semitic audience of 1598. He could have contrived a million more noble causes. Patriotism. Antonio needed the money for widows and orphans, or to defend Venice against an invader. How the audience would have eaten that up. But Shakespeare refuses to make it simple. Let us discuss the play from the viewpoint of the audience, like when your children go to the movies. "The good guys" and "the bad guys." Antonio and his friends are "the good guys"; Shylock, the Jew, is "the bad guy." Now what do we have here? Antonio's friend, Bassanio, one of the "good guys," is in debt to Antonio. He wants to pay back and he has a scheme. Portia just inherited a wad of money. If he can get Portia and her dough all his troubles would be over. But Bassanio says the project needs some front money. You need money to woo a rich girl like Portia. So he says to Antonio, lend me just a little. He says that when he was a youth and when he lost one arrow, he shot another one in the same direction and often retrieved both. So now. Lend me some dough so I can make love to a rich lady who has just inherited a vast fortune, and with good luck I'll not only pay you back what you advanced me but I'll give you all back debts I owe you.

This is the deal the two noble "good guys" in Shakespeare's play made. Antonio says, "It's a deal, only all my ready cash is tied up in my ships, and I'll not be able to lay my hands on ready cash for ninety days or so."

And so they go to Shylock to borrow the money.

How could we help but sense that Shakespeare was writing an indictment of the hypocrites who vitiated every precept taught them by Christianity? Shylock is a widower. He has only one daughter, Jessica, who falls in love with Lorenzo, a Gentile. "The good guys" induced her not only to desert her widowed father but to rob him, and dressed in boy's clothing (a third crime in Jewish law), Jessica steals away in the night to elope with Lorenzo.

> I will make fast the doors, and gild myself
> With some more ducats, and be with you straight.

Based on Western law Jessica has committed the crime of theft. She has also committed the moral crime of stealing out of her father's house during the night and deserting him, and as the young thief comes away with her father's money, what do "the good guys" say? Gratiano exclaims:

> Now, by my hood, a Gentile, and no Jew.

Can you imagine how that audience howled with glee as Jessica was leaving Shylock's house with his caskets of money? Shakespeare probably figured that during this howling the audience would miss the follow-up line. You have deserted your father, stolen out of his house during the night dressed in boy's clothing, and robbed him of his money, and *now* you are a Gentile, and by my hood, no Jew. The playwright set his 1598 audience to howling. The poet-philosopher wrote for all future generations.

Later on, "the bad guys," Shylock and his friend Tubal, are discussing Jessica's theft and desertion. Tubal tells Shylock that Jessica had exchanged one of the rings she had stolen for a monkey. Says Shylock, "I wish she hadn't taken that ring. That was Leah's turquoise. That was my wife's ring; she gave it to me before we were married. I wish she hadn't pawned that ring for a monkey." This from a Jew moneylender in the anti-Semitic atmosphere of the sixteenth century. For the first time in seven hundred years of "Jew literature" in Europe, a writer had given the Jew a motive. Then he put the cloak of "human being" around him. "I wouldn't have taken a whole wilderness of monkeys for Leah's ring," says Shylock.

Bassanio invites Shylock to supper and the Jew replies:

> Yes, to smell pork; to eat of the habitation which *your prophet the Nazarite conjured the devil into.*

The italics are mine and I say that no Christian writer, before or since Shakespeare, has dared to put such "blasphemy" into the mouth of a "heretic." Nor has a Christian writer shown such cynicism about the hypocritical setup, as when Shakespeare has Launcelot, one of "the good guys," say that we had better be very careful about converting so many Jews to Christianity; all we'll be doing is raising the price of pork.

But it is in one of the subplots of the play, with the three caskets and Portia's suitors, that Shakespeare gives us the key to his purpose. One of the suitors is Morocco, a black man, and in the year 1598 Shakespeare has him speak these amazing lines:

> Mislike me not for my complexion,
> The shadow'd livery of the burnish'd sun,
> To whom I am neighbour and near bred.

"Bring me the fairest blond from your northern forests, make the incisions and you'll find my blood as red as his," says Morocco. Thus Morocco's brief part in the play unlocks the door to the whole business. Shylock asks, "When you prick us, do we not bleed?" Morocco, Shylock, Antonio— under the skin all men are brothers.

Shakespeare leads us up to the clincher. The audience and the players are now waiting for the big moment before the court where Shylock is bringing his suit against Antonio, the merchant, for his pound of flesh. Portia enters, disguised as a lawyer, and what does she say? What are her first words at this final showdown between "the good guys" and "the bad guys"? Portia asks a most natural question:

Which is the merchant here, and which the Jew?

Both the plaintiff and the defendant are standing before the court. Portia has never seen either one of them before, but as an educated gentlewoman she has behind her the culture of many centuries of the stereotype Jew. If not actually with horns, you certainly can recognize the "devil" a mile away. And there he is ten feet away—she has a fifty-fifty chance at making a guess between "the good guy" and "the bad guy," but she won't risk it.

Which is the merchant here, and which the Jew?

And when it all goes against Shylock, Shakespeare seems to go out of his way to give us a frightening picture of the "victors." He has them standing together pouring out a stream of vengeance. We're not through with you yet, Jew, and the money we have left you after you have paid all these fines, you must leave that to Jessica and your son-in-law who robbed you. Shakespeare keeps them hissing their hate. Tarry yet awhile, Jew, we're still not through with you. You must also become a Christian. The final irony. The gift of love offered in an atmosphere which is blue with hatred. And as all of this is going on, Shakespeare leaves only Shylock with a shred of dignity!

I pray you, give me leave to go from hence.

Galli-Curci lingers

"ALL things are transient; art alone endures."

A man may live a full life of, say, fifty years of adulthood, with all its problems, worries, ups and downs, love, marriage, children, illness, surgery, deaths, reverses, successes, promotions, disappointments, joys, sorrows, and tragedies—and yet, in a sentimental mood, when he's sitting around with friends, what will he talk about? He'll tell about the time he heard Caruso sing, or the night he heard the Philharmonic Symphony, or the thrill of seeing Ethel Barrymore, or Jacob Adler, or Galli-Curci.

I heard Galli-Curci in the old Hippodrome in New York. Up to the time the new Madison Square Garden was built, the Hippodrome on Sixth Avenue and 43rd Street was the largest enclosure in America. I think it seated about seventeen thousand with room for about three thousand standees. Very few "single" acts could fill the Hippodrome. It took a great "spectacle" or "extravaganza," like the circus or a great sporting event. Billy Rose produced one of the last spectacles there, and it was a dismal failure despite his tremendous cast of elephants, Jimmy Durante, and a dozen other famed actors and musicians. The name of it was *Jumbo* and after opening night there were acres of empty seats in the great auditorium.

Caruso filled the Hippodrome by himself, so did John McCormack, and so did Galli-Curci. The picture of this tiny Italian woman standing in front of twenty thousand music lovers with a lone pianist on the tremendous stage I can never forget. I sat way up in the last balcony and the artist looked as though she was a mile away, which, come to think of it, was not far off, at that. The moment she came out to sing her famous encore, "Annie Laurie," was enough to send a shiver down your back. I doubt whether a month has gone by in all these years that I haven't thought of tiny Galli-Curci singing, "Maxwelton's braes are bonny, Where early fa's the dew, . . . 'twas there that Annie Laurie gave me her promise true. . . ."

Need we defend books?

TODAY there seems to be a conspiracy against books, or I should say against bookish men. One of the accusations made against a Government employee I know was that "he reads too many books." They made a movie recently with the great actress, Helen Hayes, and the picture was about an American family with three sons, and the eldest son turns out to be a Communist spy. When this information is revealed the father tells the FBI man, in effect: "I always knew something like this would happen. My other two boys were out there playing catch in front of the house, while this fellow (the spy) was always readin' books."

It was amazing that a man like General Eisenhower, who had been president of Columbia University, should have readily joined in this age-old bit of stupidity. In a speech in Cincinnati, Ohio, the General said, "We want men of action and not words—certainly not Harvard words." If you analyze this statement carefully you will see it for what it is: a subtle piece of demagoguery, no loftier than Westbrook Pegler's— "I have no use for intellectuals."

History shows that the educated man—the intellectual— has given the best government and achieved the best results when given the opportunity. Alexander the Great was an intellectual. His teacher was Aristotle and he acquired all the learning of his day. After talking with Diogenes in his tub at Corinth he remarked, "Were I not Alexander, I would wish to be Diogenes." Caesar was a learned man. His *Commentaries* had not been excelled for two thousand years until another intellectual came along to make history and record it—Winston Churchill. Marcus Aurelius was a great scholar and intellectual. He had a true conception of the universe and his idea of God would be acceptable to most people today above the second-year-high-school level. Napoleon was a prodigious reader. It is recorded that in his headquarters at Waterloo, with the weight of the entire world on his shoulders, he had a mobile library of some eight hundred books—most of them on history, science, and philosophy.

Queen Elizabeth I, who ushered in the era of Britain's glory, understood the value of education and learning. Frederick the Great was a scholar. He kept Voltaire by his side and subsidized as many men of talent as his coffers would allow. England put emphasis on intellectuals, and elevated her educated men to positions of highest power—Burke, Disraeli, Gladstone, Balfour.

The victory of six hundred thousand Israelis against twelve million Arabs was won by a group of intellectuals who laid the foundation of that great nation. George Washington's greatness was due in no little measure to his tremendous respect for intellectuals. Franklin, of course, stands out. Jefferson and Hamilton, bitter political enemies, had one thing in common. They were both learned men in history, political science, and philosophy. It is interesting to read the titles of the books Franklin had in his library. There was the Bible, Euclid, Shakespeare, Homer's *Iliad*, and Plutarch's *Lives*. A man could spend two lifetimes studying those five books.

You licked the honey

FOR many years only two types of literature came out of the Lower East Side of New York. First were the fellows who made an easy buck writing about violence and gangsters, and then there were the "class-war" boys who used the poverty and the early struggle as the basis for their special pleading. There was some truth in what each set of writers put into their books, of course, but it was only a very small part of the story. It was like telling the story of the South in terms of *Tobacco Road*, or relating the sad tale of Lizzie Borden and saying: "This is all there is to the culture and the tradition of old New England."

Neither set of authors made any attempt to speak of the people, nor of the drive which obsessed those people—the yearning for EDUCATION.

Now that I have looked into the state of education in the United States in the year 1907, I would be willing to bet that between 1905 and 1914 there were more classrooms in operation in the fifteen square blocks of the Lower East Side than in some of the States of the Union. It was amazing; night schools, day schools, before-going-to-work schools, private schools, business schools, schools for learning English, and classes in "Civics" (protocol for learning to be a citizen). There were schools in tenement houses conducted by fellows who had come to America only a year before, and schools in settlement houses conducted by eighth-generation Christian social workers. And classes of one sort or another in the union halls.

I was never enthusiastic about the checkoff system for collecting union dues. And if the truth were known I suspect that this system has cost the unions more than if they had gone to the expense of collecting the dues as they did in the early days of their movement. I say this because of the classes, the lectures, the fellowship, and the loyalty the union-hall system brought about. Once a week the fellow told his wife: "I am going to the union hall." This did something for the man's morale and self-esteem. And after he took care of his business, he made an evening of it.

Education was the key to everything. You walked up to your flat in a tenement house and from behind every second door would come the shouting and the arguments over the issues of the day; while the kids emptied out the library, reading books. "Have you started it yet?" That meant *Les Misérables*, by Victor Hugo; a sort of graduation. There was a legend that it took six months to read it. You went into training for *Les Misérables*.

It was down there that they established this "off-Broadway" theatre. There was an American theatre, of course, before the Jewish immigrants of 1880-1920 came here, but the real awakening in America of the serious modern drama came out of the Lower East Side. The Neighborhood Playhouse between 1908 and 1915 put on the plays of Ibsen, Sudermann, Pirandello, and Shaw; and some of them, FOR THE FIRST TIME IN AMERICA.

Even the folk songs were concerned with *education*. Your mother or your teacher dropped a bit of honey on the first book that was placed before you. You licked the honey to associate forever *sweetness* with *learning*.

I remember a song that would go like this in English (the words left untranslated are letters of the alphabet):

> By the fireside where the embers glow
> Through the wintry days
> There the teacher softly, with the little ones,
> Chants the A-lef Beys.
> Learn your lessons well,
> Remember, precious ones,
> The letters of God's law
> Chant ye once again and yet . . . once again
> "Kometz A-lef Aw."
>
> When you are older grown,
> Oh, my little ones,
> You will one day know
> All the tender love and all the burning hope
> That in these letters glow.

Chopped chicken liver and schmaltz

THE other day a cooking competition in a North Carolina community was won by a Methodist lady with a recipe for chopped chicken liver.

This is a further confirmation of a theory I advanced some years ago, that we made the public-relations mistake of our lives when we threw overboard the wonderful art of Kosher Cooking. If we had only used one side of all the goodwill pamphlets for the listing of some recipes! As soon as we learned to speak English we went looking for Chinese restaurants. It was a big deal for a young couple to announce: "We are going to Second Avenue for sharmayne." Another impressive thing was to go to some "Ye Tea Shoppe" where they served stuff that looked like birdseed.

And the Automat, the biggest of all deals. If that Automat on East 14th Street and Fourth Avenue could talk, you'd have the story of all the social revolutions of the century. This is where the "freethinkers" used to go on Yom Kippur. They'd stand around the entrance to the synagogue, talk about the Third International, and urge you to come to the Automat for pork and beans. They said this was better than listening to the cantor in the synagogue. They should live so, wherever they are today. Someone started the rumor that the Automat had "the best coffee in the world." And this became the smart thing to say. Why? No one ever explained it. What did they know so special about coffee? What did they know about anything when it came to good eating? Now, my mother made coffee. She ground the coffee by hand and sprinkled the chicory, served it with boiled milk and sugar in a large cup about the size of a bowl. Some preferred it with "shmates," but I liked it without "shmates" (the "skin" of the milk after it comes to a boil). I had this for lunch nearly every day—the coffee and a loaf of Tip-Top Bread, and butter, and, of course, the penny to spend at "Cheap Habers."

Actually, we did nothing to encourage this Methodist lady with her chopped chicken liver. These folks literally had to drag it out of us and even then we were oh, so very reluctant. We had such things as kreplach and varnishkas and holishkas to give to the American civilization, and all we kept talking about is that fellow who loaned money to General Washington.

You cannot blame this Methodist lady because she made her chopped liver with one of the commercial cooking oils. Think what it would have meant to her and generations yet unborn if she had known about "schmaltz" (chicken fat)! The immigrant mothers were terribly worried about "schmaltz." If a son, married an "American" girl, the mother walked a couple of miles every week to deliver a jar of schmaltz to the new bride and encouraged her to use it.

But this chopped chicken liver prize has greater significance. When you think of French cooking, you always think of a chef—a male. Ah, that Adolphe, you say; how wonderful that Pierre, Pea-air, and you go into ecstasies, and the same with Italian cooking. It's Luigi, how he cooks, that Luigi; and with the Germans it's the same thing, the big chef with the huge apron and the chef's cap as high as a kite; and the Swiss, also—it's Oscar.

Oscar, Shmoscar; but now when you speak of KOSHER COOKING, you speak only in terms of A WOMAN—your mother, your sister, your aunt. There wasn't a man big enough to set a foot into a kosher kitchen. All the philosopher, Talmudist, or scientist could do was stand on the other side of the threshold—and watch. They should build a statue in Washington to the Jewish immigrant mother and show her in bronze, standing over the stove, in the act of sprinkling or—tasting. She worked entirely by ear, like Toscanini, who used to listen to the single note coming from the most remote bass viol. If it didn't satisfy him, the whole one-hundred-and-twenty fellows had to start all over again—from the beginning, too.

But just think of what America has missed; and it is our

fault. Why do you suppose he spends four dollars for whiskey and fifty-five cents for lunch, which includes a hot dog or a hamburger, a cola, and a B.C. headache powder? We could have reduced America's whiskey bill by one half if that fellow could sit down to a piece of nice cold gefilte fish with a strong red horseradish, followed maybe by a huge bowl of golden chicken soup with matzoh balls made of eggs, and light as a feather. And what about the Jewish potato latkes (pancakes)? What a wonderful remedy for an "Age of Anxiety."

How many of my readers remember how often they ripped their knuckles on the "reeb-eisel" as they grated the potatoes for their mothers? The hand-grated potatoes were mixed with flour and shortening and fried schmaltz. But what's the use of giving the recipe? It just won't come out the same. And then how about a "symphony" like boiled beef flanken in horseradish sauce with a boiled potato, or a "grand opera" like holishkas—a dish which was probably invented by those alchemists of the Middle Ages who were trying to make gold out of the baser metals—ground meat and spices wrapped in cabbage leaves and cooked in a sweet-and-sour raisin sauce, which you eventually sop with a big hunk of rye bread.

And knishes? We left the poor Gentiles on their own, and so many of them step up to a counter and ask for a NISH, not even being aware of the fact that the K is part of it—of spiced potatoes or buckwheat groats in thin brown wrappers of dough.

The new immigrants, the Puerto Ricans, are smart. They caught on to this quickly and now there are establishments on the East Side selling "Puerto Rican Knishes." And what about the blintzes? How does one go about describing them? All you can do is wait for the next holiday and throw a garland into the air in memory of those Delancey Street blintzes —those flat squares of dough folded lovingly over cottage cheese or jelly and fried in butter; and eaten as you prefer, plain or with sour cream.

And I have only touched on this wonderful culture which has been lost to America because of our negligence. I have spoken of "operas" and "symphonies," but I haven't even touched on the "overtures," such as kishke (stuffed goose-neck) and derma, and helzl; and what about the "nocturne" like med, a drink of hops and honey which the Jews learned about when they were still on speaking terms with Jupiter, Juno, Venus, and Adonis.

And so, instead of telling all these wonderful Methodists, Presbyterians, Baptists, Catholics, and Lutherans about chicken schmaltz, we told them about Judah P. Benjamin; may he rest in peace already.

No more newspaper extras

IN the old days the newsboys came running at you from all directions, "Extra, Special Extra." Today this is a thing of the past. Today they call this great business, "media."

Years ago, a reporter on a big story could take his time; maybe hold back a few pertinent details for the next day, and the day after. Maybe on the fourth day he'd bring out a photographer to get some local color and that would give him still another story. Today a story breaks, and the TV and radio people move in with a mobile unit and photograph everything for miles around, and a staff swoops down and covers every angle including the innocent bystander—and then the networks begin to repeat the story every half-hour and by the final midnight newscast, the story has been literally chewed to death. Not even bones are left for the next day.

This accounts for the fact that the newspapers are filled to overflowing with "features," and why so many great managing editors have to sit around and wait for the morning mail—Dorothy Thompson, Walter Lippmann, Walter Winchell, and a few hundred others who imitate them and each other.

Think of the wonderful newspaper stories of old, such as

the Hall-Mills case, which had everything—murder, sex, a clergyman, a millionaire stockbroker, and a family of great wealth. This story ran for three years. And the Stillman divorce case. Stillman, president of the National City Bank, and his wife and the Indian guide. Ah, what a story!

Recently I spent some time looking up an old story in the files of *The New York Times;* a story that ran in the newspapers of New York for three years. It was the story of Ruth Cruger and Cocchi.

On February 13, 1917, a pretty seventeen-year-old girl, Ruth Cruger, left her home in midtown Manhattan to take a pair of ice skates to be sharpened. She never returned home. After some frantic inquiries among her friends, her parents reported her disappearance to the police. What happened next is difficult to understand. The police did not seem to be interested at all. Two witnesses had seen the girl in a basement of a motorcycle shop owned by one Alfredo Cocchi, who also repaired skates; but the police simply refused to investigate further. The Cruger family was suspicious of this Cocchi (pronounced kotchie). They had learned that several other little girls in the neighborhood had complained that Cocchi had "tried to get fresh." The police told the Crugers that it would be impossible to question Cocchi because "he was a respectable businessman," and the police captain even intimated that Ruth was a "wayward" girl and had probably run off with a man.

In the midst of this Cocchi disappeared. His shop was padlocked and his wife and children claimed they had no idea what had become of him.

And now the fates that have guarded Tammany Hall since the days of Aaron Burr took a hand. It happened that at this time a Fusion-Reform administration was in City Hall. So Tammany struck a righteous pose and demanded that something be done in the cause of justice. How do you like that? All the organ-eye-zation had at the time was the office of district attorney, Mr. Swann, who was making it hot for the Reform police chief, Arthur Woods. Mr. Swann intimated that Cocchi was a police pay-off man for a vice ring which sent hundreds of girls out of the country each year to brothels around the earth. And this was the beginning of the end of the Reform administration of Mayor Mitchel. It always works. Prosperity, depression, war, corruption; no matter what the real causes, the faction that is *in* must take the blame, just as it is willing to accept the credit and acclaim.

And then an unusual thing happened.

A lady attorney, Grace Humiston, interested in justice, made a private investigation of the case completely on her own. She enlisted the services of a fellow attorney, Julius Kron, and they both raised such a rumpus about the case that permission was given to dig up Mr. Cocchi's cellar. And thus, one hundred and twenty-four days after Ruth's disappearance, the girl was found buried in a hole in Cocchi's basement. An attempt had been made to rape her, but she had put up a fierce battle and was knocked out with a blow on her head. However, she was still alive when he buried her as it was ascertained that death was due to strangulation. The public now directed its sense of outrage against the police department. Grace Humiston told the press that the police had not pursued the investigation because Cocchi was indeed the pay-off man in a numbers game, and that is why two previous complaints that the man had molested little girls had not been investigated.

And what about Cocchi? The American ambassador to Italy reported that the fugitive was living in comfort in the city of Bologna and that he appeared unconcerned about the accusation against him. President Woodrow Wilson did something no other President had ever done. He personally signed a request for the extradition of the murderer. But there was no extradition treaty with Italy at the time and Cocchi was tried in the Italian courts. We sent over all the important witnesses, but his lawyer quickly pleaded him guilty of the murder of Ruth Cruger "by reason of insanity," and he was sentenced to twenty-five years in jail.

Grace Humiston, who had broken the case, continued to be active in New York affairs for a few years. Tammany rode back on the crest of the wave of her popularity, but once

Tammany got back into power she was slowly but effectively shunted to one side as a "meddler" in police administration——a man's business.

Caesar the humanist

THE creative writer who writes of *people* must do so in humanist terms. When he ceases to do so, he ceases to be a writer. He emerges as a propagandist or a public-relations man. And this is where we encounter confusion because we have often mistaken the rhetorician for the writer. They are of a different breed. The rhetorician is the enemy of humanism. Since the beginning of history the rhetorician has called the writer "a fuzzy-headed intellectual." He has fooled us often. For instance, take this fellow Cato. Every schoolboy will repeat to you—"Delenda est Carthago" (Carthage must be destroyed), and all the after-dinner speakers use this Cato phrase as the symbol of persistence, patriotism, and character. That is how easy it is for the rhetorician to pull the wool over our eyes.

Cato was a combination of Mussolini, McCarthy, and Cotton Mather. Carthage had ceased to be a "threat" to Rome years before, and did everything humanly possible to save herself from Cato's rhetoric. Every concession Carthage made, such as disbanding her army, made Cato angrier than ever, and at the end of every speech he shouted, "Carthage must be destroyed." He said it so often that no one stopped any more to ask why. Why should Carthage be destroyed? Carthage, of course, was destroyed, completely, and years later the Romans under Caesar were ashamed of the whole thing and tried to rebuild the famous city, but a million men and women and children had been killed and a whole civilization crushed.

Cicero is another one who has fooled us for centuries. He

was a super-duper combination of William E. Borah and
Colonel Robert McCormick. Cicero was a rhetorician. Julius
Caesar was a writer.

In the year 46 B.C. Caesar invented the "Congressional
Record" which we use today. To bring the Roman Senate
under public scrutiny he established the first daily newspaper.
He had a dozen editors make a record of the senatorial doings.
The newspaper was called, literally, *Daily Doings,* and Caesar had it posted all over the Forum for the folks to read.
Cicero did not like that at all. It was a straw on the camel's
back. Caesar's liberal farm bill was next—straw number two.
The final straw was his proposal to have the provinces send
senators to Rome so that all the people in the Empire would
have a voice in the government. The Senators under Cicero's
leadership operated a closed corporation. They owned all the
concessions in the provinces, made a business of selling offices
and honors, and controlled most of the trade. Cicero made
money hand over fist. Caesar was killed before he did any
more damage.

The excuse that he wanted to be king is a joke. A few
disgruntled army officers who had served Caesar's enemy
Pompey were easily persuaded to do the job. For "respectability" they sold the idea to Brutus, a neurotic who spent his
entire life worrying about whether Caesar was his father.

He had a big and understanding heart, Caesar, with a huge
capacity for what the French call "the love." Brutus' mother,
Servilia, had been one of Caesar's mistresses, and unfortunately for Brutus all of this happened just about the time he
was born. The military junta which murdered Caesar was
thus able to "dress up" its claim by telling Brutus that he
could now stop worrying about Caesar's bone structure. Behind it all, however, was the rhetorician—Cicero—who, like
all rhetoricians, can just as easily shout "FREEDOM" as chop
your head off if you disagree with him.

Alexander Hamilton and
Mrs. Reynolds

THE late Claude G. Bowers, in his fine history, *Jefferson and Hamilton,* makes the important point: you had two mental giants, each fighting to establish his own economic philosophy as the basic foundation of our country. America was wise. In the end she took half of Hamilton and half of Jefferson, which is probably what they were fighting for in the first place. But this was no kid-glove affair.

Hamilton was the rough-and-tumble type, maybe even hit you below the belt when desperate. Jefferson would wait for the clinches to deliver a rabbit punch and then look as innocent as a newborn babe.

Now we come to the night of December 15, 1792. Hamilton is at home in Philadelphia. His wife, the daughter of General Philip Schuyler, is the absolute ruler of American society, a combination of Mrs. Cornelius Vanderbilt and Mrs. John Jacob Astor, only prettier. There is a knock on the door. Three gentlemen enter. Hamilton knows them all—they represent a Congressional committee investigating some rumors that Hamilton had been paying out large sums of money under most "mysterious circumstances." Hamilton is Secretary of the United States Treasury. The rumors, backed by an affidavit, had to be looked into. Mind you, there was no evidence that Hamilton had done anything wrong.

The Congressional investigating committee was composed of three Jeffersonians, a "coincidence," I suppose; Mr. Muhlenberg, Mr. Venable, and Jefferson's hatchet man himself, Senator James Monroe.

Hamilton greeted the men cordially and took them into his private study. He knew, of course, what they had come for, but he was up against a peculiar situation. Hamilton had indeed paid out large sums of money under "mysterious circumstances," but it was his *own* money, and he had every scrap of paper, deed, and bank notice to prove beyond a shadow of doubt that as far as the Government was concerned, he was the soul of honor and integrity. But Hamilton also knew that it was not as simple as that; not with Mr. Monroe sitting there. Hamilton knew that Monroe was not there to play tiddlywinks. And so he (Hamilton) decided to shoot the works, tell them everything. There were many friends of Hamilton who later thought he had made a mistake, that he did not have to tell the committee everything. Be that as it may, he decided to take them into his confidence. He asked Mr. Muhlenberg, Mr. Venable, and Mr. Monroe to listen to his story—with the understanding of men of the world. He asked for tolerance.

The money Hamilton was paying out went to a Mr. Reynolds. It was blackmail money. Mr. Hamilton had been intimate with Mrs. Reynolds. He had called on her at her lodgings on the waterfront of Philadelphia. Her husband was a drunk who had deserted her, but eventually this drunk heard that his dear and loving wife was the sweetheart of America's most influential citizen, Alexander Hamilton, and Mr. Reynolds began to cash in on it. Hamilton told this story to the three members of the committee. We can well imagine what Hamilton was going through. Mr. Muhlenberg and Mr. Venable tried hard to stop him—they had heard enough; they were sorry for the intrusion upon his privacy, but not so, Mr. Monroe. Oh, no. Mr. Monroe sat there without a smile or a frown, or a word of any kind.

Hamilton told his story from the beginning. He was sitting with his family in their Philadelphia home and the servant announced that a Mrs. Reynolds wanted to see him. This was nothing unusual. Dozens of people—men and women—requested an interview with Mr. Hamilton every day. Mrs. Reynolds' story was that her husband had left her stranded; she needed some money to return to New York, and since she knew no one in Philadelphia, the only one she could think of was Alexander Hamilton, and if he could help her, she

lives at such and such a place, at the top of the landing, first
door on the right. That same night Hamilton brought her the
money. This is interesting. Mrs. Reynolds did not have a
brain in her head, and she was not half so pretty as the cul-
tured daughter of General Philip Schuyler, Hamilton's wife.
Who can explain it? Hamilton was not the first man, and
he'll not be the last. It gets into your blood—men have given
up beautiful and educated wives, fine homes and wonderful
children—all for some ignorant and perhaps even homely
tramp. Why? No one knows, and you'd better not be a wise
guy about it, either. Hamilton saw Mrs. Reynolds regularly,
but eventually his interest began to wane. Now here's another problem which no man has been able to answer satis-
factorily. Is it better to break off all at once, or to ease it off—
gradually? Hamilton saw Mrs. Reynolds less and less. She
wrote him letters, illiterate letters. Frantically she even called
at his home and demanded to know why he was neglecting
her.

No one knows whether Mrs. Reynolds called in her husband to put the squeeze on Hamilton or whether the bum
just stumbled onto the situation by himself. Anyway, he called
on Hamilton at his office and demanded money—a thousand
dollars to begin with. Hamilton paid. He paid and paid until
a crooked employee, Mr. Clingman, thought he had a scoop.
He wrote to Jefferson. Jefferson, with a raised pinkie, said
in effect: "Do not talk about such terrible, terrible gossip,
but maybe a Congressman from Pennsylvania . . . what's his
name . . . a Mr. Frederick Muhlenberg, may be interested
(and listen, Bud, get the hell down there as fast as you can
and tell him quick!)." Mr. Muhlenberg refused to make a
public issue of it until he had given Mr. Hamilton a chance
to explain those "mysterious payments," and that's how he
and Mr. Venable and Mr. Monroe came to be listening to
this great Hamilton pour out his heart to three "understanding" men.

Mr. Muhlenberg and Mr. Venable were apologetic; Mr.
Monroe was unbending, yet nothing happened. All was silence. Then in 1797 when things were again getting hot be-

tween Hamilton and Jefferson, there suddenly appeared a book, *A History of the United States*, prepared by a Mr. Callender, whom the historian McMaster called a "Jeffersonian hack." Callender told the whole story about Hamilton and Mrs. Reynolds. The point Callender appeared to be making was that Hamilton had invented the Mrs. Reynolds story as a cover for the frauds against the Government. Then, as before, no one had ever produced a scrap of evidence that Hamilton had ever done anything wrong as far as the Government was concerned. At this moment two honorable men came to Hamilton's defense—Mr. Muhlenberg and Mr. Venable—both Jeffersonians, but this was just a little too much for them to stomach; they revealed that Mr. Hamilton had made a forthright presentation of his case and that since there had been no evidence that he (Hamilton) had violated his trust of office, they were chagrined to see this strictly private affair paraded before the public. Not a peep out of Monroe, who was safely in France.

Hamilton lived to see the Federalist Party overwhelmed, although he made his archenemy, Jefferson, President of the United States, not because he had any use for him, but the alternative would have been the election of Aaron Burr, whom Hamilton hated even more.

Later, of course, Hamilton was killed in a duel with Burr, which I covered in a previous issue of my paper.

Mr. Reynolds was arrested for blackmail, but Hamilton did not press the charges and the drunk passed out of history. No one knows what happened to Mrs. Reynolds after public airing of their relationship. Hamilton's wife lived on into a new American era. She saw the nation expand beyond the Mississippi River, the coming of the railroad, and the Dred Scott decision. She died at the age of ninety-eight. Did she ever think of Mrs. Reynolds, or was that affair just a small detail in the life of her husband?

The journalism of Joseph Pulitzer

At the height of its power, the influence of the New York *World* in American politics was tremendous. Mr. Pulitzer left some twenty million dollars in assets, not including his newspapers, his yacht, and his homes. Out of that vast estate, which included thousands of shares of securities in American industry, they found only twenty shares of stock which had not increased in value from the time of purchase.

During a depression in the administration of Theodore Roosevelt, Mr. Pulitzer became mindful of the declining prices on the stock exchange. He called in his editor, the great Frank Cobb, and said to him: "Boy, I am, as you probably know, a large owner of stocks. Some of them are bound to be affected by public action. I might give way some day to such a feeling and send you an order that would mean a change in the paper's [liberal] policy. I want you to make me a promise. If I ever do such a thing, swear to me that you will ignore my wishes." The promise was made, but no such order ever came.

Mr. Pulitzer was totally blind for the last ten years of his life. His newspapers were read to him by relays of secretaries; everything, including the columns of want ads for which the *World* was famous. Other secretaries read history and literature to him, both in English and in German. When he ordered Stanford White, the famous architect, to build him a new home in New York, he had plaster models made of everything so that he could follow the construction with his sensitive fingers.

His editors learned quickly that he was a hard taskmaster. He communicated with them constantly, often two or three times a day. No matter how far he was from the scene, his judgment was amazingly accurate. "I can see that you waited a day before commenting on such and such. Remember, follow the news. Comment editorially the same day that the news breaks; the same day, not twenty-four hours later." "What have you read?" was his first question to anyone whom he considered hiring as an editor. "What have you read?"

Mr. Pulitzer understood that the most important requirement of an editor was that he should be a well-read man. It is quite possible that the schools of journalism (categorizing the profession as one which merely requires a diploma) may have had a reverse effect. Without going to a journalism college, a fellow knew that the only chance he had to become an editor was to read, read, and read—religion, philosophy, history, politics, mythology—but if the profession can be picked up during a four-year course, that's that. Certainly our editors of today are not as well-read as those of a previous generation. I'll give you an example. There was a serious incident, recently, in the Gaza Strip between Egypt and Israel. It was very important, attracted the attention of the world, and was discussed by the United Nations. There were editorials on the Gaza incident in most of the newspapers in the country. How many told of the campaign at Gaza conducted by Alexander the Great in the year 331 B.C. at the time he captured the city of Tyre? And you can't say this is not important. The people eat that up when they get it.

Joseph Pulitzer was a Democrat, too, with great big capital letters, and took part in every political campaign on the city, State, and national levels. He loved nothing better in this life than campaign-time, and he really gave it all he had.

He thought Theodore Roosevelt was a "phony liberal" and William Jennings Bryan was an eccentric who wanted to destroy capitalism. Mr. Bryan was the only Democrat whom Mr. Pulitzer did not support. Do not get the idea that Mr. Pulitzer was one of these *status-quo* reactionaries. Listen to this letter to his editor in 1907: "If we are to prevent the spread of socialism, capitalism must assume the responsibility for the more just distribution of its wealth."

William Randolph Hearst was publishing a newspaper in California and rented an office in the New York *World* building as a New York office for his San Francisco paper. It turned out that Hearst, who had already made up his mind to enter the New York field, was using that office to learn all about the highly successful *World;* getting to know the staff, who were the men of talent, their earnings, hobbies, and everything else that he needed to know about how a newspaper should be run in New York. When Hearst finally broke into the New York field, he was all set—he knew just what to offer the Pulitzer men to hire them away from the *World,* and the greatest newspaper rivalry in American history was on.

Pulitzer closed the stable after the horse was stolen. Hearst had to get a new office, but he was ready to get himself a whole building.

Hearst finally took Arthur Brisbane away from Pulitzer, and Brisbane was to go on to great heights and help make Hearst's paper reach a daily circulation of over one million.

This intense rivalry gave birth to the comic strip as a circulation builder. Pulitzer ran a strip called the "Yellow Kid" and he printed it in yellow ink. Hearst outbid Pulitzer for the "Yellow Kid," but Pulitzer arranged for a substitute comic strip along the same lines and continued to use the eye-catching yellow. This gave to America the phrase "yellow journalism." Eventually, the competition subsided and both Pulitzer and Hearst went along—each one had thought New York was not big enough for both, but they were wrong, of course. The *World* went to 800,000 circulation and Hearst's *Journal* sold over a million. In a letter of instructions to editor Frank Cobb during the 1908 campaign, Mr. Pulitzer said:

> Don't cease vigorous opposition to Rooseveltism [Theodore] in all its phases, ditto Republicanism.
> Don't say an unkind word unnecessarily about Mr. Taft [the candidate]. Not a word of untruth under any circumstances against him or Bryan, or anybody else, not even Hearst.

Mr. Pulitzer had agents all over the world. If a news story broke in the United States which had any connection with a European figure, Mr. Pulitzer had men around the globe who could be digging the facts a few hours after the story broke. One such story led to a far-reaching Supreme Court decision regarding the freedom of the press. Mr. Pulitzer was sued for libel; libel against the United States of America. During the closing days of Theodore Roosevelt's second term, Mr. Pulitzer broke a big story in which he questioned the transaction connected with the building of the Panama Canal. In order for the United States to go ahead with the canal, it was necessary to buy out the interests of the French investors in the de Lesseps project which had failed. The Congress had authorized a payment of forty million dollars to buy out the French and clear the way for the American canal. Mr. Pulitzer claimed he had information that this forty million dollars was paid to a few Americans, who had previously acquired the French interests for three million dollars. Mr. Pulitzer wanted to know, "Who Got the Money?" He hinted that among those involved were a lawyer, Mr. Cromwell; C. P. Taft, brother of William Howard Taft; and Mr. Robinson, brother-in-law of President Theodore Roosevelt. This created a great sensation. While neither the outgoing President (Roosevelt) nor the incoming President (Taft) was named in the story, each felt himself personally involved. Mr. Roosevelt was raging mad and at one time said, "I'll see to it that Mr. Pulitzer goes to a nice Democratic jail."

Eventually, Mr. Pulitzer, his editors, and his company were indicted for libel against the United States Government. Mr. Pulitzer's lawyers alleged that the Federal courts had no jurisdiction, that libel can only be charged by individuals with specifications as to damages suffered. The lower court decided in favor of Mr. Pulitzer and finally the Supreme Court confirmed the decision. By that time Mr. Roosevelt was out of office; interest in the case died down, and no suits were entered by "individual" plaintiffs. In closing the matter, Mr. Pulitzer asked editorially: "Who Got the Money?"

Exit the intellectual, enter the leader

DURING the past twenty years the Jewish intellectual has all but disappeared from the American scene. In his place has come a new figure in Jewish life, one whose influence is so complete that he dominates the scene. He is the "Jewish leader."

This was not a deliberate movement by men of bad will. The Jewish intellectual was simply another casualty of the anti-Semitism of the Hitler era. The resulting need for vast fund-raising and vigilant "defense" organizations threw the entire Jewish culture of America into the hands of the "big givers" and the more articulate laymen. In short—the Jewish leaders. It has even crept into the obituaries, "He was a Jewish leader"—the opposite number of the "civic leader" in the Gentile obits.

This development is why the intellectual everywhere has nearly always been a pacifist. In war he is the first one to be declassed. The truck driver becomes a major. And there is no greater leveler than a continued crisis of fund-raising and defense work. A chalk mark on the sidewalk, "Down with the Jews," and all the years of study and thought are worthless. The Jewish leader takes over, and in the process he becomes both sociologist and philosopher. "You shouldn't have written that article," he says, or, "You should have written that poem from a different angle," or, "That will hurt us," and finally, "Why don't you consult?"

But the rabbi and intellectual have this one big thing in their favor, as indeed the intellectuals have had in all the eras of history. They have the satisfaction of knowing that they can thrive only in the absence of war and crisis; and that, my friends, is a tremendous thing to have in your favor. Once the "crisis" is over and the captains and the leaders depart, the only ones left are the few fellows who can tell a story, write a critique, or deliver a message.

Belshazzar's Feast—with real cannon

Two of my closest friends, Dr. Raymond Wheeler of Charlotte, and Joe Morrison of Chapel Hill (associate professor of journalism) are great ones with the phonograph records. It's a religion. Wheeler has what is called a "Hi Fi," and the minute you enter his home you are greeted with a blast that sends your eyeglasses flying off your nose. I am not sure whether Morrison's is also a Hi Fi, but if it isn't, he certainly doesn't need one. Right now he is engaged in a subtle scheme to get me over to Chapel Hill to hear Walton's *Belshazzar's Feast*, which he recently exchanged for Fauré's *Requiem*.

Wheeler's blast and Morrison's *Belshazzar* remind me of my landsmann Moishele Halperin, on the Lower East Side of New York. The ambition of all these folks is to get someone who likes good music and then they can really go to town. Moishele went Wheeler and Morrison one better.

He used to conduct every record he played—right down to the end, his hair flying, his finger pointing, giving instructions to the musicians—louder, faster—sometimes he'd even throw his baton down and bawl them out as the record went on and on.

When I came to Moishele's house he would literally seal off all exits including the fire escape. I do not know exactly how many records he had, but it must have been close to a million.

His great ambition in life was to hear Tchaikovsky's *1812 Overture* with real cannon. He would speak of this dream often and if someone told him of a concert which had included the *1812 Overture*, Moishele would be sure to ask,

"With real cannon?" Why this little furrier wanted to hear the *1812 Overture* with real cannon, I'll never know.

Raisins and almonds

WHEN Jan Peerce, the Metropolitan Opera star, was in the Soviet Union, the request number from his Jewish audience was for a simple folk song, "Rozhinkes mit Mandlen" (Raisins and Almonds).

Those elderly Jews in the Soviet, cut off from Jewish communal living, folkways, and culture, wanted this great American tenor to sing a folk song to bring them a bit of their past: mother, father, home, and memory.

Mr. Peerce's experience was identical with one related by Irving Berlin. It happened the day after the Americans entered Rome. Berlin and his troupe of GI actors arranged a show to which hundreds of Italian civilians were invited. This was the first free theatrical performance these Italians had seen in twenty years. Under Mussolini, as well as Hitler, their culture had been regulated. But no matter how hard Irving and his troupe tried, they received very little response from the Italians, and they could not understand it. Finally, Irving thought of the Lower East Side where he was raised, near Little Italy, and he had an inspiration. He went to the center of the stage and in his high-pitched voice sang that old Italian song, "Oi Marie, Oi Marie . . ." The Italians rose in their seats; first they cheered, then they wept for joy. Here in Rome, the capital of the entire operatic world, the Italians poured their hearts out to a simple little folk song, "Oi Marie," just as the elderly Jews of the Soviet wanted "Rozhinkes mit Mandlen" to bring them so much closer—home.

Is Greta Garbo an artist?

THE first test of an artist—a painter, poet, writer, actor —is a dedicated and passionate desire for COMMUNICATION. This Greta Garbo has never had, and her "shyness" may be part of the story. A beauty, a personality, yes—but an artist, an actress—*no* sir.

Sarah Bernhardt was an actress. I saw her at the Palace Theatre, in her seventies, reclining on a couch and reciting from *L'Aiglon*. Helen Hayes is an actress. Last summer I saw a picture of her in a cramped, sticky, barn dressing room. She was making up for a part in a summer play. Ethel Barrymore could have quit after her famous debut in *Captain Jinks of the Horse Marines*, and she would have been remembered kindly, but she is nearly eighty and they put her name below the names of the "stars" in Hollywood; but she's there.

Giovanni Martinelli is an artist. He is over seventy years of age and teaches a whole string of youngsters. For the money? Nonsense.

Greta Garbo is pleasant and interesting. So was Maxine Elliott, a famous beauty of her day, who has a theatre named for her. You will not find her in any history of acting. And so was Lina Cavalieri. She was a pin-up girl of 1912. She used to come in penny candy and in packages of cigarettes, only in those days the pin-ups were fully dressed. But they were not *artists*.

I suspect this about Greta Garbo; she is afraid of a *test*. Many fine people possess this fear all their lives. They are willing to let well enough alone.

The desire to COMMUNICATE—is fundamental. Caruso could have retired after his first three great performances in 1905, but twenty years later he was going on stage in *Samson and Delilah* with a heavy towel in his hand to stop the flow of blood from his throat. An ARTIST.

Forget victuals

THE prettiest words in the English language begin with
the letter *m*—murmuring, Monongahela, mackinaw, Madagas-
car, maiden, majesty, Majorca, and marinated (especially
herring). The ugliest word in the language is—victuals. You
can't say or write it. The best thing is to forget it.

Monday at the "Met"

MONDAY night was called "Gala Night," because of
Enrico Caruso, at the Metropolitan Opera. He may have
given two performances during the week, but one of them was
certain to be on Monday. The fire inspector counted you off
for standing room—a dollar fifty downstairs behind the
orchestra and a dollar upstairs behind the Family Circle. The
Family Circle is equivalent to the sixth balcony and you
could hang on to a wire grill behind the seats. I got in
line right after school, about 3:30 P.M. I stood outside four
and a half hours; inside three and a half hours; and another
hour at the stage entrance, waiting for Caruso to come out,
total standing for the performance, nine hours. During the
intermission, I roamed behind the boxes of the Diamond
Horseshoe to look at Box No. 35. This was the box of
J. P. Morgan. I just looked at it, that's all. The name J. P.
Morgan was very important on the East Side in those days—
to the Socialists, who blamed him for everything, and to the
non-Socialists, who were determined to become capitalists
like Morgan as quickly as possible.

The performance which made the most lasting impression

on me was Verdi's *La Forza del Destino,* with Caruso, Rosa Ponselle, and Antonio Scotti.

What was there about Caruso? His voice? Of course. But there was something more. He had the quality that sportswriters call "color," something which does not get into the record books. Thousands of people around the world still speak of Caruso. For many thousands he represents a sort of milestone in their lives: "We did such-and-such during the week we heard Caruso."

Caruso made you feel alive.

The "workshop" is a bore

WHERE did they get that term "workshop" for so many noble projects and worth-while events? The schoolteachers get an invitation to "come to a workshop on reading." Now, what does a workshop have to do with reading? Isn't reading in a deplorable enough state without associating it with a workshop? A workshop is where you make book ends or candlesticks, or file down your handcuffs.

Greatest single moment in music

I THINK the home run of music, the photo finish, the winning touchdown with a minute left to play, the raising of the American flag in center field—is that moment when the principals and the chorus burst forth into Schiller's "Ode to Joy" in the fourth movement of Beethoven's Ninth Symphony—"Alle menschen werden brüder."

Shakespeare wrote the works of Bacon

It was Delia Bacon, of Boston, who started all this business about Bacon having written the works of Shakespeare. After Delia came a host of fellows with other theories as to who wrote the works of Shakespeare.

At the bottom of all the arguments is one basic theme—Shakespeare did not go to college and therefore could not have been the author of the plays. And since Bacon, Oxford, and Marlowe went to college, it had to be one of them.

All of which is highly encouraging. Since four million boys took advantage of the GI Bill of Rights and went to college, all we need do now is sit back and wait for the literature to roll off the presses.

I think the time has come to re-examine the whole proposition. I think these debunkers of Shakespeare have hit upon the right idea but have not focused it properly. A careful study of the college situation may very well lead us to a new conclusion. We find that thousands of men and women are receiving college degrees without ever opening a book by Draper, Hume, Lecky, Cervantes, Rabelais, Plutarch, Cellini, Reade, Gibbon, Heine, Goethe, Chaucer, to mention only a few of the great classics of thought. Reasonable men will begin to argue that, since Bacon, Oxford, and Marlowe went to college, they could not have possibly written those plays; that they could have been produced only by a fellow who stayed home, read some books, and studied life.

They never met a payroll

1. Copernicus
2. Galileo
3. Newton
4. Einstein

PART 6

Tammany, Tammany

~~~~~~

How Tammany Hall did it

> Tammany, Tammany,
> Big Chief sits in his tepee,
> Cheering braves to victory.
> Tammany, Tammany,
> Swamp 'em, swamp 'em,
> Get the wampum,
> Taaammmaaannieeee.

Big Tim Sullivan was the Tammany Hall power on the Bowery of New York. He was a tremendous man, physically, and a tremendous man, politically. He made a fortune out of his position as a Tammany district leader—principally from "concessions" to gambling houses—and "Raines Law" hotels.

What was a "Raines Law" hotel? John Raines, a member of the New York State Legislature, was a strict Prohibitionist who unwittingly established hundreds of brothels in New York.

Raines tried and tried, in the State Legislature, to restrict the use of Demon Rum. Finally he succeeded in putting across a bill prohibiting the sale of intoxicating liquors on Sunday throughout the State, *except in hotels*. So what happened? Every saloon became a "hotel." The saloonkeeper knocked out a few walls upstairs and advertised rooms for rent. And what decent family would occupy rooms above a saloon? So pretty soon the rooms were rented out to prostitutes and the money just rolled in for everybody concerned (according to the Lexow and the Mazet investigations).

The police got their share, the politician his cut; the saloonkeeper was able to buy a five-thousand-dollar pew in his church, and good old Mr. Raines had his "Prohibition" on Sunday.

Well, what I started out to tell you was about Big Tim Sullivan, as colorful a character as ever wielded political power in this republic. During one of the periodic investigations which revealed some of his vast wealth, Big Tim made a speech to his constituents: "The trouble with reformers is that they don't know our traditions down here.

"That's why the reformers think just because I have a little money, there must be something wrong. I say 'to hell with reform.'" The crowd cheered. "And," continued Sullivan, "if I have done wrong, I have always thought I have done right, and I was always good to the poor." The women in the crowd wept openly and most of the men were dabbing their wet cheeks with handkerchiefs.

Big Tim gave us kids on the East Side a trip up the Hudson River every year. A trip to Bear Mountain; and the name "Big Tim" was blessed in thousands of households.

In his report to the Tammany Hall chieftain, Richard Croker, at the end of one election day, Big Tim Sullivan wrote: "Boss, Grover Cleveland, 938—Benjamin Harrison, 3. This is one vote more than I expected Harrison to get, but I'll find the guy who did it if it's the last thing I do."

Big Tim's greatest contribution to Tammany power was his organization of "repeaters." He had hundreds of Bowery bums organized in one or two places on election day, and he waited for the reports—"The Fifth District needs two hundred," etc.—and, as each "requirement" came in, Big Tim dispatched a truckload of the required number of bums to the polling place where a henchman went down the line and gave each the name under which he was to vote. The names were usually of those voters who had died between registration day and the election, or of those voters who had not yet voted an hour before the closing of the polls.

Big Tim also had about fifty student barbers working for him on every election day. These barbers performed a great service for Tammany. Here is how it worked. Along about August Big Tim sent word around the Bowery flophouses for the bums to let their beards grow. By election day, Big Tim had at his disposal several hundred Bowery bums, each with a full-grown beard. First, each bum would vote with a full beard under one name. He would then rush to one of the stand-by barbers who immediately clipped off the chin fuzz. So then the bum voted under another name with sideburns, like the Emperor Francis Joseph of the Austro-Hungarian Empire. Then he would rush back to the barber who shaved off the sideburns, and now the bum would vote for the third time with just a moustache; and finally that came off and he would go forth to vote for a fourth time —plain-faced, as Tammany called it.

For this day's work the bum got one dollar, three meals, a pint of whiskey, and, of course, a lesson in civics and good government.

Big Tim and the other Tammany district leaders were careful to keep in the good graces of the foreign-born. The Tammany sachems had henchmen roaming the districts looking for bar mitzvahs, weddings, fiestas, and funerals, but mostly funerals. The presence of the district leader at one of these functions made the voters very proud and they talked about it for years to come. "Just think, Patrick Divver, the leader, *himself*, was at the funeral of my father, God rest his soul."

Sometimes there was lots of trouble at these functions when two Tammany factions were fighting each other, as often happened. Big Tim Sullivan, Tom Foley, and Patrick Divver attended all the funerals and christenings they could find. Each leader had a man stationed at the marriage-license bureau to telephone whenever an Italian couple from the district came to get married. They had a whole system of espionage to find out what kind of present each camp was buying the couple. If the word went down that Foley is giving earrings to the bride, then Divver would give earrings *and* a set of cups and saucers.

Tammany leaders rarely made speeches. The henchmen went down the line getting out the vote and the "repeaters," and that was all that was necessary. Once, however, the Bowery Congressman, Tim Campbell, did make a speech. His opponent in the race was an Italian named Rinaldo. Tim's only political speech was: "There is two bills before the country—one is the Mills bill and the other is the McKinley bill. The Mills bill is for free trade with everything free; the McKinley bill is for protection with nothing free. Do you want everything free, or do you want to pay for everything?

"Having thus disposed of the national issue, I will now devote myself to the local issue, which is the Dago, Rinaldo. He is from Italy. I am from Ireland. Are you in favor of Italy or Ireland?

"Having thus disposed of the local issue and thanking you for your attention, I will now retire."

Do not think for one moment that the Tammany men spent their own money on political campaigns. Everything followed a system, and one thing had nothing to do with the other. They were uncouth, but not so uncouth as they wanted to appear. These Tammany sachems could very easily relax of an evening at one of the fashionable university and millionaires' clubs on Fifth Avenue, during the course of which they might receive a big campaign contribution from a financial tycoon, a traction magnate, a paving contractor, or a manufacturer. The Tammany men in Congress and in the State Legislature were in particularly favorable positions to deliver what they promised, because their constituency was composed mainly of "new citizens," who were concerned with one thing—survival. These new citizens were still struggling to gain a foothold in the new country, and if some politician helped along the way with a ton of coal at an opportune moment, or working papers for a young son, or took the kids off the street for a boat ride, it was all right with them.

This left Tammany Hall politicians with complete freedom of movement in those economic and political areas which were, as yet, of no vital interest to the voters in their districts. It was a two-way street. The Tammany men were not so uncouth as they appeared to be, and the new citizens were not so naive as they appeared to be either.

Pretty soon the sons and grandsons of these new citizens would be forming committees and sending Tammany sachems to jail. But, after all, Tammany had been at it since Aaron Burr had founded the "Columbian Order of St. Tammany," and they were highly resourceful. Thus, when the new citizens themselves became aware politically, Tammany entered upon new schemes: alliances with gangsters and other resourceful measures.

Tammany is still strong, but at least it is no longer necessary for an Orthodox Jew to buy two five-dollar tickets to "Big Tim Sullivan's Chowder and Pigs' Knuckles Party" at Ulmer Park.

The death of Senator McCarthy

THE conservatives nearly always tolerate the demagogue while he is destroying liberals. The conservatives may even know that their turn will come next, but they usually take this calculated risk. "Let him knock their heads together," they say, "we'll take care of him in good time." ("Let him keep going," said Senator Taft. "He's hurting the Democrats.")

But it never works out the way the conservatives would like to have it; especially if the demagogue knows how to consolidate his position before he finally goes after his early "allies." Hitler understood the mechanics of perfect timing. The Thyssens and the Krupps loved him because he was destroying the Weimar Constitution, the liberals, the trade unions, the political heretics—all in one shot. But the conservatives made their move too late. They fell before him like ripe apples off a tree.

But how did McCarthy know to use this oldest, most heinous, and most effective weapon of the demagogue? "I hold a piece of paper in my hands with some names on it . . ." and here his voice trails off to another subject with perfect timing; and suddenly this blank piece of paper becomes a living document, a terrifying document. It becomes a document of potential destruction because *my* name is on it; and so is *yours;* and so are the names of Senator Taft, and Dwight D. Eisenhower. We are all on it, because none of us is on it.

Do you remember that slightly ajar brief case always resting on its haunches in front of his right foot as he stood on the platform? "I have in my brief case a list . . ." and again the voice trails off to something else, but every eye rests on that brief case which now may hold our political destiny and our human dignity. Soon, soon, it will become the symbol of the New Order; instead of a swastika, this time it will be a brief case.

"Let us see that list," asked one or two of the more courageous reporters of those days.

"What do you take me for?" replied McCarthy. "Do you expect me to betray America to these razor-at-the-throat Reds?" And indeed how can you induce a man to betray America?

But how did McCarthy know to use this oldest gimmick of the demagogue? Had he also read the history of the world? Or do these fellows come by all of this stuff by instinct?

"The High Sheriff will come next week with his list of the traitors [Puritans]," said the notice on the bulletin boards of England after the Restoration. There was no list, of course; but when the Sheriff came he knew exactly whom to pick up. He picked up the wives of the men who weren't home. The men who had run away included "real" Puritans, fellows who had an enemy in town, and men who get scared when the

Bill of Particulars is a blank piece of paper on which the sheriff may improvise as he goes along.

What makes a McCarthy tick? It is one of the oldest stories of mankind. When you have succeeded in creating a devil, the people begin to lose faith in themselves. They even begin to despise their intellectual selves in dealing with the devil who is closing in on them from all sides; and now they are literally pleading for help—anything and anybody, even a young squirt of a lawyer, and his side-kick, a young assistant hotel clerk; these will now lead America by the nose, the America of Franklin, Adams, Jefferson, Pinckney, and Robert E. Lee.

And so the liberals of America hoped for a miracle. They hoped that the conservatives would come to their rescue before it was too late. And this time they prayed for a miracle, and they got the miracle. Senator McCarthy overplayed his hand. At that single moment when he said that General Zwicker was not fit to wear the uniform of the United States Army, that was the precise moment of McCarthy's destruction. He had made a move against the "nobility" a year, maybe even two years, too soon; and they knew they had to finish him right then and there. A few necessary formalities were all that remained.

The politician-women

LIKE the perfume saleswomen on the Tiber in ancient Rome, the cosmetics and plastics women of modern Charlotte, North Carolina, play an important role in the political destinies of their community. In each of the sixty-eight voting boxes (precincts) of the county, there are two, three, or four women who hold the political balance of power in many a close election. Some of them are housewives, but the majority are door-to-door saleswomen.

In fact, their door-to-door selling has given them the

confidence and, experience to handle the primary and run-off elections each year for practically all the candidates. Among them are mothers, wives, widows, and spinsters.

Their respective sales managers know that, come April of each year, the sales of plastic kitchenware, vanilla extract, lipstick, and greeting cards will fall off considerably. April means that the politician-women of Mecklenburg have taken to the political wars. Individual candidates hire the women to do missionary work, hand out circulars, marked ballots, and do a selling job in general. All the regular candidates know the most experienced women in this field, and the new candidates learn very quickly. Because of their wide acquaintance in their respective districts, the women find the doors of the electorate open to them as they distribute the campaign literature and plead the cause of their candidates. In working for the various candidates, they also serve the city in getting out the registration and the vote. On Primary Day they drive groups of people to the polls, serve as baby sitters while the housewife goes to vote, and perform many other quasi-official functions. Come April the potato peeler and the corset fittings are put aside and the phones begin to hum as they call each other:

"Working for anyone yet?"

"No, I'm waiting for Mr. X to announce."

"Do you think he'll announce?"

"Sure, did you see who else announced today?"

"I'm not interested in him announcing; I'm waiting."

"So far I'm working for four."

"Is Mr. Z paying any more this year?"

"No, he says to wait till he's elected sometime."

"I only had three calls so far."

"Listen, by the way, will you look up the paper later and let me know what Mr. X, Mr. Y, and Mr. Z are running for. I'm working for them. I always like to know what they are running for, when I work for them."

Causerie on the death of Mrs. Leo Frank

I RECALL the headline in red ink—"Leo Frank Lynched
In Georgia." I sold hundreds of papers on my regular corner
on Delancey Street near the corner of the bridge-local which
took the factory workers across the Williamsburg Bridge to
Brooklyn.

Forty years later Mrs. Leo Frank was in the audience when
I delivered an address to the Hadassah society of Atlanta,
Georgia. Recently Mrs. Frank died in an Atlanta hospital. She
was sixty-nine years old. In 1913 she was a young married
woman, the former Lucile Selig, who had come out of a
substantial and honorable home, only to be caught up in a
great human tragedy that wrecked her home and her chances
for future happiness; caused untold distress to the Jewish
community of Georgia; and brought immeasurable harm to
the great State of Georgia.

Leo Frank was born in Brooklyn and went to Atlanta
where he was the foreman of a pencil factory in which his
rich uncle had substantial interest. He married an Atlanta
girl, went to concerts and operas, and at the time of his
arrest was president of the local B'nai B'rith. He was not
what you would call a handsome man. He had protruding
eyeballs with heavy lids; he was extremely shy, a bit nervous.
(This made it simple for the yellow journalism of the day to
put his picture without the thick eyeglass lenses in the
paper, under a caption: "Monster.")

The factory was closed on Confederate Memorial Day in
April, 1913, but Frank had gone there to do some paper
work. Around noon, Mary Phagan, a fourteen-year-old girl,
came to get her pay for a day's work. Some of the girls had
been laid off early in the week because the factory had run
out of metal for the erasers. According to Frank he gave her
the envelope out of his cash box and she went away. Late
that night the night watchman found the girl on the coal

heap in the cellar, strangled. An attempt had been made to rape her, but it was never ascertained whether this part of the crime had been completed.

A week later Frank was arrested. The feeling against him was hostile from the beginning and the newspapers had a big time with him. As I have already pointed out, he was far from being photogenic. In addition, he was a Northerner and a college graduate. (In 1913 it was not too difficult to call a man a pervert on the evidence that he had gone to college.) Furthermore, very few women were as yet employed in industry. The agrarian South did not take kindly to the idea of their women working in factories. The accusation against a factory foreman confirmed their worst suspicions of this new development. One tent evangelist told them that the factory was a sort of "Jewish" Catholic monastery with all the same "goings-on." And, finally, what may have hurt Frank most was that his family was rich.

There was a terrible depression in Georgia at the time—in the entire Southeast. Only a year or two before, a man ran for Governor on a platform promising bread ("Brown for Bread"). This is hard to imagine in these days of country clubs and electric dishwashers. The prosecutor, Mr. Dorsey, in his summation to the jury, sneeringly referred to the Frank family as "capitalists." Today an up-to-date Dorsey would probably call him a "Red." The world turns upside down every forty years or so, doesn't it? It reminds me of the Japanese mission that went to Berlin to sign the Axis Pact in the late 1930's. The Japanese were enormously impressed with the success Hitler was having with this "gimmick" and when they left for home one Japanese was heard to sigh, "Ah, how I wish we had some Jews in Japan."

Frank was convicted and sentenced to death. The Supreme Court refused to open the case (Justices Holmes and Hughes dissenting).

Governor John M. Slaton commuted the sentence. He had become convinced of Frank's innocence. So had many other Georgians in high places. They had learned the full details of the confession of Conley, the Negro janitor, the principal witness against Frank. The Governor felt that a commutation would provide a cooling-off period to allow the truth to come out. A self-righteous cellmate slashed Frank's throat from ear to ear, barely missing the jugular vein. It would have been much better if he had not missed. Before the wound had healed the mob came to get Frank out of jail and they hanged him near the home of the murdered girl.

For a long time the young housewife, Lucile Frank, stood "alone" beside her husband, and she acquitted herself with wisdom and dignity throughout the ordeal. I say she stood "alone" because, contrary to the stereotype of "sticking together," the real truth of the matter is that the Jewish people are highly sensitive to a situation of this kind—when a member of their community gets in trouble. This, of course, is not true in the very large metropolitan cities where they achieve some degree of what I might call "civic anonymity." But it is true everywhere else. I have observed it a hundred times and more. The immediate reaction—"I am a citizen like everybody else; I am not responsible for the acts of someone else." In his attempt to appear nonchalant about the whole thing, the Jew often overdoes his "aloofness" and his "indifference." Often he outcondemns the condemners of the accused. He has been criticized by well-meaning Gentiles for being too sensitive; but you cannot argue with history. The Jewish communities stood aloof in both the Dreyfus and Frank cases, but they most certainly were made "co-defendants" in each case. Thus when a member of the Jewish community is arrested, it is not a moralistic indignation that the man has betrayed all his people; but rather that he has exposed them all to the danger of mass guilt. Christianity is rooted in this concept as it concerns the Jewish people, and it has never been too difficult to use it.

The Jew tries desperately to break off any identity with the accused; but he hopes that, if the man is really innocent, his "allies," the Gentiles of Reason, will come to the rescue. The fact that these Gentile allies have never failed him is not adequately emphasized in Jewish history or in our sociological studies.

After the real traitor, Major Esterhazy, had been exposed and the French General Staff still refused to acknowledge its error, world opinion cracked down on France very hard. But at this moment an editor who had been a Dreyfus supporter all along wrote: "Today I am proud to be called a Frenchman." That newspaperman was a philosopher. It is true that France had falsely accused an innocent man, but it was also true that France had created the atmosphere which led to the man's vindication.

It was certainly true that Georgia's Tom Watson, the anti-Semitic journalist, had incited a mob to lynch Leo Frank, but it was also true that the same Georgia produced Governor John M. Slaton. The mob violence did not end with the lynching of Frank. They turned upon the Governor who had commuted the sentence and literally drove him out of the State. If I were to write a play about the Leo Frank case, I would call it "Slaton," just as the best book written on the Dreyfus case was properly called *Zola*.

If we are to ask ourselves whether all this could happen again and we study all the factors involved, we immediately come upon an amazing parallel. In France it was the anti-Semitic journalist Edouard Drumont and in Georgia it was the anti-Semitic journalist Tom Watson. Almost immediately after the arrest of Dreyfus, Drumont's *La Libre Parole* made all the Jews of the world codefendants and immediately after the conviction of Leo Frank and the beginning of the long fight to save him, Tom Watson struck with unmitigated venom against an entire people. Both journalists were talented. In recent years we have come to underestimate the power of the newspaper.

And the reason, I suspect, is that Roosevelt won at least two of his elections against the overwhelming opposition of the press. But no matter how we expand our systems of communication, nothing can touch the newspaper for power. There's magic in it. The editors of the South smashed the Ku Klux Klan of the late 1940's, and the editors are the men who still keep the ragtag elements of bigotry outside the pale of respectability.

Could a Tom Watson make any headway today? I cannot answer.

There are times when resistance to demagoguery is low, and no one knows how much good will can be swept aside in an atmosphere of poverty and hopelessness such as Georgia experienced in 1913. But we are certain of one thing—there will always be a Zola or a Slaton or a Clemenceau or a Balfour.

In understanding the Frank case in Georgia and the Dreyfus case in France, an interesting conclusion impresses itself at once. Each of these cases involved *one man* (and each rather an unpleasant fellow), yet the *entire world* wrote editorials and held mass meetings in their behalf. The States of Texas and Tennessee passed resolutions urging Georgia to "save Leo Frank." Emile Zola and Major Georges Picquart gave up their careers and went to jail because they said, "Save Alfred Dreyfus." Governor John M. Slaton gave up his home and his law practice to "save Leo Frank," and Fernand Labori, France's greatest lawyer, took a bullet in his back because he shouted in the courtroom, "Save Alfred Dreyfus." Sir Winston Churchill writes that Stalin told him to his face that he had killed five million landholding peasants in the Ukraine. Churchill was stunned, but they finished the bottle of vodka anyway. Hitler killed six million men, women, and children in gas chambers and death camps, and Dorothy Thompson, in a Zionist discussion, sneered at me in front of the Davidson College audience, "There he goes talking about those six million Jews again." Just think how deeply concerned the world was because of the ordeal of each of these *two men*—and Jews, at that. Who cares about *one man* today—any kind of a *one man?*

Leo Frank and Alfred Dreyfus were at least fortunate in this—they lived in what was probably the last era of *humanitarianism* in world history—an era in which *one man* was still important.

How Pompey lost an empire

RECENTLY some Republican Party stalwarts went up and down the country accusing the Democrats of "treason." All eyes were on the President to see how he would react. The disclaimer was not as forthright as one issued by the late Wendell Willkie. Willkie demanded that Father Coughlin should *not* support him.

Mr. Hoover was up against the same thing when his assistant attorney general, a lady, told a convention of Protestant clergymen to work against Alfred E. Smith because he was a Catholic. No one in his right mind can accuse Mr. Hoover of bigotry. Yet he did not exactly pounce on this subordinate, Mabel Walker Willebrandt.

William Shakespeare gives us insight into this political problem in his drama, *Antony and Cleopatra*. Octavius, Antony, and Lepidus have divided the world after defeating Brutus and Cassius. Octavius took Rome and the west, Antony took Egypt and the east, and Lepidus ruled over Africa. But they had a new problem. Sextus Pompey had a huge fleet and was blockading the ports on the Adriatic. Sextus Pompey was the son of the great Roman general Pompey whom Caesar had defeated. Now the son wanted part of this Roman Empire; he also wanted the vast wealth Caesar had confiscated from the Pompey family after the defeat and death of his father.

This young Octavius was a genius. He was only eighteen years old but his granduncle Julius Caesar had trained him well. He figured that this was no time to have a showdown with Sextus Pompey. He needed time to prepare; and in his own good time he would pick off each of his rivals one by one, which is exactly how it turned out in the end.

But let us return to this triumvirate, Octavius, Antony, and Lepidus, in the act of appeasing Sextus Pompey. Octavius arranged a meeting on Pompey's flagship. This was like our diplomats in Berlin holding a meeting in the eastern zone in a Soviet building. Sometimes that's good diplomacy. It worked for Octavius.

Now they are on the ship and they agree to the truce and they are drinking to it, and for one of the few times in his entire life Octavius himself has taken a little too much wine. He is ashamed of himself. He is trying to shake himself sober. But of course Mark Antony and Lepidus are roaring drunk.

During these festivities, Menas, a subordinate of Pompey, takes Pompey aside and says, in effect, "Pompey, I can make you the master of the entire world. All I need do is cut the cable and slit the throats of these three drunks here; and in five minutes you rule the world." The funny thing about this proposal is that it was absolutely true.

Now what does Pompey reply? This good loyal Menas could have learned from Miss Willebrandt and from some of our Republican politicians. What does Pompey tell him? In effect he says: "Why the hell didn't you go ahead and do it without telling me, you dope? Now it's too late."

> In me 'tis villainy;
> In thee't had been good service.

That's what Sextus Pompey says. "Why didn't you just go ahead and come to me when it was all over? How can I possibly sanction such an act, now that you put it up to me?" What a situation! Here Shakespeare is paying his compliments to the fatuousness of a humanity that can dedicate all its power to three drunks on a boat and let its destiny depend on the slender thread of a cable and the still slenderer string of one man's honor. But Shakespeare was showing us, too, how some subordinates are smarter than Menas. They just go ahead and do the dirty work without asking. Sometimes the boss is even grateful.

When adultery was proof of "loyalty"

WHEN Charles II was restored to the throne after the death of Oliver Cromwell, the five judges who had sentenced Charles I to death were arrested and convicted of treason against the Crown. This was the official sentence:

> You shall go from hence to the place from whence you came, and from that place shall be drawn upon a hurdle to the place of execution, and there shall hang by the neck till you are half dead, and shall be cut down alive, and your privy members cut off before your face and thrown into the fire, your belly ripped up and your bowels burst, your head to be severed from your body, your body shall be divided into four quarters, and disposed of as His Majesty shall think fit.

Thus began an historic era, which interestingly enough has had its parallel in our own day. We have all seen how folks have become superpatriots and vigilantes out of fear that they may be suspected of subversion.

This happened in a more interesting way at the beginning of the reign of Charles II. The Puritans (who were now the traitors) had imposed a very strict moral code upon the people, which brought in its wake that same old villainy which has oppressed people through all the ages; being reported by friends, neighbors, and their own children for violating Puritan taboos against sex, dancing, kissing on the Sabbath, play acting, and gaiety of any kind. Thus the best way you could now show your loyalty to the Crown was—to have fun.

Adultery was the most convenient way to prove that you had never been a follower of Oliver Cromwell, and the folks went—all out. If a man and woman were on a journey and they suspected the coachman of being a Government agent, they went to all sorts of extremes to prove their "loyalty" and throw the fellow off the track.

And so when the coachman peeked, and saw what was going on back there, he shrugged his shoulders: "Those people are all right, they ain't no Puritans."

My sermon on informers

A FEW years ago Senator Langer turned down the request of Paul Crouch—a former Communist turned informer—to investigate the then Attorney General Herbert Brownell for being a Commie-sympathizer. Thus the greatest American Attorney General since McGranery learned the hard way what every rookie cop knows from the very first day on his job—to make sure that the informers he uses never see him (the cop) taking a beer while on duty.

The former Communists turned informers tell all; they mention every name, describe every incident. They become big shots. Demand for their stuff increases. Now they must begin to invent, improvise, and embellish. Since their word is law, and all they need do is crack the whip for the entire machinery of government to snap into action, they can get away with it. And if they are tripped up, they can always turn on their employers. So if you must use an informer you had better stay away from him. Do not even take him to lunch. He'll watch every move you make; it will all go down in his diary. Remember you have taught him an easy way to make a living and he will not give it up and go back to work without a struggle.

And, my friends, it does not stop there. We have built up a whole new class of "experts" and "lecturers" on the same basis. There are a dozen men and women on lists of various lecture bureaus, all making a good living, talking about Russia, and who know as much about it as they know about the

Galaxy of Andromeda. One fellow I know has been on the air
for years now as an "expert" on how to fight Reds, and each
time he goes on the air he is introduced as an "expert who
was there." I once checked up on this fellow and found
that the guy had visited in the Soviet Union for a period of
ten days—in 1926.

Should housewives be in politics?

DURING the heat of the Punic Wars, the Roman magistrates and consuls set up what was known as the Oppian
Law, a system of rationing and other wartime measures of
austerity. One of the provisions stated that "no woman should
possess more than a half ounce of gold, or wear a garment
of various colors, or ride in a carriage drawn by horses in a
city, or in a town, except on occasions of religious solemnity."
The women of Rome kept clamoring for repeal of this
law and thousands of them organized a sort of League of
Women Voters and knocked on the doors of all consuls,
praetors, and magistrates.
Marcus Cato, one of the great orators of the day, took the
platform of the Roman Forum in 215 B.C. to speak against
repeal. He made an impassioned plea for continuation of all
austerity measures to help win the war. He understood, he
said, how rich women feel about wearing the same kind of
clothes as the poor, but this is much better than knuckling
under to Hannibal.
But Cato's real fire was directed against the principle of
women in politics. His position was, if women go around
asking special favors of strange men, who knows what this
could lead to. He urged the Romans not to lose control
over their households:

> If, Romans, every individual among us had made it a
> rule to maintain the prerogative and authority of a

husband with respect to his own wife, he should have less trouble with the whole sex. But now our privileges, overpowered at home by female contumacy, are, even here in the Forum, spurned and trodden under foot; and because we are unable to withstand each separately we now dread their collective body. I was accustomed to think it a fabulous tale that in a certain island the whole race of males was utterly extirpated by a conspiracy of the women.

Cato was *not* against political freedom for the women of Rome, but exactly 2,173 years ago this politician raised a most valid argument. He said this: If the women are so eager to win a point in law or legislation no one stops them. Let each of them stay home and convince her own husband, and since all the consuls are married men, this should make it comparatively simple to achieve the desired result. But *no,* they cannot convince their own husbands and so they come out in the streets and importune strange husbands. This, said Cato, was an unfair advantage—men being men. He made the point that, when a wife urges her legislator-husband to vote for or against a certain measure, the husband will think only in terms of the law in question. He will weigh the pros and cons. But when a strange woman solicits the vote of someone else's husband, she may be talking about repeal, but he's already thinking of something else.

And think of something else they certainly did, because the law was repealed. Livy writes that the day after repeal the women "went in procession through the streets and the forum, bedizened with their now legitimate finery."

The impeachment of Governor Sulzer

A LONG-TIME friend, retired Judge Aaron J. Levy, died in Florida at the age of seventy-four. I was surprised that *The New York Times'* column-long story did not take advantage of the tremendous file which that great newspaper must have in its morgue on Aaron J. *The Times* told of the elevation of Judge Levy to the State Supreme Court, his two successful campaigns for re-election, and the several inquiries and investigations in which he was involved, but the obituary did not mention the biggest story in the history of the State of New York, the only legal removal of one of its Governors— the impeachment of Governor William Sulzer, which Aaron J. Levy (representing Boss Charles F. Murphy of Tammany Hall) managed from beginning to end.

Boss Murphy of Tammany controlled the Legislature of New York State, of course. Alfred E. Smith was the Speaker of the House; Robert Wagner was Leader of the State Senate, and Aaron J. Levy was Democratic Leader of the House.

Governor Sulzer of New York was an interesting politician. He was a Protestant of an old family who, like Franklin D. Roosevelt, a quarter of a century later, was very popular with the Irish, Jewish, Italian, and Slav minority groups of New York City. Sulzer, Tammany Hall's best orator, was the image of Henry Clay. The resemblance was so striking that he affected that great statesman's manner and dress, down to the underwear, some said. Sulzer, too, like Clay, was brilliant and resourceful on the platform. This phenomenon of Tammany politics was also an ardent Prohibitionist of all things—"The great curse of mankind is RUM, RUM, RUM." But he had developed a good system in public. He drank white likker like a Southerner and everybody thought it was water.

Sulzer was elected Governor at a time when Tammany needed a man to dress up the ticket after one of the periodic graft scandals. And Sulzer beat two good men, too. One was Oscar S. Straus, running for Governor on the Bull Moose ticket with Theodore Roosevelt, and the other was Job E. Hedges, the Republican, also a fine man. The Republicans too needed some window dressing that year after a graft scandal of their own upstate; and so Sulzer became Governor and Murphy immediately sent for him and gave him the list of "his" appointments. Murphy, in all seriousness, once gave his idea of political science. In discussing a previous Governor, he said: "Governor Dix is a great statesman—he does as he is told." But Governor Sulzer *refused* to do as he was told this time and that was the beginning of the end of his political career. Indirectly, Woodrow Wilson caused Sulzer's destruction.

Without Wilson, Sulzer would have followed the instructions of his boss, Murphy. Wilson had been a professor at Princeton University. The political bosses of New Jersey also had had a big scandal on their hands and rather than lose the State they decided to take a chance on the professor. *Maybe* he'll be grateful. So when Mr. Nugent, the political boss, came to Governor Wilson with *his* list of appointments, the professor threw him out of the office and told his secretary, Joe Tumulty, to have the political boss arrested if he ever showed up again. A few years later Wilson became President of the United States, on the same day that Sulzer became Governor of New York.

The lesson was not lost on Henry Clay-William Sulzer. Why not do to Charley Murphy in New York what Wilson did to Nugent in New Jersey, and become President maybe? There were two things wrong with this reasoning. Sulzer was not a Woodrow Wilson and Charley Murphy was not a Nugent. Wilson could thumb his nose at the political machine because he had come from a university campus—he owed the politicians nothing. They took a chance when they picked him, and they lost. The politicians gave up gracefully and waited patiently for the day when they could get rid of Wilson by sending him to the White House. But Sulzer was not "unspotted from this world," as the Methodists would say. He had indeed supped at Tammany's table, to borrow a phrase from John L. Lewis, and it is not easy for a man who had *used* Tammany to tear up Murphy's appointment list.

Sulzer was impeached on charges that he diverted campaign funds for personal use, but Sulzer could have had a

thousand times the amount charged against him if he had
played along.

Murphy decided to impeach him and he wanted it done
immediately. And Aaron J. Levy was to manage the proceedings in the Legislature.

Murphy knew that Smith and Wagner were aiming for
higher offices. Therefore, while Smith in the House and
Wagner in the Senate smoothed the way for the impeachment, Murphy saw to it that the most important name connected with the prosecution of the Governor was Aaron J.
Levy. All that Al Smith and Bob Wagner did was wake up
the members of the State Legislature when it came time to
vote. But this was not the whole story on Aaron J.'s importance in the proceedings. The Jews on the East Side
literally worshipped Sulzer. When Sulzer was a member of
Congress he fought against an early proposal to restrict
immigration and his fight had been successful. You can well
imagine what that meant to a million naturalized citizens in
the City of New York. Aaron J. Levy was himself an immigrant and active in Jewish fraternal affairs and with him
acting as the "prosecutor" there would be no question in
anyone's mind that Sulzer was being impeached for his
ideals. Louis Marshall, the leading Jew in America, and one
of our greatest Constitutional lawyers, defended Governor
Sulzer and the witnesses called were Jacob H. Schiff, Herbert
Lehman, the broker Louis M. Josephthal, and Thomas
Fortune Ryan. These men had made sizeable contributions
to Sulzer's campaign. Mr. Marshall raised a very interesting
point in the defense of Sulzer. He said that all the alleged
acts took place *before* Mr. Sulzer was Governor and therefore could not be used as the basis for his impeachment.
However, the ruling was made that campaign contributions
were part of the "acts" of the office involved. (This has
been upheld since then in several similar cases.) The con-
tributors to his campaign had done nothing wrong. Contributions of $2,500 to $5,000 from these men were not considered unusual. But Sulzer was charged with using some of
this money to pay off his personal debts, and when it was

brought out that he had personally solicited a $10,000 contribution from Thomas Fortune Ryan, his case collapsed completely. After the Ryan testimony the liberals, independents, as well as all the civic groups interested in "better government" lost interest in Sulzer. They now took the attitude of "a plague on both your (Tammany) houses." Sulzer was convicted; Lieutenant Governor Martin Glynn took over the office; Aaron J. Levy became a judge; and Alfred E. Smith and Robert Wagner went on to the highest political honors and worthy public service: Governor four times and United States Senator for three terms, respectively. Mr. Wagner's son is now Mayor of New York.

There is a bit of irony in the name of Thomas Fortune Ryan who helped bring down Governor Sulzer. This was the same man who helped make Woodrow Wilson the President of the United States! There was a moment during the Baltimore convention when William Jennings Bryan knew that he couldn't make it. But he also knew that no one else could make it without his support.

A point came up during the early proceedings with respect to the seating of Thomas Fortune Ryan with the New York delegation. Bryan sent a telegram to the three leading contenders, the favorite, Champ Clark of Missouri, Mr. Wilson of New Jersey, and Judson Harmon of Ohio. The telegram said: "If you were a delegate to this convention how would you vote on the question of seating Mr. Thomas Fortune Ryan?" Mr. Clark, who had Murphy's support, did not reply. Mr. Harmon was ambiguous in the word he sent to Bryan. Wilson did not reply directly, but one of his floor managers, Josephus Daniels of North Carolina, a close friend of Bryan, told the Great Commoner just how Wilson stood on both Tammany and Thomas Fortune Ryan. At that moment Woodrow Wilson was as good as in the White House.

Sulzer had everything it takes to become a President. Some men muff the chance. He was very popular with women. At the beginning of the impeachment proceedings, some woman came along and sued Sulzer for "breach of promise." She remembered that the Governor had "ruined" her ten years earlier. When Charles Francis Murphy of Tammany Hall went after a man—he surrounded him.

Bloc voting

DURING the run-off primary between Dr. Frank P. Graham and the late Senator Willis Smith, the latter's campaign headquarters issued strong statements to the effect that "the Negroes voted as a bloc for Graham." This double talk represents a renunciation of logic whereby it is assumed that the best way to show your patriotism is to vote against your own interests. Who does that? Suppose a candidate was unfriendly to banks; would a banker vote for him? Our democracy is made up of dozens of sectional, industrial, ethnic, and religious groups; and somewhere a balance is struck between the demands of the farmers' Grange and the labor unions; between the huge industrial and financial lobbies and the group which is demanding a change in the calendar. The Irish indeed tipped the scales in two presidential elections; each case involved Grover Cleveland. In 1884, the Republicans ran James G. Blaine ("The continental liar from the State of Maine"—Democratic campaign song), and the Democrats nominated Grover Cleveland of New York "Ma, Ma, where's my pa, gone to the White House, ha, ha, ha"—Republican campaign song alluding to Cleveland's alleged illegitimate child).

The election eventually turned on New York State, which Blaine seemed to have in the bag. Three days before election day, the Reverend Samuel D. Burchard, leader of a delegation of clergymen who called on Blaine at his headquarters, referred to the Democrats as the party of "Rum, Romanism, and Rebellion." Blaine's failure to disavow the remark cost him the Irish vote in New York and therefore the Presidency.

The Irish again swung the election in 1888, this time against Cleveland. Benjamin Harrison was the Republican nominee. On the eve of the election, the Republicans produced a letter written by the British Ambassador, Sackville-West, in reply to an inquiry from a naturalized Englishman. The letter said that he (the British Ambassador) recommends voting for Cleveland. The Irish in New York "saw red" at this British "interference," and voted for Harrison. Again the election hinged on New York's big electoral vote, and Harrison carried it by 3,490 votes, and by that margin won the Presidency.

The Republicans did a little bloc voting themselves on occasion. The Republican Party we know today had not yet been constituted; but under the banner of the Whigs were to be found all the big-business conservative people who are today Republicans. They were out to break the Democratic hold in Washington, and went all-out in the campaign of 1840 with their candidate, William Henry Harrison (who probably was the least qualified man ever elected to the Presidency). His opponent was Democrat Martin Van Buren. During the campaign the Whigs distributed hundreds of thousands of circulars throughout the country with this notice: "$5 a hundred for pork if Harrison is elected; and $2.50 if Van Buren wins."

Again in 1896, the Republicans were genuinely alarmed by the popularity of William Jennings Bryan, and many industrial firms put a printed notice into the pay envelopes on the Saturday before the election: "If Bryan is elected on Tuesday, do not report for work on Wednesday morning." McKinley won by less than four hundred thousand votes out of a total of twelve and a half million ballots.

The Democratic Party and the South

THE time has come for a new approach; a sort of reappraisal of the position of the South in the Democratic

Party, and the position of the South in its relationship to the entire American dream of individual freedom.

Over the years, I have written many articles in my paper to admonish Southern politicians that their chairmanships in the Congress and their power and influence in the nation is due, to a large extent, to the fact that up in the North, the Poles, Greeks, Czechs, Jews, Irish, Negroes, Italians, and trade-unionists vote the straight Democratic ticket. But the coin has two sides. The time has come to tell the Northern liberals that their own success, from time to time, in effecting economic reform—yes, even the expansion of the labor unions, and the establishment of collective bargaining—is due, to a large extent, to the Southern habit of voting the straight Democratic ticket. If the truth were known, the Southern contribution may have been a little greater. In the first place (and despite the meanderings of some officials), the Populist tradition is just as strong in the South today as it was fifty years ago. I have spoken to farmers in eastern North Carolina who would make F.D.R., Jr., sound like a William McKinley Tory. Basically, the South has not had a good press, not by a long shot. Even the Ku Klux Klan after World War I was just as ugly in Freehold, New Jersey; Binghamton, New York; Berkley, Michigan; and Kokomo, Indiana. Neither did the "Christian Front" terrorists of Boston, nor the "America Firsters" of New York, Pennsylvania, Michigan, and Ohio, make the slightest dent in the South. Without the South there probably would have been no Lend-Lease Act, or at best, it would have been delayed precious months. The Selective Service Act, which was extended a few weeks before Pearl Harbor by the margin of one vote, had the support of 96 per cent of the Southern delegations in the houses of Congress. It is well to think about these things clearly, and weigh their importance. For the Democratic Party to cut itself off from millions of these "individualists" because they don't like Jimmy Byrnes would be the height of stupidity, and fraught with serious danger for the future of the nation and the Democratic Party and the United Nations.

Let us consider, for instance, that neither the Ludlow Bill of 1937 nor the Bricker Resolution of 1953 came out of the South, and any important Southern support for such isolationist measures is remote. It is here in the South that Presidents Wilson, Roosevelt, and Truman won almost immediate (and unanimous) understanding of America's position in world affairs, and America's obligation in assuming her world leadership. It was not in the South, but in Massachusetts, Connecticut, Idaho, and California, that the plots were hatched to destroy Woodrow Wilson's dream of a concert of nations to preserve world freedom and peace. In the area of America's world leadership, every Democratic President appeared before the Congress with the almost unanimous backing of the South to start with—quite an advantage in the march of events.

But that is not all. Here in the South, a Senator McCarthy couldn't be elected to the town council.

If ever you liberals in the North needed an ally with the individualistic cussedness of the Southerner—it is now.

When it's raining, have no regrets

TAMMANY HALL knew how to handle the many religious, ethnic, and cultural groups which make up the population of New York. Tammany always put "balanced" tickets into the field. If an Irish Catholic headed the ticket, a Jew was number-two man, and an Italian was not far behind. Sometimes, depending upon the stature of the individual candidates, this order was rearranged. (The Protestants? Unburdened by minority status and therefore relieved of the terrible pressure of trying to prove individual worth, they were busy making money in the banks, insurance companies, and brokerage houses.) On the basis of the "balanced" ticket, a young Jewish lawyer once became a magistrate because it was raining.

It was the night of the meeting in Tammany when designations for public office were announced. Three candidates for magistrate were to be named. They named the Irishman and the Italian, but, when they called out the name of the Jew who was slated for the job, there was no answer. It was a night unfit "for man or beast." The fellow made a mistake in thinking that the meeting would be called off. An alternate name was called out; still no answer. Finally Charley Murphy, the Tammany boss, a bit nettled, called out: "Is there a Jewish lawyer in the house?" A young fellow who had passed his bar examinations a few weeks before stood up.

He was named magistrate. Turned out to be a darned good judge, too.

Crime investigations

THERE are many interesting characters answering questions and refusing to answer questions in Senate committee investigations. But no one can ever hope to match the good old Tammany man, Sheriff McQuade, during the Seabury investigations which threw Mayor Jimmy Walker out of office. McQuade's salary was $9,000 a year, and Judge Seabury's investigators found that McQuade had banked $350,000 in the three years preceding the investigation. McQuade was asked to explain how he secured this vast amount of money. This is how he explained it (the official record):

"I need $1,000. I borrow it from say, John Brown. Then John Brown wants his money back, so I go to say, John Smith, and borrow $1,000 from him and pay John Brown. I borrow another $1,000 from say, Bill Jones, to pay John Smith. In this way, by borrowing from every Tom, Dick and Harry, I keep paying back Smith, Brown and Jones, and all the time I have in my possession these other thousands which I borrowed from Tom, Dick and Harry, and that's how I get the money. If I am short, I have a tin box at home with money, and I also take from that tin box and make deposits, and that's how I come to have so much money in the deposits, taking it out of the tin box."

McQuade was re-elected the following year.

The lawyers got a break

It was more or less an unwritten law. The magistrates in New York always gave the lawyers a break. When the magistrate knew that he had to dismiss a complaint for lack of evidence, he always allowed the lawyer to make a speech defending freedom, using a few ideas from his bar examination papers, plus a closing quotation from de Tocqueville. Always de Tocqueville (a Frenchman who recorded some of the most incisive observations of the American way of life).

So the police would swoop down on a gambling den after they had been tipped off. These gambling dens were usually set up in temporary quarters—in the back of a stable or in an empty factory loft. The managers of the gambling den would be tipped off, too, usually by the same one who had tipped off the police. (Both sides paid him.) Thus, when the police hammered down the door, all the money had been taken off the tables and the gambling equipment and paraphernalia had been stashed away. And there they were, sixty people standing shoulder to shoulder, and just looking at each other. In Magistrate's Court the police had to admit that they saw no money and they found no gambling equipment. Then the young lawyer took over and the magistrate gave him a break. The lawyer would blossom out with a big speech about the right of peaceful assembly. Then came the quotation from de Tocqueville, followed by the magistrate's crisp order, "Cases dismissed." Then the sixty people carried the successful lawyer out on their shoulders, and for the next ten years each of them spoke of the brilliant defense that had electrified the court and swept the magistrate off his feet.

Negroes on the ballot

THERE were two Negroes running for a place on the Charlotte City Council. Not only the liberals, but leading citizens of every shade of political thinking felt that the time had come for a Negro to have one of the seven seats. It was felt, however, that, with two Negroes in the race, they would split the vote and cancel each other out. Interested citizens tried to get one or the other of the Negroes to withdraw. I joined in these attempts, but I pulled up short.

Wasn't I doing something that we have fought against for so long? Who am I—who, indeed, is anyone—to say, "Here, gather yourselves into one mass and give us 'one' of you." Luckily, I stopped in my tracks, silently apologized to the Negroes for even thinking of such a thing, and went about my business. Certainly, we must think of each other in terms of "individuals," and hope to be judged by our individual actions, and stand on our individual efforts. If two Negroes want to run for office, all right. Suppose fourteen Negroes decide to stand for public office. Why not? I realized then that a victory for an indiscriminate "representative" was far less valuable than the defeat of two individualists.

We hate our own

HERE was the chairman of the South Carolina delegation shouting, "WE WANT KENNEDY!" Kennedy? In South Carolina? In Mississippi, too? This is no reflection on the ability and charm of the young Massachusetts Senator. I wish all my good friends to have sons like Jack Kennedy. But neither should young Kennedy take this thing seriously.

We hate our own much more than we hate "outsiders." There were Americans who hated Roosevelt much more than they hated Hitler, and I daresay there were others who hated Hoover much more than they hated Stalin.

We can never forgive our own. The feeling against Kefauver, bone of the bone and blood of the blood, a Southerner, was strong because of his liberal views on the race question. The Southern delegations, therefore, wanted Kennedy, a New England Roman Catholic, who writes articles in the *Atlantic Monthly* against the Southern textile industry. How do you like that for the renunciation of logic?

The Southerners had no way of knowing how Kennedy stood on racial segregation. I'll bet anyone fourteen to one that his position is far to the left of Senator Kefauver's, but that does not matter. Kefauver is one of our own and therefore you must never forgive him. "North Carolina, Alabama, and Texas vote for Kennedy."

Now we've seen everything!

Shakespeare knew all about politicians

"THERE shall be in England seven halfpenny loaves sold for a penny: the three-hooped pot shall have ten hoops; and I will make it felony to drink small beer: all the realm shall be in common; and in Cheapside shall my palfrey go to grass: and when I am king, as king I will be, . . . there shall be no money; all shall eat and drink on my score; and I will apparel them all in one livery, and they may agree like brothers and worship me their lord."

—Jack Cade in *Henry VI*, Part II, Act IV, Scene ii

PART 7

Merry Christmas,
Billy Graham

~~~~~~

Mayor William J. Gaynor

THE first time the name Gaynor began to mean more to me than that of another politician was when I was a kid on the Lower East Side. One afternoon I saw a cop beating up a bearded old peddler. I remember the peddler rolling in the gutter, holding his head, and, as the night stick kept crashing down again and again, the policeman was screaming: "Gaynor ain't mayor any more! Gaynor ain't mayor any more!"

Let me tell you about Mayor William J. Gaynor.

He was an irascible old cuss, a bearded Unitarian, who got himself elected mayor by the Catholics, Protestants, and Jews of New York in November, 1909. The reason behind his election followed a general pattern. Whenever Tammany Hall was exposed in some thievery, the sachems picked an "independent"; a man as "unspotted from the world" as it is possible to be in public life. In other words, they were always willing to take a chance on a man who was nominally a Democrat, rather than allow the opposition to beat them. On this occasion they picked a judge of the Appellate Division of the Supreme Court, a man with an international reputation as a jurist.

After he was inaugurated, they wished they had let the Republicans capture City Hall.

Mayor Gaynor fired every Tammany officeholder; tore up every Tammany Hall recommendation; and once sent word that he would arrest any Tammany politician found loitering around City Hall. In the process, however, Gaynor threw overboard any chance he may have had to become Governor of New York, and perhaps President of the United States. When the Democrats were preparing for their 1912 convention (which resulted in the nomination of Woodrow Wilson), the national party leaders kept coming to New York's City Hall to see Gaynor.

Late in the year 1911 Colonel Edward Mandell House of Texas began his career as a political "power behind the throne." In order to achieve this goal you must first go out and get yourself a "throne" to be a power behind—or at least help make someone the President of the United States. The first man to interest Colonel House was the amazing Mayor Gaynor. And so House went to New York and formally invited Gaynor to make a speech before the State Legislature of Texas. A high honor. On the appointed day Gaynor did not show up in Texas. When the frantic House finally reached him, Gaynor said, "Haven't the faintest idea what you're talking about. This is the first I know anything about a visit to Texas."

But House was not ready to give up. He still thought Gaynor would make a wonderful candidate, and so he went to New York again. And it turned out to be one of Gaynor's better weeks. On Monday he made a speech in which he insulted the members of the press. He was talking to the Board of Estimate and made a reference to the Roman Senator, Cato. Gaynor leaned forward to the press table and repeated to the reporters: "Cato— I said, Cato— Has any one of you ever heard of him?" On Tuesday he attacked a bishop of the Roman Catholic Church—said if the priest continued to hang around City Hall he would have the sergeant-at-arms throw him out. On Wednesday Gaynor delivered a blistering attack on Rabbi Stephen S. Wise as a meddler; and that same night in a public address he told an audience that the great publisher William Randolph Hearst was "the most heinous force in American life," and to round out the week, Mayor Gaynor told the Protestant clergyman, Dr. Parkhurst, "You are not pious, you are merely bilious." By this time Colonel House was already swimming across the Hudson River to Governor Woodrow Wilson. He wouldn't even wait for the ferry.

When a group of reformers sent him a list of small hotels in New York where (they alleged) unmarried couples could get accommodations, Gaynor sent the list back with the notation: "Why isn't the Waldorf-Astoria on your list?" When an evangelist applied for a license to preach the gospel in an all-Jewish neighborhood, Mayor Gaynor returned the application with the following remarks: "Please attach a list of the Jews you have already converted, and I'll give your application further consideration. In the meanwhile do not annoy these people."

Nothing escaped Mayor Gaynor. Once he sent a memorandum to his street-cleaning commissioner, Bill Edwards, after the Mayor had seen a group of men shoveling snow while the driver of the truck stood idly by: "Do you want the driver to freeze to death? Give him a shovel."

Mayor Gaynor was so free with advice on any and all matters, trivial or complex, that a popular retort of the day to anyone with a problem was, "Tell it to Gaynor." The opposition *Tribune* wrote, "Nothing that does not concern him is too difficult for his brain."

Today the mayors of our cities hand the "complaint" to a secretary who writes: "Your letter has been turned over to the proper department for study." Individualism is gone. The day when the mayor locked himself in his office and had all visitors screened for whips, guns, knives, and clubs is gone, and that's a pity, too.

In answer to a letter from the National Publicity Bureau asking him for a statement, Gaynor replied, "You ask me to give an interview saying, 'What would I say to the readers of your three thousand newspapers.' I would say to them to be very careful about believing all they see in those news-papers."

To a fellow who complained about the danger from hatpins in women's hats in the elevated trains and streetcars, Gay-nor replied: "Why do you get so close to a woman that her hatpin becomes a threat to you? I hope the next woman uses her hatpin to good effect."

To a letter complaining about a stiff fine for spitting on the platform of the elevated station: "Spitting is a nasty habit and therefore you must be a nasty fellow. You are lucky I wasn't sitting as the Magistrate in your case."

To a Greek Orthodox priest who complained that he was ridiculed when he walked along the street because of his black beard, he wrote: "How is it that they take notice of your beard? Have you trimmed it in some peculiar way, con-trary to the Scriptures? . . . Are you certain it is your beard which is the cause of the trouble?"

To a Republican politician who had misquoted him, he wrote: "I am glad to perceive from your letter, just received, that I have already cured you of your propensity to make false statements, that you drop your forged quotation from my letter to Mr. Ridder, and use the correct quotation. While the lamp holds out to burn the vilest sinner may return."

A year after he took office a discharged city employee shot Mayor Gaynor. He came up behind the Mayor on the deck of an ocean liner, where Gaynor stood talking with friends who had come aboard to see him off to Europe. The would-be assassin held the pistol close to the Mayor's head and fired. The bullet entered the back of his right ear, and passed through the throat, and was never extracted. His voice was permanently affected, and the wound hastened his death which occurred a few months before the end of his term, when he was running for re-election, as an "independent" this time, of course. Incidentally, the photo of Mayor Gaynor staggering to his feet after the attempt on his life is in every collection of the famous news photos of all time.

Throughout his career as a judge and mayor Gaynor kept his private life strictly to himself. Few people knew that he had been born on a farm, that he had once studied for the priesthood, and that he had been married twice. Photographs of his wife and children were nonexistent as far as the public was concerned. He went home every week-end to a farm on Long Island, at St. James, and tolerated no intrusion except for neighboring farmers with whom he would discuss crops, weather conditions, and purely local affairs. He was a political and mental giant among pygmies. Compared to Gaynor, Jimmy Walker was a department store floorwalker; La Guardia, an opportunist whom Gaynor would have given the back of his hand; and Impellitteri would have done well to have been allowed to tie Gaynor's shoelaces. (About La Guardia, I can never forgive him for having withheld the salary of Professor Bertrand Russell when the mob was hounding the British philosopher out of the City College of New York for teaching "advanced" ideas. One may well imagine what Gaynor would have done in this case. He probably would have delivered Russell's pay envelope himself, and with his cane carved a path through the mob of shouting obscurantists.)

But with all of Gaynor's notable achievements, his greatest talent was his remarkable use of the English language. Professor Brander Matthews read Gaynor's letters in his class at Columbia University, and so did the English masters at Oxford and Cambridge. Gaynor was one of the most widely read political figures in our history. His knowledge of the religious, philosophical, and literary classics of the world was phenomenal. Time after time, as he delivered a lecture and quoted from Marcus Aurelius, Cervantes, Shakespeare, and the Bible, he would turn to the reporters and give them the volume and the chapter of his quoted reference so that their account of the occasion would be complete.

His written opinions as a judge were full of references and quotations from the great minds of our civilization. One of his decisions is known to this day as the "Pater Noster Case." It was a divorce case against a man. The evidence showed that he met the woman at a railroad station, that they came together in a hack with their baggage to the hotel, that the man registered them as man and wife, and that they went to the bedroom assigned to them. One of the judges wrote an opinion that this evidence was not sufficient. Gaynor wrote an opinion that the legal inference of misconduct could and should be drawn from it, that they did not go there to say their prayers, and he cited that passage from Burton's *Anatomy of Melancholy*, which says of a man under such conditions, "It is presumed he saith not a Pater Noster."

One of the best Gaynor episodes concerned the Protestant clergyman, Dr. Charles H. Parkhurst, and the "Leapfrog Dance" in a New York brothel. Dr. Parkhurst felt that the city had too many prostitutes and that Gaynor wasn't doing anything about getting rid of them. So to gather evidence, he hit upon one of the most interesting experiments ever initiated by a man of the cloth. He went out to gather the evidence himself. He hired a private detective companion. Dr. Parkhurst, head of the fashionable Madison Square Presbyterian Church, trimmed his fine beard, put on old waterfront clothing, a turtle-neck sweater, and off he went. Dr. Parkhurst insisted on "a full investigation." The companion, a Mr. Gardner, wrote a book about it in later years. First they visited some Bowery saloons, but each time Dr. Parkhurst said, "This is bad, but I want to see worse." Then Gardner steered the doctor to the five-cent lodging houses where the reek of perspiration from the naked sleepers was enough to knock you down. A few more lodging houses, but the clergyman still wasn't satisfied. "I want to see the worst." Gardner finally got the point. He and the doctor then made a round of the brothels, plus a few opium houses as a bonus. Dr. Parkhurst was all the time taking notes, and, on the third night, says companion Gardner, he took the clergyman to the one and only Hattie Adams House, where Gardner says he arranged with the madam for her girls to perform their famous "dance of nature" for the edification of Dr. Parkhurst.

Gardner records that they first had to blindfold the "professor" as they called the piano player in these places, because the girls were shy and would perform only for strangers. The "dance of nature" included a "leapfrog" sequence during which Gardner writes he was the frog and the others jumped over him, with Dr. Parkhurst taking it all in.

This was where the clergyman made a serious blunder. When he made his report from his pulpit and demanded that the district attorney close all the places he had visited, Dr. Parkhurst, to emphasize the degradation he had seen, mentioned this "leapfrog" sequence in the "dance of nature" up at the Hattie Adams House. Well, don't ask! The newspapers immediately picked that up, and the whole town was buzzing—jokes by the million and saloons were advertising special leapfrog concoctions. So by the time Dr. Parkhurst appeared before the Society for the Prevention of Crime, the dignity had gone out of the whole thing and the opposition papers called it "Dr. Parkhurst's Leapfrog Investigation." It blew up in ribaldry and jest.

In the end, however, the brothels and joints were closed by the reform Mayor John Purroy Mitchel. But to this day no one has adequately answered Mayor Gaynor's original statement to Dr. Parkhurst: "If you secured for me the authority to take the prostitutes down to the river and drown them all, I would see a point to your demands, but you don't want that. What you want me to do is to chase them out of New York and you would feel better, I suppose, if they were walking the streets of Philadelphia, New Haven, and Jersey City."

A day with Carl Sandburg

I SPENT eight hours with Carl Sandburg.

Except for a short walk around his Connemara Farm at Flat Rock, North Carolina, we sat on his porch and exchanged stories. But mostly we laughed just as the poet Blake imagined it—" . . . we laughed and the hills echoed."

Carl Sandburg and I spent eight hours together, and the sapphire mountains of North Carolina cast echo and shadow of Lincoln, of Swedish immigrant farmers to the broad plains of the American Midwest, of pushcarts on the Lower East Side of New York, and of a long-ago place in the province of Galicia in Austrian Poland—and this could happen only in America.

And when we rested from our labors, Margaret, the charming daughter of the Sandburgs, read to us out of George Ade, a household favorite.

Nor did even the dinner bell intrude upon us. "Bring it out here on the porch," said Mr. Sandburg; and I reflected later, with considerable chagrin, how I had not offered to help Mrs. Sandburg and Miss Margaret when they lugged the side tables to us; and they tried hard not to disturb us.

And when it was all over, Sandburg said, "Harry, it's been about fifty-fifty, you talked half and I talked half."

I am certain that Carl Sandburg had thought of this appointment as just another interview. Just another newspaper fellow, standing first on one foot and then on the other, asking how do I like North Carolina; what am I writing now; a question maybe about Lincoln, or Nancy Hanks, or Mary Todd; who is my favorite novelist; what do I think of *Andersonville,* etc.

I shuddered at the thought that he might associate me with such nonsense.

Nor did I carry a book for him to autograph, or a camera to snap his picture, or a manuscript for him to read in his "spare time." All I brought was a bottle of whiskey.

Whiskey? Who ever heard of bringing a bottle of whiskey to Carl Sandburg? Well, I figured that, even if he doesn't drink, he probably would not think it in bad taste if I drank a few toasts to him—right on the spot. Margaret Sandburg kept us supplied with fresh North Carolina branch water.

I had planned the appointment for a long time. Several years ago Don Shoemaker, the Asheville *Citizen-Times* editor, had introduced Mr. Sandburg to *The Carolina Israelite* and we exchanged a few letters during the past five years. Several months ago I wrote him for an appointment, and received a note:

> Brudder Golden: All signs say I'll be here April 3 and if you're here we won't expect to save the country but we can have fellowship. Carl Sandburg.

I arrived about noon and as I got out of the car I heard Sandburg's voice through the screen door of his porch: "That must be Harry Golden; I want to see what he looks like." There are about ten steps leading up to the porch of the old plantation home and when I reached the top Mr. Sandburg was already outside to greet me. He wore a Korean army cap low over his eyes, khaki shirt and work pants. I turned from him to take a long look at that breath-taking scene, the acres and acres of lawn as clean as a golf course in front of the house, the heavily wooded areas to the right, the majestic North Carolina Rockies in front—the whole thing like a Christmas card without snow, and I greeted Sandburg with the first thought that came into my head: "Well, I wonder what old Victor Berger would have said if he had seen this place." (Victor Berger, the first Socialist ever elected to Congress, was publisher of the Socialist paper *The Leader* on which Sandburg had worked in his early newspaper days.) Sandburg threw his head back and roared; called back into the house to Mrs. Sandburg, "He wants to know what Victor Berger would have said if he had seen this place," but then he motioned me to a chair on the porch and began to apologize in all seriousness for a proletarian's ownership of an old Southern plantation. "When did I get this place—1945, right? And how old was I in 1945—seventy years old, right?" But I told him he had nothing to worry about; that from some parapet in heaven Victor Berger and Eugene V. Debs look down upon Carl Sandburg with love and devotion and by now even the writer of Psalms has memorized a bit of Carl Sandburg:

> There is only one man in the world
> And his name is All Men.

We discussed socialism, of course, the American Socialist movement and the tragedy of so many, many uneducated editorial writers who speak of "Communism, socialism, etc." as though they were the same; and this, the supreme irony: wherever the Communists have conquered, the Socialists, the Social Democrats were *always* the first ones they killed. We spoke of the days when the movement was at its height, when Walter Lippmann was secretary to Socialist Mayor George Lunn of Schenectady, New York; and the party stalwarts included Margaret Sanger, Heywood Broun, Morris Hillquit, Algernon Lee, Alan Benson, August Claessens, and Charles P. Steinmetz, the electrical wizard.

We swapped tales of the Lower East Side of New York, the *Jewish Daily Forward,* and Morris Hillquit, who, foreign accent and all, was one of the best orators I ever heard. And Sandburg brought out a volume of his poetry, *Smoke and Steel,* and read to me of the East Side:

HOME FIRES

> In a Yiddish eating place on Rivington Street . . .
>   faces . . . coffee spots . . . children kicking at the
>   night stars with bare toes from bare buttocks.
> They know it is September on Rivington Street
>   when the red tomaytoes cram the pushcarts,
> Here the children snozzle at milk bottles, children
>   who have never seen a cow.
> Here the stranger wonders how so many people remember
>   where they keep home fires.

We talked of the poor immigrants and how much more it cost them to live than the rich. They bought a scuttle of coal for ten cents; a bushel was a quarter. This in the days of five-dollars-a-ton coal, and they were paying thirty-five dollars a ton in dribs and drabs the way poor people have to buy. I told about how the Germans paid no attention to bare floors, concentrating on overstuffed beds; but that the Irish were nuts about carpets and curtains even if they had no other furniture; and how the Jews paid little attention to either carpets or beds, and concentrated their all on *food* on the table, the carry-over from centuries in the ghetto and the will to survive, to survive at all costs.

Sandburg brought me a little volume by the late August Claessens, *Didn't We Have Fun!* Claessens was one of the most famous Socialists on the East Side, a man with a brilliant mind and a wonderful sense of humor. This little book · is a humorous record of thirty years on a soapbox. Mr. Sandburg inscribed the book: "For Harry Golden, whose heart is not alien to agitators." Interesting, I had once carried the American Flag for August Claessens at one of his street-corner meetings.

This charming Claessens had represented his all-Jewish district in the New York Legislature and eventually joined the Arbeiter Ring (Workmen's Circle). A Roman Catholic, Claessens said that he joined the Jewish fraternity because of its cemetery benefits: "The last place in this world the devil will look for a Gentile is in a Jewish cemetery."

And, of course, Sandburg and I exchanged anecdotes about Emanuel Haldeman-Julius, the Little Blue Book fellow. Haldeman-Julius was a feature writer on Victor Berger's Socialist paper at the same time that Sandburg was a reporter. Later, Haldeman-Julius went to California, Sandburg went to the Chicago *News,* and thereafter wrote his CHICAGO, "Hog Butcher for the World," which started him on his way into the mind and heart of America.

We swapped a dozen stories about this interesting Emanuel who published and sold three hundred million books in his lifetime and was the father of America's paperback book industry. Emanuel would watch the sales of his Little Blue Books carefully. If a book sold fewer than 10,000 a year he gave it one more chance. For instance, Gautier's *Fleece of Gold,* sold less than 10,000. The following year he changed the title to *The Quest of a Blonde Mistress*, exactly the type of story it is. Sales jumped up to 80,000.

Late in the afternoon a car drove up with Florida license plates and Mr. Sandburg went down the porch steps to greet the visitor. I followed a step or two behind. The fellow wanted to know something about Lincoln's money policy. Mr. Sandburg was gracious in his greeting, but told the visitor, "It's all in my books; look in the index." An hour later a phone call for Mr. Sandburg, and through the open window I heard: "It's all in my books; look in the index." And after another phone call: "That was Senator Johnston of South Carolina; his daughter is writing a term paper on me and wants to come out. I told him to call me some time after May fifth."

We discussed Oscar Ameringer, Herbert Hoover, Richard Nixon, Clarence Darrow and the famous trial of the Mc-Namaras, and Mr. Sandburg had a few new facts about Darrow's trouble with labor after the Los Angeles tragedy.

I was happy when he agreed that Anzia Yezierska and Abe Cahan were among the best "Jewish" writers of modern American literature. We discussed Chapel Hill and Sandburg told me that he has known Phillips Russell for over forty years. I told him that a literary columnist had included his name among a list of North Carolina Writers, and how someone disputed it as a bit of provincialism. Sandburg was indignant. "I pay my taxes here; and I shall die here; *indeed I am a North Carolina writer.*" He was genuinely sorry that he had not met Jimmie Street after I had told him all about the late novelist. "He was over here in Asheville, speaking one night, and if I had known about him then, I would have gone over." Street was a much greater writer than his books indicated, and we discussed how completely true that has been of others; and, of course, how it happens in reverse, too.

When Margaret Sandburg excused herself, she shook my hand with the best goodbye I have ever heard—"I wish we had put this day on a tape recorder. I would love to have had a playback of your conversation with my father."

But it was hard to break away, and finally after the second goodbye, Sandburg brought me another book, *Home Front Memo,* being a hundred or more newspaper columns Mr. Sandburg had written during the America First and phony war period. And Mr. Sandburg inscribed this book, too: "For Harry Golden, who is also slightly leftish, and out of jail, and loves the Family of Man."

At home the next day I thumbed through the volume and came across a paragraph in which Mr. Sandburg describes a parting with a close friend and how he had put his arms around him and kissed him on both cheeks: "the second time in my life I have done this."

I closed the book. I did not need to read any more for a little while. I recalled how the night before, as I was leaving, Carl Sandburg had put his arms around me and kissed me on both cheeks.

William Travers Jerome

In some of the brothels in New York, the immigrant panderers who could not read and write used pins as a book-keeping system. They watched their establishment and for each customer the panderer stuck a dressmaker's pin in the lapel of his coat. At the end of the day he demanded his share of each pin. "The Brass Check" however was more or less in general use during the heyday of the "wide-open" city. It played its part in a most heinous system of human slavery. The madam gave the girl a brass check, which was about the size of a poker chip, and its denomination varied with the type of brothel. On Allen Street in New York there were some fifty-cent houses and the brass checks given to the girl could be redeemed at the rate of twenty cents. In these places there was a strip of black oilcloth at the bottom of the bed so the men would not take their shoes off. The girl, however, seldom got any cash. The main idea was to keep her in bondage, and often even her clothes were kept from her. When she came to cash her checks all the "expenses" were taken out, including a share for the man who had seduced her into the profession. This fellow was called a "cadet." The pimp or panderer could run an entire brothel, but the cadet had an interest only in the girl he "contributed." These people, if we may call them people, gave money to the police and the politicians who protected them and who usually said, "Don't tell me where the money is coming from."

Then one day a courageous man came along. A truly great man, William Travers Jerome, and he ran for district attorney of New York against the political machine and against the whole rotten business of police protection and the degradation it involved. Today this William Travers Jerome is remembered only for his part in the prosecution of Harry K. Thaw, who killed the architect Stanford White in a controversy over the virtue of the "Girl in the Red Velvet Swing"—Evelyn Nesbit. This famous case has obscured the rest of the career of this remarkable man.

Mr. Jerome was a "blue blood," as the class distinctions were known in the first decade of the twentieth century. He was an aristocrat who soon showed Tammany Hall that he could leave the Yale Club and get into the gutter with them and trade blow for blow. He scared the daylights out of the big boys. The first thing Mr. Jerome did when he ran for district attorney was to call together all the fellow aristocrats of New York, the clubmen and the clubwomen and the folks with the parterre boxes at the opera. These people settled back comfortably in their seats in Carnegie Hall and prepared their lace handkerchiefs to wave with gentility at appropriate pauses in Mr. Jerome's speech, and this is what William Travers Jerome told them: "My friends, you are of my own class. I was born and bred with you. But I want to say to you that you are of no use to this city. I feel bitterly against you because of your heartlessness. Morally, you are as bad as the people I am fighting in the lowliest dive. Morally, you are not worth the powder to blow you out of

existence. You are too respectable to care about the teeming
tenements and the hovels where crouch in darkness a million
people of this city. It is you, the better people, who are
responsible for the conditions in this city today. Every dollar
you have laid by, every step you have climbed in the social
scale has laid upon you an obligation of civic leadership, and
you have failed. You are not bad people. You are heartless
people, and, above all, stupid people. And you came here
tonight to get from me some words of assurance that I shall
do nothing to ruffle you. Do you think I want your votes?
Take your votes to Tammany, that is where they belong, but
remember this: by reason of your neglect of your civic
duty, your lack of civic pride, you have also shown your lack
of patriotism. You should be ashamed of yourself. The only
civic and welfare work being done in this city today is being
done by the Irish Catholic Charities, the Russian Jews, and
the Socialists. Shame on you. When I look around in the
clubs of social position I have not yet found a single man
who, from the point of view of civic honor, is worthy of a
decent burial."

Mr. Jerome was elected and gave the brothels, the pimps,
and the politicians a very bad time. He tried desperately to
reconstruct the whole structure of the city government but
he was only one man. He was beginning to "hurt" business,
and people wanted to forget all the disturbance. Soon a big
Tammany politician was to shout at a mass meeting, "To
hell with reform," and the crowd cheered itself hoarse. But
when one man plants a seed such as William Travers Jerome
planted in New York in 1900, it is impossible to stop its
development, and to Mr. Jerome must go the major credit
for the genuine reform movements that followed.

Another interesting story of the William Travers Jerome
campaign was the publication of a campaign newspaper in
Yiddish. A fellow named Fred Stein, whose father owned a
rich woolen concern, became a journalist by accident. He
saw a good chance for public service by supporting Jerome.
He went to see the candidate and wanted to know how he
could help. After a lengthy conference they decided that,

since some of the Yiddish press (as well as the English newspapers) were pretty close to Tammany because of the advertising support, the Jerome candidacy needed a campaign paper of its own to reach the great mass of Jewish voters. He published ten weekly campaign editions of 100,000 circulation each. Mr. Stein, a rich boy, had traveled around the world and the temptation was now too great for him— he began to use a couple of the columns for other than campaign propaganda; literary criticism, and a sort of log of his travels. This actually added to the value of the campaign journal. So successful did this sheet become that Stein captured for Jerome seven out of the ten "Jewish" districts, all normally Tammany. Eventually the newspaper began to publish regularly as *The Jewish World,* privately subsidized without advertising, and it went along for a few years.

And so an interesting episode in the history of American politics. When you see a four-page political tabloid during a race for Senator or Governor, remember that the first ever produced was called "William Travers Jerome," and was published in Yiddish.

Judge Otto A. Rosalsky

PUSHCART peddlers warming their hands in front of a street stove would pass the time of day— "Did you see what Rosalsky did yesterday?" Elderly Jews walking toward the synagogue for morning prayers would smile with pride if one of them happened to mention the name Rosalsky— Otto A. Rosalsky, Judge of the New York State Court of General Sessions (the criminal court).

This was during the days of heavy immigration to America. Every day there were streams of immigrants walking down the middle of the street with tags around their necks. They were accompanied by relatives or looking for addresses on slips of paper. And for the moment we had Otto A. Rosalsky.

We are probably the only people who came so close to making a folk hero out of a judge of the criminal court.

It is true that there had been other Jews who had reached high political office in America, including a Cabinet officer in Theodore Roosevelt's administration. These men were Strauses, Guggenheims, Sulzbergers, and Adlers, respected names; but for the new immigrants from Eastern Europe they were as distant as the names Salvidor and Emanuel who had held public office in South Carolina and Georgia in Colonial days. Rosalsky was different. He was—ONE OF THEM. They felt a kinship with Rosalsky which they could never feel for the famous Spanish or German Jews who had preceded them to America years before. They could identify themselves with Rosalsky; he was a familiar figure on the East Side. He maintained an office there and attended all their fund-raising meetings, fraternal banquets, and synagogue services.

And Rosalsky was not an ordinary judge. He soon earned a national reputation for severity in his judgments. A prisoner before him was terror-stricken—a marked man, an unfortunate man. Ten, twenty, thirty years in Sing Sing! The electric chair! (If the man at the bar was a Jew, Rosalsky always tacked on a few extra years.) The newspapers began to keep count each week like the box scores of the baseball games. On days when Rosalsky's sentence was less than ten years, the newspapers used a new head— "Bargain Day in Rosalsky's Court." Lawyers who had sharpened themselves on the points of law governing postponements were sought after by men under indictment to swing a touchy case away from Rosalsky if at all possible. (Rosalsky watched for this like a hawk.) And during the process he built up a huge population in Sing Sing and another huge "alumni" of men who had completed their sentences. These men, "inside and out," and their families, became his very bitter enemies. After several attempts on his life, his colleagues on the bench convinced him that he must have police protection. It was not publicly revealed at the time but for the last ten years of his life

Judge Otto Rosalsky had an around-the-clock police guard stationed outside his apartment door.

But convicts were not the only ones who had become the enemies of Rosalsky. The social workers, intellectuals, and Socialists began to look with mounting chagrin at his work. In addition, there were many whispers about the man and his personal life.

Finally all the whispers, legends, and tales about him were put between the covers of a book, a novel by Sam Ornitz, *Haunch, Paunch, and Jowl.* The author left little doubt that his leading character, Meyer Hirsch, was Otto A. Rosalsky, and his book created a sensation. Ornitz, who became a good novelist, had been a Protestant probation officer in the New York criminal court. The Roman Catholics and the Jews had probation officers to handle cases involving their co-religionists in trouble. The Protestants had none, and the court usually appointed a Jew to handle those case histories. The novel form, of course, gave Ornitz the opportunity to widen the scope of his probing into Rosalsky's judicial career and personal life. The novelist claimed that the fabled severity on the bench was merely a cover-up for favors which Rosalsky performed for political henchmen, rich men, and higher-ups. The book portrayed a hard-hitting opportunist who did not care how many lives he blasted as he clawed his way to the top. It also expanded on a tale that had been bandied about in a hundred East Side cafés for many years to the effect that the judge had been financed through law school on the earnings of a streetwalker who had fallen in love with the law student. (I look upon this in an entirely different light. The story, if true, is wonderful! He married the woman and lived with her all his life. How many men, who never got to be a judge, have done much less.)

When I was going to school I detested Rosalsky and his judicial philosophy, but today I look upon him with more tolerance and understanding. Rosalsky's severity could not be explained in such pat and simple terms—as a cover-up for political favors. This severity was really part of the whole story of the immigrant in America—the attempt to accelerate the process of integration, of becoming an American as quickly as possible. This leaning backward was an attempt to prove individual worth and was not a Rosalsky trait at all. It was an immigrant trait. (Negro evildoers feared no one so much as they feared the pioneer Negro policemen in Harlem. These men were merciless in their handling of arrests and interrogation of suspects.)

The idea that Rosalsky had clawed his way to the judgeship was probably true, but again this was not unique. It was impossible to achieve political success in New York without clawing. What Charles Murphy, the Tammany boss, overlooked, the Republican boss, Sam Koenig, put into operation. Political power in New York, then as now, meant the expenditure of a budget second only to that of the United States Government. The system produced many good men, some truly great men. I am sure that none would have been happy to reveal the steps it was necessary to take in their upward climb and the compromises they were called upon to make.

I also look with greater understanding at the pride that the East Side Jews felt for this Otto A. Rosalsky. The immigrants had come from a society of Czarist oppression. Often it was the police themselves who started the pogrom. Then, as they got off the boat, they were told this incredible tale —that in America there was an immigrant Jew sitting on the highest criminal court bench handing out judgments and holding the power of life and death over the men who stood before him.

A man could go to the sweatshop and work torturous hours with the knowledge that his son could get to be (as we used to say on the East Side) "an anything"—even a judge.

Soon, very soon, the children of the immigrants began to talk of new heroes: Ty Cobb, Bronco Billy, and Christy Mathewson.

Perhaps someday there will be a definitive biography of Otto A. Rosalsky. It is an important story of the growing pains—the story of growing up to be an American.

Merry Christmas, Billy Graham

FROM Madison Square Garden, on June 1, 1957, the Reverend Billy Graham brought his "New York Crusade for Christ" to a nation-wide TV audience. Mr. Graham said: "Seated on the platform is my old mentor, the man who gave me the inspiration to become an evangelist."

The name of this "old mentor" is Mordecai Ham, one of the South's most fiery revivalists, and the fact that Mr. Graham did not mention that name may be the essence of the Billy Graham story.

Before discussing Mordecai Ham, let us take a look at Billy Graham's second mentor—none other than the late William Randolph Hearst. Graham had had some success in conducting a revival in Grand Rapids, Michigan, when he decided to make Los Angeles his next stop. It was at this moment in 1949 that Mr. Hearst sent a telegram to his editors, "Plug Billy Graham" (several of those editors had to ask each other, "Who is Billy Graham?"). But with the Hearst press behind him, Billy Graham was soon on his way to fame and influence. Yet I am certain that if the fabulous William Randolph Hearst had been seated on the Madison Square Garden platform, Billy Graham would have merely added another sentence to his announcement: "And sitting beside my old mentor from Charlotte is another old mentor from California."

Thus the phenomenal story of Billy Graham is that the two mentors completely misjudged their man. Mordecai Ham was the South's most conscienceless anti-Semite of the 1930's, and William Randolph Hearst was America's number-one isolationist at the time of his "Plug Billy Graham" telegram. And whatever else Billy Graham may be, these are the two things he definitely is *not*.

Mr. Hearst, of course, had every reason in the world to

believe that he had latched onto the logical successor to
the Reverend Billy Sunday of the 1920's, whose gospel of
"America for Americans" and snide comments about aliens
had given considerable aid and comfort to the hatchet men
who buried the League of Nations. But not three weeks
after his Los Angeles revival Billy Graham spoke from the
steps of the Capitol in Washington, D. C.— "We must hold
to our communications with the peoples of India, Indo-
nesia, the rest of Asia, the Middle East, and all the peoples
of the African continent." It was not that Graham was un-
grateful for Mr. Hearst's support. The chances are that he
had no idea at all that the publisher was even an isolationist.
It is more than likely that Billy Graham had merely accepted
the Hearst plug as evidence that the Lord of San Simeon had
seen the light and, like the actress Jane Russell, had come
forward to be saved.

Mordecai Ham, the original mentor, was not a theological
anti-Semite along the lines of the average tent evangelist
with his stock phrases: "the synagogue of Satan," ". . . the
Jews scourged Him," etc. Old Mordecai was right out of
Europe's Middle Ages. He did not rail against a few of the
Hebrews of the Bible. He reached right down to the local
level to heap calumny upon the one or two Jewish merchants
in whatever town he happened to pitch his tent.

One wonders what Mordecai Ham was thinking when, at
the moment of Billy's greatest triumph, before an audience
of untold millions of Americans, the protégé did not mention
the name of the mentor. And yet it was not as if Ham had
not been adequately forewarned long ago. After Graham's
first success, he had taken over the "Youth for Christ," a
postwar movement which had been causing considerable concern in liberal circles. This was an entirely different brand of
"nativism." The thousands of boys and girls a-hootin' and
a-hollerin' "for Jesus," to the beat of a drum and to the orders
of a few spielers, posed a serious problem to the Jewish
"defense" organizations right after World War II. Every
soldier on every front had heard the same rumor, about
what would "happen" to—you-know-whom—"when we get

home." The big question was, "Is this then the *movement?*" And with its emphasis on "religion," the challenge was a highly delicate one in that period of 1945–50.

The first thing young Billy Graham did when he assumed leadership of the Youth for Christ was to tone down its entire program. He suggested that the organization could do its best work as separate units in their respective churches.

I asked Mr. Graham the questions suggested in this article, questions about Mordecai Ham, William Randolph Hearst, Youth for Christ, and the Jews. I was following him around the toy department of the J. B. Ivey store. It was a day or two before Christmas, 1954, and on the eve of his departure for the European "crusade."

The evangelist listened carefully and finally said that he believed that one reply would answer all my questions, and so I took it down: "I will say this about Jews and all other non-Christians; we must lead millions of Gentiles to Jesus Christ, who then by their example of love will eliminate the need for evangelists; each Christian by the manner of his living will be a missionary himself."

Saying "halevei," I wished Mr. Graham a merry Christmas and many happy landings.

James Street

IT is hard to write about the death of an artist, and it is harder still when the man was a close personal friend. I never met anyone with a bigger heart than James Street. But Jimmie, who gave more of himself than most men of talent, was as ashamed of his good deeds as most men are ashamed of their sins.

There was this business of "I write only for the money." This was the first thing he told his audience of newspapermen, writers, or would-be writers. He shot it right out as if to say, "You think I'm soft, do you; well, I'll show you." He used the same gimmick on his friends. With one novel on the best-seller list; with *The Biscuit Eater* translated into most of the foreign languages; with *Hazel Flagg*, an adaptation of another one of his stories, on Broadway; with a completed history at the publishers; and another novel half-completed; he would greet me—"Harry, the money is piling up." But the front was beginning to wear thin, and even he was slowly coming to the realization that it was just no use. If the invitation had the word "press" in it, or "writer" or "forum," Mr. Street was off like a volunteer fireman. Where most of our artists keep themselves aloof from the public, jealous of every intrusion upon their privacy, indignantly rejecting every inquiry into their method or style, Jimmie would tell you anything you wanted to know and volunteer more. He was one of the most successful professional writers in the country, yet I have seen Mr. Street sit with his palm under his chin enraptured by the "remarks of the chairlady" announcing the award of a fifteen-dollar prize "for the best short story of the Amateur Writing Club of such-and-such county, North Carolina."

Indeed, is there a man anywhere in this great country of ours who "did it" *less* for the money than the late James Street?

He died of a heart attack during a heated political exchange with a correspondent (who was promising us a "preventive war") at an Associated Press function at Chapel Hill.

What happened was that James Street "exploded" with the things the speaker of the evening said. The speaker was Yates McDaniel, chief Associated Press representative at the Pentagon, and this is what he said, as summarized by the *News-Leader* of Chapel Hill, N.C.:

> One statement was that the Pentagon habitually issued confusing statements in order to mislead U. S. enemies. Another was that despite Pentagon denials that a preventive war is being contemplated, "the United States will not wait to be attacked."

Another version of the McDaniel speech was given by Scott Jarrett, a Chapel Hill radio newscaster, who received an award at the AP dinner:

> Actually the reporter from the Pentagon didn't say it in so many words. But the impression I got, and one I will swear Mr. James Street got, was that, through some miraculous means the Pentagon, or the chiefs of staff, or the Central Intelligence Agency, or somebody, will determine the precise moment our potential enemies plan to attack us . . . and beat them to the punch in time to win.

> The Pentagon hadn't only confused the Communists. It had confused James Street. He couldn't understand how the United States could prevent a war by starting one. In the best democratic tradition, James Street got up and made his stinging protest.

Mr. Street died a few minutes later.

James Street was not the man who is usually honored at interfaith or intergroup meetings, nor was he the man whose name adorned a lot of fancy letterheads, as a front for a lot of talk. James Street instead fought in the front ranks, not for any group or sect, but for the fundamental American principles of complete freedom of expression and complete dignity of the individual. Yet somehow I always sensed that this former Baptist missionary from Mississippi had a special warm spot in his heart for the Jewish people. He saw the Jews as a glitter on the horizon of man. What surely intrigued him no end was that the Jews have been contemporaneous with all of recorded history. When he discussed Jesus with me, or Caesar, or Augustus, he gave the unmistakable impression that he was talking to an eyewitness.

He was my special champion. He was so generous that he kept reminding me of all I had "done for him." Luckily, I told him a few weeks before he died what he had done for me, although from the twinkle in his eye, he probably knew it all the time. I have no hesitancy in revealing the fact that no man can publish an offbeat, unorthodox, little newspaper like mine in this day and age, unless he has a few influential men like Jimmie Street in the editorial offices and university towns of the State.

He sent me a post card about once a week, and usually put an air-mail stamp on it. In one of his post cards he said that he "liked" me because I represented for him the "traditional American Populism, which of course is Hebraic in all its essentials."

Here again Jimmie was trying to excuse his generosity. In this great commercial age he felt it to be a little too risky to reveal himself as so completely a man of sentiment. I think he loved his friends because he loved people. Obviously he couldn't get all the people into his kitchen, so he used a few of us as representatives of the mass. After one meeting, I saw him stand around talking with a refugee for two hours and then take the stranger home for lunch. And when James Street liked you, he went all out. He liked your family, your business associates, your employees, and all your friends. Characteristic of the man was his relationship to his closest friend, the Chapel Hill writer, Noel Houston. Argue? Why, you've never seen anything like it in your life. And often the arguments reached the fever pitch of table-pounding and door-slamming. Thoroughly exhausted, Jimmie Street would always say, "Noel and I have nothing in common except we love each other."

One of the nights I sat up with him till about four o'clock, we took a one-minute rest during the proceedings. I happened to mention that Dave Wallas, my closest friend, was having trouble with his home office up in Yonkers, New York. It seemed that my friend's employer was not giving him his rightful earnings. Jimmie got mad. He hopped around that kitchen madder by the minute! I thought he was ready to pack two suitcases and drive on to Yonkers to demand justice for my friend whom he had never met.

Jimmie Street left a wonderful legacy to North Carolina.

It is remarkable that a man could stamp his personality upon a society so thoroughly and within so short a period. His memory and his influence will live a long time in the editorial offices of this State, and in the hundreds of homes in every corner of North Carolina where live the men and women who put thoughts and ideas on paper.

His death struck me as particularly tragic aside from the personal loss, because he was doing the best work of his brilliant career. He had a book on the Revolutionary War all finished; another novel, *Acts of Love*, on the way; and he was making plans to visit Jerusalem next spring to work on his novel, *Hillel the Pharisee*. He had done a lot of planning on that book and we had discussed it on numerous occasions. He pointed toward it with the hope that it would be his life's greatest work. And he told me that he intended to dedicate it to me.

Which reminds me of the time my old father went to hear Enrico Caruso sing the role of Eleazar in the opera *La Juive* (The Jewess). And then Caruso died; and my old father said: "You see, my son, the Jews have no luck."

Walter Hampden

AND so this fine actor died at the age of seventy-five. Hampden was a truly great artist. One of the best America has produced.

He had just come from a great success in England and he played Cyrano de Bergerac on Broadway, a very long run. Later I saw him in *Othello* with Ian Keith as Iago. Memorable performances. I met Mr. Hampden through a friend. On two or three occasions, we sat in his dressing room and discussed politics. I was fascinated, of course, when I learned that this "Englishman" was a New York Irishman by the name of Daugherty, and his father had been a Tammany bigwig on the West Side. He continued his

successes on Broadway. He played Shylock with Ethel Barrymore in the role of Portia. That was something to remember.
Then came *The Immortal Thief*, and several others. By this
time Hollywood was clamoring for Walter Hampden, but
he would have none of it. Hollywood offered him one million
dollars for any three pictures he would choose. Instead, Mr.
Hampden took all his earnings and staged a drama called
The Light of Asia, and that wasn't a success. He lost all his
money. Eventually Mr. Hampden did go into the movies
and you can understand the feelings of one who loved Mr.
Hampden when I first saw him on the screen dressed as an
Indian saying "Ugh."

But I'll never forget him as Cyrano.

Sweet are the uses of adversity

I WAS thinking of that line from Shakespeare when I
thumbed through Lillian Roth's book, *I'll Cry Tomorrow*. The
story of a "fallen" woman who made a comeback. Lillian
was in musical comedy when she became a lush. She deserves
a lot of credit. According to her photographs, she is still
handsome; she has a successful book and they made a movie
of her life.

The point I want to make, without detracting from Lillian's
comeback, is that right now is her biggest professional success.
The advantage of adversity is that you can build up your
"former" status. When you survive a fall, you may as well say
you fell from the twelfth floor instead of the fifth. The rich
and successful men always exaggerate their lowly beginnings
and the same is true in reverse. Many refugees claim they
owned big factories or operated banks in the old country.

This is harmless. It represents the basic drive for self-
esteem.

It just so happens that during Lillian Roth's best days, I
was a man who went to the theatre twice a week, and Lillian

Roth was all right. She had a flash there for a year, maybe, but she was no Fanny Brice, or Marilyn·Miller, or Ann Pennington, or Louise Groody, or Jeannette MacDonald, or Ruby Keeler, or Grace Moore, or Ruth Etting, or Edna Leedom, or Irene Bordoni, nor any one of another fifteen or twenty musical comedy stars. Lillian Roth deserves a lot of credit, but we always go overboard on these things. The point from which Lillian "fell" was not as high as she would like us to think and this is not fair to these other great performers of her era who played the boards like troupers; went on to greater heights on the screen or made a graceful exit in favor of a new crop of stars.

A wonderful newspaper interview

SOME years ago *The New York Times* sent a reporter to interview Mr. Roebuck who had reached his ninetieth birthday. The reporter started out in the usual way: "To what do you attribute your longevity and good health?" But Mr. Roebuck cut him short with these few well-chosen words: "Son, I sold out to Mr. Sears; Mr. Sears made ten million dollars and now he's dead. Mr. Sears sold out to Julius Rosenwald, who made three hundred million dollars and now he's dead. All I want you to tell your readers is that, on his ninetieth anniversary, Mr. Roebuck took his usual·walk in Central Park."

Albert Schweitzer

WE are a people who go overboard about everything. As soon as *Life* magazine said that Dr. Albert Schweitzer is the "greatest living man"—presto, that's it. Now I am not trying to debunk a truly great soul. I have read a few articles by the renowned scholar-physician. I have also read a few articles about him when he visited in the United States a few years ago. But what strikes me about this "greatest living man" is the fact that Dr. Schweitzer has not been on the firing line during the past two or three decades.

He did not "man the lifeboats" or risk the give-and-take of political controversy in the national or international arena. How we have needed his voice of reason during the three decades that he has been in Africa! It is wonderful and admirable that Dr. Schweitzer lives in Africa and brings spiritual help and medical attention to the villagers. But thousands of priests and missionaries have done as much, and their names will never leave the musty records of church and diocese. And so, long life and good fortune to Albert Schweitzer, but the greatest living men are those who are in there all the time, raising their voices in a world which seems to have lost faith in itself.

Where Irving Berlin wrote
his first song

I WALKED over to Pell Street, in the heart of China-town, and stood in front of Number 20. The glass in the window was black with the dust and grime of years, but, after a few minutes, the door opened and I was able to peek. Inside was a group of ragged old men, including a Chinese, picking over some rags and paper. It looked like some sort of salvage business.

This was where Irving Berlin wrote his first song. It was a saloon in those days, known as "Nigger Mike's." "Nigger Mike" was not colored, but a Roumanian Jew, who was given the name because of his dark complexion. His real name was Mike Salter. Irving Berlin, as Izzy Baline, got his first job there as a singing waiter. It was while working for "Nigger Mike" that he wrote his first song, "Marie From Sunny Italy."

A few years later, Berlin got a job with the famous prize fighter, Jimmy Jelly, who owned a café of his own. Soon thereafter the entire world was humming "Alexander's Ragtime Band," and Irving Berlin was on his way.

Millions of American boys have marched off to three wars singing Berlin's tunes: "Oh How I Hate To Get Up In The Morning," "A Pretty Girl Is Like A Melody," "God Bless America," "Remember," "White Christmas," "There's No Business Like Show Business," and hundreds of others. From a singing waiter in a Bowery joint to the position where he earned $15,000,000 for Army relief with his show, *This Is the Army*—all within the lifetime of an immigrant boy. You can say it again, "God Bless America."

PART 8

The Frozen Rabbi

~~~~~~

We would be nothing
without each other

THE Greeks came, then the Syrians, and then the Romans, and against them all the Jews kept alive the faith in Israel, for they were custodians of civilizations yet to come.

But many centuries before, the first thought of the human intellect had been in terms of the family and the clan. He did not think it wrong to attack someone who was not of his clan.

Then the clans formed a community and the town was born; but still the conscience of each man was confined to his own place. Law was based solely on family responsibility. Each father was responsible for the delinquency of all the members of his family. The law did not seek the murderer or thief; it called only upon the head of the household.

But the frontier of this respect for law reached only as far as the city gates. Beyond were neither safety—nor conscience. It was yet impossible for the human intellect to extend this respect for the father beyond the community. No one was called to account for inflicting a wrong against an outsider. Travel, except in armed bands, was almost unknown.

Then out of the East, out of the Hebraic milieu of Palestine, there came a strange figure, a fellow with neither sword nor protecting outriders. And he wasn't afraid to travel. And he was left unmolested. He wore a black robe and hood and carried a walking stick in the shape of a cross, and he found himself going in and out of cities' gates without inquiry, negotiation, or discrimination.

Thus the Roman church "universalized" the religious philosophy of the Hebrews and created for us a new idea in human relations, the idea of *communication*—between *all* families, communities, and cities, and it was made possible only in these specific terms—a mutual interest in an *idea*—an idea that had come out of Israel.

And later there came a group of men who called themselves "Protestants," and their "protest" was based on a different interpretation of that same Hebraic philosophy out of Palestine, and these Protestants now extended the "city's gates" to the actual physical person of the individual; and gave us *habeas corpus*, trial by jury, the ballot, and the free public school.

And so, as we sit in the comfort of our homes in Charlotte, North Carolina; Paris, France; Minneapolis, Minnesota; or in any other city of the civilized world, we know that none of us could have achieved the life we have today without— each other.

And all of this began in the desert of Sinai where a wandering Hebrew by the name of Abraham gave maturity to the human intellect with the discovery of Jehovah; and immediately the habits of centuries upon centuries were shriveled; and the god Ra grew old and his bones turned to silver; and neither Zeus nor Jupiter would ever again descend from their mountains; and Osiris, Tammuz, Adonis, Horus, Attis, Mithra, and even the Great Goddess of the Vestal Virgins died without any hope of resurrection; and this Jehovah of Abraham elicited such an amazing response from mankind that to this very day we know that none of us, nor our children, nor our children's children, would be what we are, and what we hope for them to be, without each other—all of us together.

This you call "bringing Christians"?

For about a month the Jewish community in a large
Southern city had seethed with dissension and anger. When
it was all over, one family resigned from the temple and the
widow of one of the charter members publicly declared that
she would "never set foot into this temple again." The
rhubarb started with the preparations for Brotherhood Week,
1953, and while I am not mentioning any names or places,
I am leaning backward in my effort to give a concise and
accurate report of the events as they occurred.

To begin with, Brotherhood Week in this particular Southern city has always had its ups and downs. The ups had
occurred when the "exchange-of-pulpit" speaker happened to
be the pastor of one of the big Presbyterian churches; while
the downs were on those occasions when all the temple could
get was the Unitarian minister. The day when you could
fool the congregation with the Unitarian minister is a thing
of the past. They are up on the theology; and they know
all about Episcopalians, Methodists, Presbyterians, and Baptists, vis-à-vis the Unitarians ("They're practically Jews themselves").

Only three months before, when the Temple Sisterhood was
preparing for its annual Book Review Night, the secretary
had pointedly read the minutes of a gala meeting of a few
years back when the previous rabbi had actually succeeded
in bringing *all* five Gentile board members of the local
Civitan Club to a temple function. This had been read for
the benefit of the new rabbi who hadn't shown the same
enthusiasm for this type of activity; but the ladies were now
determined to set the matter right again and to get a few
outstanding Gentile guests for Book Review Night.

The new rabbi went about his task with diligence and
sincerity. He sent out twenty invitations, each individually

typed, to as many religious, civic, and political leaders of the community, but—you've got to have luck, too. It was one of those bad nights, and only two non-Jews showed up— the ubiquitous Unitarian minister and the Regional Director of the CIO. Nu, nu, all our enemies should go through such a night. I honestly felt sorry for the ladies—they had gone to so much trouble—but I also felt sorry for the new rabbi. All evening he was dodging the Sisterhood ladies, but the presidentke finally cornered him in the foyer, and in a voice throbbing with disappointment and dripping with sarcasm, she said, "Rabbi, this you call 'bringing Christians'?"

But that was three months before and had all been forgotten in the new excitement and happy anticipation of big things to come during Brotherhood Week, 1953. As usual the Sisterhood and the Brotherhood of the Temple agreed to a joint interfaith meeting, to be featured by a short invocation by the rabbi, reports of their stewardship by the presidents of the two organizations, a piano interlude, the speaker of the evening, and the social hour.

At the board meeting of the Sisterhood, the rabbi was asked to suggest a "suitable Christian speaker of the evening." It happens that the rabbi teaches a class in Hebrew once a week at a Negro divinity school not far from the city (under the auspices of the Jewish Chautauqua Society), and when he was asked about the speaker of the evening, he suggested that the dean of this Negro theological school would be the logical choice to deliver the Brotherhood message this year. After a few moments of shocked silence the suggestion was "thrown open for discussion." To be perfectly fair, let it be said that two of the ladies were highly enthusiastic, but soon each of the other ten ladies voiced her opposition, some giving no reason beyond saying, "It is not practical." Others went into some detail. One lady said that since the temple is situated in a very fashionable white section, "how will the neighbors react?" Another member said, "Suppose the Negro should decide to bring some of his students, or a few members of his staff, how would it look if a dozen Negroes were seen walking into the temple building?" Then there was the matter of the social hour. How about that? Who would serve and how? Suppose the Negroes brought wives along, what then? These were all matters that had to be thought out carefully, and the Sisterhood ladies thought they had bitten off more than they could chew. They decided to refer the whole matter to the governing board of the temple itself.

Meanwhile the matter had snowballed into a communal controversy, and with Brotherhood Week creeping up on them, the temple trustees knew they were confronted with a red-hot issue. A few hours before their meeting a member of the congregation, who had discussed the matter with several of his friends, called the president of the temple and told him that unless the Negro educator was invited, at least four members of the congregation would feel themselves duty-bound to resign from the temple. This put the matter in an entirely different light and the trustees now made short work of it. They handed the project back to the Sisterhood with explicit instructions to invite the dean of the divinity school to speak at the temple on Brotherhood Thursday.

And now there was little time to lose. Unless arrangements were made at once, Brotherhood Week could actually slip away before they knew it. The Negro was called long distance and he gave them some very bad news. He was delighted with the invitation; but arrangements had already been made for all his evenings during Brotherhood Week; if he had only known about it a week before, he would have cancelled one of the other appointments, etc. Many of the members were relieved by this—they had invited the Negro and at the same time they had won their point; but wiser heads knew that at this stage it was far more complicated than that. Who would believe them that the Negro had indeed taken himself out of the controversy? The president of the temple acted quickly and forcefully with the only logical decision left to him: "Change your meeting to suit the convenience of the Negro college dean, and no matter when it is to be, he is the one who makes the Brotherhood speech this year." The Negro accepted at once and the meeting was set for that Thursday week—a sort of chol-hamoed Brotherhood Week.

The vestry room looked very nice. The buffet tables were tastefully decorated. Everything went off smoothly. The dean made a pretty fair speech, too. "Those who love Jesus as I do never cease to be grateful to the Jewish people for having given us so noble a dream and so exalted a hope as Christianity." The social hour was also pleasant. By an amazing coincidence, the three ladies selected by the Sisterhood to serve the refreshments (completely out of the normal rotation) were the only members of the temple who (with their husbands) belong to the local chapter of the Americans for Democratic Action.

There is one more interesting item to report. After one of the ladies had been introduced to the Negro educator she was heard to remark to one of her Sisterhood colleagues: "Did you notice what small ears he has?"

The best sermon—give 'em hell

WITH the advent of the fall and winter seasons, the Protestant and Jewish clergymen are busy preparing sermons, but there has been a great change during the past twenty-five years. And this may be one of the reasons for the poor attendance on Friday nights and Sunday mornings. Since the beginning of history, we have found that the best sermon, indeed the most welcome sermon, is a warning to the congregation to mend its ways, and a threat of the dire consequences to come.

The reason for this is obvious. Few people really feel that they are worthy of heaven, and so, when they are scolded and warned and threatened, it takes a terrible weight off their minds. And when they leave the church or temple it gives them the feeling of having done penance, and the exhilaration of expiation. To talk of heaven only adds to the terrible sense of guilt which weighs down upon us so heavily.

Any student of history and religion knows this. Yet the question remains, why do clergymen of today avoid these highly effective "Give 'Em Hell" sermons? The answer is the Board of Trustees. The Board of Stewards. The Elders. These fellows have taken over; they build the edifice, support the institution, and have a strong voice in hiring of the clergyman. Under these circumstances it is very difficult. Every time the minister or the rabbi feels like a real "give 'em hell" sermon, he sees two trustees sitting behind him, and four or five of the elders right there in the front row, and so it is the better part of valor for him to review the poetry of T. S. Eliot, or talk about juvenile delinquency.

This is the reason for the success of the unaffiliated evangelists. Billy Graham can give 'em hell every night because he has no board of trustees.

The board of trustees, usually big businessmen, like to consider the sermon as part of the entire operation. Therefore, instead of the books of collected sermons of the old days, the sermons are included in the annual report of operations: "Sermons preached, 51; Rotary speeches, 6; TV appearances, 3; panel discussions, 2; Chamber of Commerce meetings, 4; exchange of pulpits with the Unitarian minister, 2," and so forth.

Bigger and better invocations

THE practice of full-length invocations and majestic benedictions at Jewish communal functions is the result of three basic developments: *a.* the attempt to reflect the habits of the Protestant society in which we live; *b.* the expansion of the middle class; and *c.* the natural result of *b* with laymen taking full advantage of the opportunities for self-expression, for which there is so great a hunger in the breasts of men everywhere. So, instead of the short blessing before the bread is broken, you now have a complete invocation with notes, lectern, microphone, and sound effects.

The powerful invocation and the majestic benediction came out of a long succession of committee hearings—the Committee on Arrangements. At a historic moment during one of these deliberations, the chairman, in a terrible swivet, with his voice shaking, asked, "What will we do with the two rabbis who are coming?" That did it! A pall settled over the whole committee. Wistfully each member fondled the program—the president will introduce the toastmaster; the toastmaster will introduce the chairman of the committee on arrangements, who will present the president of the Sisterhood. The president of the Sisterhood will thank her committee for the place cards and the floral arrangements. The toastmaster will then introduce the next speaker, who will deliver "remarks"—just plain remarks. Then comes the fellow who will introduce the guest of the evening, and after the main address comes the member who will express thanks to the main speaker. Everything so nice and smooth, and now this—this problem. What to do with the two rabbis who are coming? No one will ever know who spoke up, but it electrified the committee: "Let's give one rabbi the invocation, and the other rabbi the benediction, and that takes care of the two rabbis."

Thereupon the committee sat the two rabbis at opposite ends of the dais to wait for the bell. This gave the fellows in the center of the dais a free hand with few complications—or so they thought. It wasn't long before they were in for a rude awakening. The clergymen were beginning to feel their way; warily at first, until the *invocation* burst forth as the major address of the night, as it should be, and while the invocation was going on, the frustrated fellows in the middle of the dais began to look toward the benediction rabbi at the other end, who was literally licking his chops—you haven't heard anything yet, boys.

Don't tell them about shrimp

WE made a wonderful deal when we got the Christians
to accept HAM as the basis for our piety. Ah, if, God forbid,
they also knew that shrimp, crab flakes, and lobster ther-
midor are as unkosher as HAM! But let us be grateful for little
favors and tread lightly. As long as they continue to concentrate on HAM, all is well. Often I speak at a luncheon or
dinner meeting of a Christian fellowship or society, and I
see the chairman and his assistant in a huddle and then with
the graciousness for which Southerners are known, they say
to me: "Mr. Golden, we know you do not eat ham, so we
have arranged for a special plate of fried chicken for you."
I thank them profusely for their thoughtfulness, and I look as
innocent as a newborn babe when one of the ladies of the
church puts the shrimp cocktail in front of me.

Now if we can only get the Christians to accept the community center as the temple, all would indeed be well.
Handball, massage tables, and bingo! But I'm afraid they'll
never agree to this. "M'ken leben ober m'lust nisht." (You
can live but they won't let you.)

The Frozen Rabbi

IN a small Southern community, the congregation was
trying to "make a change." For one thing, the rabbi had asked
for a raise, and it seemed to be a good opportunity to "adjust"
and sever the contract. But the rabbi did not resign and his
contract had two more years to run at eight thousand dollars,
plus the annual dues to the Kiwanis Club. Meanwhile the

important wing of the congregation was getting restless. All sorts of complaints were bandied about, and I shall only list the more serious ones: (1) The rabbi was seen uptown without a necktie. (2) The rabbi's wife is too stuck up. (3) The rabbi doesn't visit the members often enough. (4) The rabbi refused to follow the rules of the ritual committee about the length of time the Torah should be kept out of the ark on Friday nights.

Finally the rabbi decided that he would like to resolve the matter, too. But, during the course of the negotiations, they arrived at an unimportant impasse. It wasn't serious and it involved only a difference of eight hundred dollars additional moving expenses. The congregation wasn't being unreasonable either, but you know how people are—they like to "discuss" it—sleep on it for a day or two. This was a fatal mistake—because Uncle Sam stepped in and settled everything.

What does Uncle Sam have to do with all of this?

The rabbi was drafted for the chaplaincy—and immediately became *frozen*. The congregation can get its new rabbi all right, but, according to the rules, they must pay THE FROZEN RABBI the difference between his Army pay and his contract pay—all during his term of service—*and*, listen to this—for one additional year after he is mustered out, and while he is looking around for a new post. Address all mail to THE FROZEN RABBI, care of my office.

Brotherhood Week

"DID you count the three in the back?"

"Yes, but I still say there were only eleven."

"But how about the two sitting behind Irene and the one up front?"

"Maybe you're right. Maybe there were fourteen. I thought there were only eleven."

It is the morning after the annual Brotherhood Week meeting, and the ladies of the Sisterhood are discussing the number of Christians who were present! This is the big headache connected with the annual event (I have managed a few)—the great gap between Jew and Christian attendance. Practically all the Jews seem to be for it.

The problem, of course, goes much deeper than the mere "counting of the house." In appraising the "results" of nine or ten of such annual observances, we have to think in terms of that legendary rabbi, who, told that the Messiah had indeed come, looked out the window and said, "I see no change."

There has been no change. The daily devotionals and religious (Protestant) instruction are still part of the public school program. The public water fountains are still labeled "white" and "colored"; the atmosphere of separateness and almost complete social segregation between Jew and non-Jew is still as rigid as ever.

In the first few years of the Brotherhood Week observance, the rabbi made a determined effort to establish an annual "exchange-of-pulpit" custom.

Where the invitation was met with a favorable response, the Protestant minister invariably sent an assistant to speak at the temple, and the "exchange" was usually an invitation for the rabbi to speak at a men's club or Sunday School group of the church, but never from the church pulpit itself. An incident connected with one of these exchanges is worth repeating. It involved a young minister with a pastorate in one of the suburban communities. After the usual introduction the young preacher took his place before the ark to deliver the Brotherhood sermon. Stating that his appearance before a Jewish congregation was part of God's plan, the preacher delivered one of the most impassioned "Come to Jesus" sermons ever heard outside of an evangelist's tent. When none of the "flock" came forward to be "saved," the preacher informed the rabbi that we were a bunch of atheists.

Since then the Brotherhood Week exchange program has proceeded along safer lines, and now our pulpit is turned over to the Unitarian minister for the event. However, since neither the rabbi nor the Unitarian minister is eligible for membership in the local Ministerial Association, this could hardly be called an exchange at the level of interfaith.

"Not the real thing, of course," but to most of the congregation a half a Christian is better than none, and every effort was made to make it a pleasant evening.

It is important to emphasize at this point that there is a healthy reservoir of Christian good will in every Southern community. These groups include editors and publishers of the daily press, many of the Protestant clergymen, as well as all college professors and civic leaders. They are our allies in the sense that they are the allies of democracy. But this strong core of Southern liberalism in no way has been the result of, or associated with, organized good will.

I cannot speak strongly enough of the sincerity and honesty of the purpose behind Brotherhood Week and its sponsors. That the idea has not caught on at all (in the South, at least) is certainly not for any lack of integrity or hard work on the part of its promoters and officials.

There is one highly encouraging aspect of the future of the American-Jewish community in the South. On the occasions when the Jewish community or the synagogue itself has conducted public projects at the civic levels (such as a temple anniversary celebration, or a banquet for a rabbi), response from the Christian fellowships has been sincere and enthusiastic. It seems as though the Christian clergyman or the Christian layman wants to be able to say to himself: "The Jews want me to come to one of their functions."

He'll stand for no other "complications."

The Ten Lost Tribes?
They are the Presbyterians

ACCORDING to a number of Midrashic sources, ten of the twelve tribes of Israel whom Moses had blessed in the wilderness were carried away by the Assyrians after the fall of Samaria in 722 B.C. Since there were numerous prophecies that they would return, there was a lively expectation that they might be found by diligent search. Many Christian scholars have been deeply concerned with this problem.

There was even a legend that Prester John would one day appear leading the ten tribes bearing the banners of Christendom. Cotton Mather and Thomas Thorowgood were convinced that the American Indians were the Ten Lost Tribes. The strange thing about it is that through all these centuries the Gentile world has been more concerned about what happened to the Ten Lost Tribes than the Jews themselves. The Jewish position, however, is most logical. Things haven't been going exactly plushly for the Jews these past two thousand years, so why should we go out and find ten more tribes for them? Look at all the additional "restricted" juke boxes and "exclusive" slot machines they'd have to make. The Ten Lost Tribes would have been the worst kind of fools if they had revealed themselves all these years. As a matter of fact, I really believe they have been lying low waiting for the time when the coast is clear.

Which brings me to my own theory. I have a strong suspicion that the Ten Lost Tribes are really the inhabitants and the ancestors of the inhabitants of Scotland. I have several reasons for my theory. First of all, we Jews have a sort of natural affection for the Scots. There must be a reason for this. I have heard epithets thrown around at every race and nationality on earth, but I have yet to hear a Jew say an unkind thing about a Scotsman. Secondly, let us consider the Presbyterian religion which at its very inception was in effect a return to basic Orthodox Judaism—sort of an Anglicized Judaism with all its laws and most of its rituals. Both Calvin and Knox emphasized a belief in the One God, Jehovah, and for the first three hundred years of Presbyterianism, *all* the emphasis was on the Torah, specifically on the Five Books of Moses. The struggles within Calvinism were identical with the various reform movements within Judaism. I have come across records in my study of Calvinism of congregations forbidding the use of as much as a vase of flowers anywhere in the church, and on one occasion a few angry covenanters in this country smashed an organ or, as they called it, "the unholy whustles." In the home country, in the early days of Presbyterianism, they did not even allow a portrait of the ruling monarch in their house of worship —identical with Judaistic tradition. It is well to remember, too, that Britain achieved her greatest hour of empire during that generation when a Scotsman and a Jew directed her destinies (Gladstone and Disraeli). And do you think it was a coincidence that Lord Balfour, the man who gave Palestine to the Jews, was a Scot? Of course, it was no coincidence. Lord Balfour may have been aware of the connection between Scotland and the Ten Lost Tribes.

In addition, my thesis is strengthened by the phenomenon that of all the civilized countries of the world Scotland is the only one without a history of anti-Semitism, and this on top of the fact that these wonderful Scots have had plenty of provocation. No one has given the Presbyterians more trouble than the Jews—on account of the Psalms of David. When we gave them the Psalms we caused many a Scotsman to lose his sense of humor. It was family against family, and friend against friend. The Psalms of David have caused more schisms among the Presbyterians than all the other theologies combined. Some said that the Psalms should be sung, but others said they should be recited. Then for another hundred years there were four or five more reform movements—all about our King David's magnificent poetry. Some Scots said the Psalms should be sung kneeling, others were against kneeling and remained seated, while in every church there was always one wonderful individualist of the Clan Cameron who said the Psalms should be sung—standing. And through all of this four hundred years of discussion, philosophy, and schism on these Psalms of our King David, they have kept their sense of honor and decency, and have remained among our best and most loyal friends.

What a dull world this would be without Scotland—and without Jews and King David!

Chocolate matzos

ABOUT forty years ago, the Orthodox Jews were prophesying that, if the United States should stop the flow of Jewish immigrants for twenty years, there would be no matzos, no Hebrew Schools, and Judaism would die.

Today there are thousands of Hebrew Schools, study groups, Talmud Torahs, Sunday Schools, kindergartens; there are Hillel Houses on every major college campus. Young Israel, organized just about the time when these dire prophecies were made, has branches everywhere, in nearly every State, and not only are there huge big-business matzoh factories, but Barton's makes chocolate matzos, chocolate hamantashen and chocolate Chanakah dradles.

Rabbi, make it short

No matter what the occasion there is always someone who says, "Rabbi, make it short." This covers sermons, weddings, bar mitzvahs, funerals, as well as circumcisions. Recently in a Southern town not far from here, an elderly gent died, a man who had been one of the early presidents of the congregation and widely respected. To honor the deceased the folks invited a distinguished rabbi who had occupied the pulpit in the early years of his career. The rabbi had flown over a thousand miles to officiate at the funeral, and, as he mounted the rostrum, one of the relatives of the deceased leaned over and whispered, "Rabbi, make it short."

I know of one incident which involved a rabbi with a sense of humor. He was officiating at a wedding and during the preliminaries the groom whispered the usual: "Rabbi, make it short."

When the couple stood before him, the rabbi said: "Do you, Milton—take this woman as your wedded wife? Do you, Anna—take this man as your wedded husband? I now pronounce you man and wife." All of this took exactly fourteen seconds, and, as the rabbi began to walk away, the groom looked pleadingly, "Is that all there is to it, Rabbi?" And the rabbi said, "That's all there is to it. You asked me to make it short so I made it short."

Unitarians wait for their first Negro

SEVERAL years ago the Unitarian Church of Charlotte desegregated its fellowship and gave public notice that Negroes would be welcomed. To date not a single Negro has applied.

But what is even more to the point is the fact that very few Negroes have become converts to Roman Catholicism, despite the fact that the Catholic Church has assumed a sort of religious leadership in the fight to implement the United States Supreme Court racial decision, and has desegregated most of its own institutions in the South: churches, parochial schools, and hospitals.

In the main, the Negroes of the South (with the exception of lower Louisiana) belong to the several Protestant fellowships: Baptist, Methodist, Episcopalian, and Presbyterian. There are, of course, independent sects, as well as adherents to various fringe cults, notably the one led by Daddy Grace. The autonomy of the individual church organization, aside from the spiritual benefits derived, is of great importance to the vast Negro memberships. The church is the outstanding social institution. It provides the Negro with the opportunity for self-esteem and self-expression which is denied to him in open society. The Negro is a truck driver, his wife is a domestic, but over the week-end they are deacons, stewards, elders, communal leaders, readers, Sunday School teachers, and choir directors. It is of particular importance for the children to see their parents, dressed in Sunday clothes, participating in the educational, religious, and social activities of the community.

The open forum discussions of the Unitarian Church, and the Mass of the Roman Catholic Church cannot, for a long time to come, offer an equal opportunity for individual and family *status*.

However, my good friend, the Reverend Ed Cahill, Unitarian minister, tells me that he has a luncheon appointment with a Negro prospect right after the summer vacation.

Eddie Fisher and Debbie Reynolds

EDDIE Fisher started a new trend in marrying Debbie Reynolds. The young Jewish girls felt scorned and hence bereft. A psychologist might call it "The Michal Complex." Michal was told by her spouse, King David, to expect him to give children to an "outsider," but never to her.

Eddie Fisher was young King David, "The Sweet Singer" to practically every Jewish girl in America. If he had married one of them, all the others would have been "fulfilled."

For the old girls, eating yogurt is enough; but for the young ones—no.

No doubt a happy compromise will be worked out and the next generation will produce Rabbis O'Houlihan, O'Brien, and O'Shea, while the devout young priests, Francis Xavier Cohen and Aloysius Goldberg, are being showered with Papal blessings.

Anyway, we are heading for a ghastly sameness in our country, in which the magnificent Latins from the Mediterranean, the wonderful Swedes from Scandinavia, the brilliant Jews from Eastern Europe, and the effervescent Irish from the Auld Sod, will soon be indistinguishable from the Cape Cod Yankees.

This is good?

Give us a blond rabbi any time

THE demand for blond rabbis, especially in the South, is tremendous. Of course, if the blond rabbi should happen to have a pretty wife, this cancels out the great advantage. We're not even talking about the brunet rabbi with a beautiful wife; that fellow shouldn't even have been born. In such a case he should start looking around for a new career. A plain-looking rebbitzen—now that's different. There's nothing the Sisterhood likes better than to work with a plain-looking rebbitzen. Ah, how wonderful! Everything she does is wonderful, and how they admire her! Everything is fine. Now if you are talking about a blond rabbi *and* a plain-looking rebbitzen, you're talking about the whole jackpot, that's all. This is a combination hard to beat. In this situation even the board of trustees is properly awed and keeps the peace. Here's a rabbi who can write his own ticket, and serve on his own terms—anywhere.

Concerning those who go to
services once a year

In recent years the rabbinate and the Anglo-Jewish press have pointed with alarm to those who attend services irregularly or only on the High Holy Days in the fall. My brother Jacob ran a few hotels in midtown Manhattan before he retired, and many years ago, in one of these hotels, I met a great big fellow by the name of Davis and we became friends. Whatever I may have thought of Mr. Davis, it never entered my mind that he might be a Jew. He looked for all the world like a big Irish detective. One day he stepped up to the desk and inquired where he could find the nearest synagogue. He wanted to say kaddish for his mother, and he said that he never missed the annual memorial prayer in her memory. That impressed me very much. Essentially it was what we would call "dos pinetelle Yid"—the spark in the chain of Jewish continuity. It was a good lesson. There are many phonies who go to temple every week, and there are many righteous people who go only once a year—and vice versa, of course. I am not talking against regular temple attendance. It is very nice and should be encouraged, but I also believe that to scold the "once-a-year folks" is both unjust and unnecessary.

PART 9

Complaints and Free Advice, or Twenty-Six Notes in Closing

~~~~~~

The saloon and the cocktail lounge

THE American people were sold a pig in a poke when they replaced the saloon with the cocktail lounge. To appease their sense of guilt after the repeal of Prohibition, they said, "Outlaw the saloon," and everybody was happy, and thus one of the great tragedies of our times. The saloon was a place of *fellowship*. No women were allowed, and the place was as light as day. In the center there was always a brilliantly illuminated chandelier. And what have we today in its place? The cocktail lounge! Dark! Candlelight business! Booths stuck away in a corner where you can plot, nay, accomplish all your illicit stratagems, and the cocktail lounges are loaded with women sitting on those upholstered stools; embarrassing the men, and embarrassing themselves. No more poetry to listen to at the saloon bar, or those fine political and philosophical disputations, and the magnificent lettering on the glass mirrors which announced the picnic or the Tammany outing, or the Christmas fund for the children of the neighborhood. I have no doubt that it was this fellowship, more than the evil of drink, that made the women rise up "against the saloon."

They wanted to go, too, but the saloons were too strict. And so the women replaced the saloon with the cocktail lounge so they could tag along. The women outsmarted themselves. They did not leave well enough alone. When their man was in the corner saloon, he was as safe as in his mother's arms. Now look at the situation—in dark corners where the man could be sitting with his wife's best friend and no one would know it, or he could be taking a shot of heroin and not attract the least attention. These things were impossible in the saloon.

But I am afraid the cocktail lounge is here to stay. Where is the politician who would have the courage to stand up like a man and say, "Give us back the old-time saloon"?

How to hire a stenographer

I PLACED an ad in the local paper for a new stenographer and received about twenty letters. As I studied the applications, I came across one signed "Carrie Ferrara."

Ferrara? In Charlotte there's a Ferrara?

I immediately put all the other letters to one side and decided to hire Miss Ferrara sight unseen.

You can always get a stenographer, but how often can you get a "Ferrara"?

What thoughts came to mind as I studied this "Carrie Ferrara" application—Donna Gracia Mendes and her nephew, the Duke of Naxos, the Marranos who practically ruled that wonderful city of Ferrara during the years of its glory; Princess Leonora who resisted that attempt of Pope Julius III to establish a ghetto in Ferrara, but finally lost through the force of arms. Yes, I certainly thought of that great city of culture, art, good wine, and beautiful women.

Miss Ferrara turned out to be a little thin girl about nineteen or twenty years old; and after a few hours of work, I knew that I had not only gained a bit of the Italian Renaissance, but a good office assistant as well. Her residence in Charlotte follows a pattern. Her brother was stationed at one of the huge infantry camps in North Carolina during the war; he met and married a Charlotte girl, settled here and raised a family. After a few years he sent for his little sister to come down and live with them and establish herself here. A very wise move; a good thing for Miss Ferrara and a good thing for Charlotte and for the State of North Carolina.

It is interesting that Italians came as far south as Richmond, then hurdled the Carolinas to establish themselves in proportionate numbers in Georgia, Florida, etc.

Now, a few more "Ferraras" and eventually Charlotte, too, will be enriched with a substantial community of these people who have given so much to the world!

If there is any truth to what the philosophers say, that the Jews represent "the salt in the stew of civilization," it certainly follows that the Italians supply the bits of "red pepper" and the dash of "paprika" which help make the whole concoction more delightful.

Protest for eleven books

ONLY eleven books out of all those millions. What does that amount to? Look at all the books that are left!

This, in effect, is what some otherwise intelligent, educated, and freedom-loving editors and commentators have said recently. The official notice from the State Department itself was to the effect that "only eleven books were burned."

There are so many ways in which you can register disapproval. You have so many chances to register your opinion. For one thing, you need not buy the book. You need not buy it as an individual, or as a school board, or as a library, or as a government. No one says you must buy it! For another thing, you can write a review blasting the daylights out of it! You can say what you want about it. You can warn others, you can do almost anything within the power of the printed word and the law. But to burn it! What good is becoming

Secretary of State, if you have to live with that thought, that during your term of office, books were burned because, as a nation, we feared printed words.

The Jews are all right. Up in the New York Public Library, they maintain an entire section of anti-Semitic writings of the world. There in New York with a population of two million Jews there are shelves and shelves and shelves of anti-Semitism gathered from all corners of the world in all the original languages; and if that represents a problem to you, they'll even get you a translation yet. Wherever some nose-running hatemonger has written himself an anti-Semitic pamphlet, they say, "Let us have a copy of it, son." Then they put it on shelves and catalogue it with index numbers and provide you with a beautiful reading room where you can read to your heart's content. All these writings are labeled "Anti-Semitic," both on the index card and on the back of the front cover, that's all. In this same way, we can label books wherever they are, "Communist propaganda," or "Anti-American," or for that matter, as I said at the outset, we don't have to buy them; but to burn books is something foreign to Americans (and Englishmen).

Book-burning is a crime—a crime against the human intellect. The most remarkable aspect of book-burning is that dictators and conquerors always have felt that, next to killing humans, the burning of books was a most necessary part of their programs. The Persians hated the Phoenicians and the Egyptians, and destroyed their books. God only knows what treasures we would possess if we had those books today. Hippocrates, he of the famous oath, was so fanatical that when various Greek communities did not follow his doctrines, he burned their libraries.

Who knows what a treasure we would possess today if Theodosius of Rome hadn't burned the Jewish books? They burned Jewish books for nearly three hundred years, first the Romans and then the Christians, and finally, along about the eighth century, the Christians began to burn the books of Rome, Greece, the Jews, and the pagans. Even within Christianity books of the Early Church Fathers were being burned continually as they failed to please succeeding church fathers. Gibbon pathetically describes the empty shelves at Alexandria after they burned that greatest of all ancient libraries:

> The valuable library at Alexandria was pillaged or destroyed; and nearly twenty years afterwards, the appearance of the empty shelves excited the regret and indignation of every spectator whose mind was not totally darkened by religious prejudice. The compositions of ancient genius, so many of which have irretrievably perished, might surely have been excepted from the wreck of idolatry, for the amusement and instruction of succeeding ages.

Thus one of the great tragedies of world history—the destruction of the Alexandria library. Did it contain some of the writings of King Solomon? Who knows? At any rate, some scholars have thought so.

The reading of the Jewish Talmud was forbidden and Emperor Justinian and some Popes of Rome put a bounty on the Talmud. Bring the book "dead or alive" and you get the brass ring or something to that effect. A few Jews made the preservation of the Talmud their life's work, a "trade" which was handed down from father to son. To them, whoever they were, we owe the possession of this documentary record of the progression of a historic people.

Dictators are as scared of books as they are of cannon. The first thing the Spanish did in Mexico was to destroy the records of the civilization of the Mexican Indians. Everything in that country had been painted—whole philosophies and histories and biographies were painted. They were burned. A few years later, after they had secured their position in the New World, the Spaniards were sorry. They would have loved to have that treasure back, worth more than all the gold in all the mines and caves of the land, but it was too late. They sent over their most diplomatic priests who went up and down the country trying to find remnants of this great treasure. It was known that the Indians had salvaged some of these paintings, but the natives were so indignant at what had happened that they remained silent. Where these paintings were hidden has never been known.

The Caliph Omar took Alexandria in Moslem times and again an Alexandrian library was put to the torch. Omar said that the Koran contained everything which was useful to believe and, therefore, commanded that all the books in Alexandria should be distributed to the masters of the baths, to be used in heating their stoves, and so another ten thousand volumes of intellectual treasures went up in smoke. Finally, Pope Gregory VII, inflamed by the apathy he felt existed with regard to the Scriptures, ordered everything else burned, and so into the flames went all the records of ancient Rome, the logs kept by early Mediterranean mariners, and autobiographical sketches of a succession of Roman emperors. All burned. The orders designating which books were to be burned varied with the age, the times, and who or what was considered unorthodox at the moment. At one time, during the Reformation, orders went forth to burn all books with words printed or written in red ink. This had nothing to do with our present-day "red" Commies. The Catholic monasteries had all developed the fine art of illuminating books in which process much red ink was used. As in our time, it was not necessary for a book-burner to know how to read. Just look inside—red ink?—burn it!

And so it has existed—this crime of crimes—book-burning.

After Henry Ford had apologized to the Jewish people for his Dearborn *Independent* campaign, a question came up as to what should be done with his vast anti-Semitic library. To further his campaigns he had combed the highways and byways of the world for this stuff. The Jews had a suggestion. Give it to us, they said. To burn the books? Of course not. They would arrange to have these writings preserved forever in the library of the Hebrew Union College at Cincinnati. But Ford's collection never got there.

He burned it himself. At least once the book-burner was the author and collector himself.

No more crying at Jewish weddings

MOST of the joy of the old-fashioned Jewish wedding has been eliminated.

Only one thing remains. The groom's mother is still the most important person at the affair. (In the Gentile world the bride's mother is the big wheel.) And if the groom's mother takes her duties a bit too seriously, which is hardly possible, someone always says, "After all, she is his mother."

But in every other way the "tomm" (flavor) has gone out of it. There's no bodkhan anymore. He was a sort of minstrel harking back to the Middle Ages, who combined the skills of poet, wit, master of ceremonies, composer, musician, and philosopher. He called out the names of the guests as they arrived, giving proper honor to each one according to his status in the community. He had the guests laughing one minute and crying the next; but the crying was the most important. The minstrel "bespoke" each of the four parents; then the grandparents; a bit of broad humor when he spoke to the groom; and finally his "instructions" to the bride for her new way of life; and at this moment the crying began, with a furtive glance here and there to see if someone important maybe was not crying. This was extremely impolite.

And the kids under foot making such a terrible racket. In those days they invited everybody—the neighbors, the landsleit, and the members of the burial society. A long table with fine herring, potatoes, and all sorts of good snacks. And you put the herring on a respectable piece of rye bread or pumpernickel. None of this fancy cracker business. On the other side of the hall was the "sweet" table with wine, honey cake, spongecake, apple strudel, glazed fruits, and candies.

Now the first thing you see when you come to a wedding is a big fountain with fruit juice pouring out of six spouts, all different colors. There is a twenty-five-foot table with hors d'oeuvres, which include puny little objects which they dare call—knishes.

It was a great honor to hold one of the four poles of the canopy under which the couple spoke their vows, but what have we today? A huge Cecil B. De Mille job, gorgeously decorated with flowers, and any minute you expect pigeons to fly out. The cantor wears a very tall, heavily embroidered yarmulka which makes him look like Cardinal Spellman conducting High Mass at St. Patrick's, and this you have to see to believe—the glass which the groom traditionally crushes under foot (symbolizing the destruction of the Temple) is now put into a little velvet bag with a zipper; and it makes a fancy little "ping" instead of that good old-fashioned masculine "crunch." And then a girl (she's a music major at Juilliard) sings "O Promise Me"—so help me.

And the fine dances are no more, the circles bigger and bigger, and finally the old bubbe (grandmother) inveigled into the center and everybody laughing as she did her few little steps. Now they all dance the cha cha; and instead of slivovitz (plum brandy) they serve Haig and Haig. "Pinch," he says yet.

And tip? Why Noel, that's just not done! What a fine feeling in those days when the big soup plates were passed around for tips to the musicians and the waiters, and everybody watched with such pride as the rich uncle dropped the twenty-dollar bill.

And, of course, now the kids are quiet; each one looks like Freddie Bartholomew, and they are all in a corner practicing the cha cha. Can you imagine what would have happened to those kids on Eldridge Street?

It is all gone. Today the Jewish wedding, hors d'oeuvres and all, is just another semiannual Chamber of Commerce affair.

Hennington Hall was a place on the Lower East Side, or I should say one of many places, where the catered weddings took place. The entire progress of the Jews of America can be traced from Hennington Hall to the Pierre, that exclusive hotel on plushy Fifth Avenue. After Hennington Hall there was an "advance" to places that had the word "casino" in their names—Stuyvesant Casino, St. Marks Casino, Prospect Casino, etc. After the casino stage came the Hotel Mc-Alpin, uptown, which everybody called "the McKaplan"; weddings every week, sometimes four or five going on at the same time in the rooms set aside by the McAlpin for the purpose. After the McAlpin era came the Astor. The Astor phase went for a considerable number of years, but finally gave way, in a burst of social glory, to THE PIERRE.

In Hennington Hall there were weddings known as khop weddings. This means "grab," but it was not quite as bad as the translation of the word implies. There was a long table loaded down with herring and huge loaves of bread. Today in the Pierre they serve herring on a little fancy cracker about the size of a thumbnail, and you can't get in there by paying hat-check either, like we used to do in the old days at Hennington Hall. And it is far from the joyous occasion it used to be.

Today at the Pierre, things are different. Instead of the glorious bodkhan, there is a headwaiter who watches to see that you pick up the right fork; instead of some old grandmother dancing with a big loaf of bread, we have a nasal soprano singing—God help us—"Trees."

From Hennington Hall to the Pierre—or—as you get bigger and bigger the herring gets smaller and smaller.

Our new breed of knuckleheads

THE Quiz Champion is the keeper of that fool's paradise, the Almanac. He represents Madison Avenue's greatest achievement in the philosophy of the "tie-in"; the association of scholarship with the sale of laxative, lipstick, and lanolin.

In order to be a Quiz Champion, you must be concerned only with that which is *past*. If Columbus had been a Quiz

Champion, he would have never discovered America. He would have been heavily laden with the words of countless *others* who said the world was flat, and he could also tell you in which cities those fellows flourished, and how many children each of them had produced.

The Quiz Champion is not a self-thinker. He is too busy trying to recollect the words and thoughts of *others*, which he has read and memorized, and thus his own words can never have any lasting value. No one ever did a considerable work in the world who was not a self-thinker. The memory of too many useless facts weakens judgment. What we absorb by reflection becomes part and parcel of our mental processes and comes forth spontaneously for use when the mind enters the society of ideas to which it belongs. Mere feats of memory are of little or no use at all. Voltaire could not recall the name of the mayor of his town. Thomas Jefferson and Benjamin Franklin, our two greatest philosophers, made a particular point of not cluttering up their minds with stuff that could be looked up at a moment's notice when, as, and if needed.

The Quiz Champion spits in the eye of the music lover who wants nothing more than to spend a couple of hours listening to the Toscanini recording of *Otello,* but who now is burdened with a deep sense of guilt because he does not know (a) when the opera was first produced, (b) who was the conductor, and (c) the name of the soprano of the première.

Albert Einstein, who never remembered where he put his eyeglasses, liked to play the violin. If you asked him where Vivaldi was born, and how many children he had, the professor would have retreated to the other end of the room, and pleaded with you: "Please, let me just play it for you on my violin."

Over the years I have known and communicated with six or seven of the leading Shakespearian scholars of our time. I do not recall that these men were particularly concerned with the given name of the fellow who printed the First Folio, or with the date on which Shakespeare's son-in-law died. All that seemed to matter to them was a study of the images in that "mirror" which Shakespeare "held up to life."

To be able to remember and repeat many names, dates, and verses may be likened to the physical feats of the acrobats we used to see in vaudeville. The Quiz Champions, like those acrobats, excite the same attention by their novelty, and are alike of little worth. The Roman general who is said to have been able to repeat the names of all of his soldiers seems to have had no other distinction. Absorption, not verbal memory, forms judgment, and judgment has shaped our world.

The Quiz Champion is part of the current decline of the intellectual and the distrust of the scholar. He is our new knucklehead. He has succeeded in reducing scholarship to the level of knowing the population of Tokyo, and the batting average of Babe Ruth—and thus, unwittingly perhaps, he has helped to shut the door a bit tighter on Original Thought and the exploration of a New Idea.

How to buy cigars

I HAVE been smoking cigars for about thirty years. I have gone without many things in my time, but I cannot recall a single day in all those years that I have been without a cigar.

Naturally during the years I have been pestered by the "why-don't-you-buy-them-wholesale" boys.

I have successfully resisted their arguments. I have never bought a box of cigars in my life. The only time I've had a box of cigars intact is when someone gave me a present. I buy three cigars at a time, and make my purchases two or three times a day at a drugstore, a restaurant, a newsstand, or in a hotel lobby. There is no "ritual" business. I buy them when I need them and wherever I happen to be at the moment. Thus, during the course of any week, I will have made cigar purchases in at least eight different establishments—the establishments of neighbors in my community, in my city. This is good. Multiply that by fifty-two weeks and you'll realize how really good it is! Over the years I've made a dozen new friends, and have seen many hundreds of new people and have heard many fine new stories and anecdotes. What in the world is better than to go into a business establishment, put some money on the counter, and buy the man's merchandise? Nothing is better than that. It is good for me. It is good for him. It does something for the morale.

I operate the same way with the newsdealers. I buy about ten dollars' worth of newspapers and magazines each week. Except for those few publications which they do not carry here, I have never bought a subscription in my life. Here again, I buy from three or four newsstands and dealers, without any set plan, just where I happen to be when I want to pick up something. Pfui on these pretty girls who come around to your office and sell you nine subscriptions for a dollar down. If I were a dealer I wouldn't handle the merchandise of a firm which competed with their own distributors under such unfair conditions.

The wise guy is the sucker after all

I REMEMBER a fellow on Broadway in the old days, and, for the moment, I'll call him Jack Duffy. Jack had been a song-and-dance man in his early days, but when I knew him, he was betting on horses and losing, of course. He was nearly always broke. On one bitter cold night Jack was seen walking up and down in front of the famous Captain Churchill's Restaurant on 49th Street. He had no overcoat, no hat, and no overshoes, despite the steady driving wind and snow. He was stamping his feet to keep them from freezing, and blowing his hands; he looked blue and miserable. Someone went up to him and asked him what was the idea, why didn't he get back to his rooming house. Jack pointed into the plush café and said, "Shh, my gal's in there with a sucker."

Inside, the "sucker" had two buckets of wine beside him and the headwaiter and two flunkies were standing at his table carefully writing down his instructions on what to bring and how to prepare it properly.

But this is not unusual. Many a man blowing on his hands to keep warm, an obscure, uninteresting individual with little hope and few prospects, will get mad as anything because the officials of the ball club insist on giving his favorite ballplayer only thirty thousand dollars, and the ballplayer is holding out for forty thousand. And our obscure, uninteresting friend is hopping mad. "The nerve of those crooks trying to put something over on Jimmy the Slugger," says our obscure friend. It is the same with movie stars, and, of course, comic strips. The "intimacy" of the masses with the great athletes, stars (and millionaires, of course), is based on a simple formula, one of the oldest of mankind—the identification with the personage they would like to be, with the status they would like to hold. Often this attempt to put yourself in the shoes of those in your daydreams even leads you to serious criticism of them. I have listened to unemployed actors hold heated conversations in the hotel lobby. "Jolson can't sing."—"Of course he has no voice."—"Who said he could dance?"—"I can name you thirty singers who can put a song over better."—etc., and they mean every word of it and continue their discussion all the way to Joe's where they'll get another cup of coffee "on the cuff." When they completed the great Radio City buildings, it was still in the depths of the Depression. Whole floors were vacant for a long time. And many people, the poorest of the poor, the most jobless of the jobless, would go through the building and sigh, "Poor Rockefeller, what a bust this thing is—poor Rockefeller—he'll never rent these offices."

Even that is part of the daydream, because the "obscure" is putting himself on terms of "intimacy" with the man he wishes to be, and he is, therefore, "assuming" some of that man's burdens and worries, or what he thinks may be his burdens and worries.

But what would we be without a daydream? Nothing. There is nothing wrong with it provided you never lose contact with reality, with this month's rent, and with your appointments today; and under those conditions a little daydreaming is a good thing. The main thing is to keep the dream as uncomplicated as possible.

Montor and Keyserling on the Stock Exchange

IT reminds me of a story. On the Lower East Side of New York in the old days a boy could enter active politics at the age of twelve. He could perform any one of a dozen valuable services for the Tammany ward heeler, the candidate for local office, or even the precinct boss. These services included running errands, distributing handbills, carrying banners, and helping to swell the audience and organize the applause at street-corner meetings. The pay for each specific chore was more or less standard—a silver half dollar. Only a Samuel J. Tilden could mount a soapbox and attract a crowd immediately. It was necessary for the speaker to start with a captive audience, and this is where the kids came in. As our boy got up to speak we lifted our faces toward him and looked enraptured. As the folks passed they stopped and joined us. I have seen speakers, however, start with four silver-half-dollar shills and wind up with the same four kids in the audience. Another chore was to harass the speakers of the opposition—by standing on the opposite curb and trying to drown out the opposition voice with "Tammany, Tammany, Big Chief sits in his teepee, Cheering braves to victory. . . ."

One of these politicians was a fellow by the name of Wronker who always wore a brown derby. Mr. Wronker went through our district "doing favors" for the people. I got to like this Mr. Wronker—there were a few moments there when I looked upon him as a statesman. It came as a great shock to me years later when I again met Mr. Wronker who was now selling electric light bulbs and marked an invoice "paid"—PADE.

Well, coming back to my story, Mr. Wronker was running for the State Legislature again and I remember that this particular campaign was tough; as the campaign got tougher I got madder by the minute at the Republican opponent. I think his name was Blechman or something like that. Every time I looked at my candidate, Mr. Wronker, with the shiny brown derby, I became furious with Mr. Blechman. I could hardly control my anger when I heard Mr. Blechman right out on the street corner call Mr. Wronker a crook. When Mr. Wronker heard about it, he did not seem perturbed at all, and this heightened my affection for him. I began to identify him with Sir Launcelot du Lake, or at least with Roland lashing out blindly at Ganelon at Roncesvalles. I do not know of any man I despised more than Mr. Blechman, not only for calling Mr. Wronker a crook, but for running against him in the first place.

Well, the election was finally over and Mr. Wronker squeezed through over the Republican and Socialist opposition, although we did hear later that in four or five voting places the cops turned out the lights every time the tide went against Mr. Wronker.

But then something happened which I could never forget, and which changed the entire course of my life. It happened by sheer accident. I was passing by Davis' saloon on the corner of Houston and Orchard Streets, and it just happened that one of the swinging doors was stuck and as I looked in I saw a terrible thing. For a moment I stood there transfixed and all the events of the previous weeks passed in review before me—the worry, the work, the emotion, and the terrible hatred for Mr. Blechman; and as I stood there, looking into the saloon, there was nothing to do but just bust out crying, because there at the bar, standing jowl to jowl, drinking beer and laughing like hell, were Mr. Wronker and Mr. Blechman, closer, much closer than Roland and Oliver, to say nothing of Damon and Pythias.

After I recovered from the shock I decided to throw in with Mr. Meyer London, the Socialist. There were no silver half dollars now, but I had the pleasure of knowing that our civilization was capable of producing men with intellects of honor and souls of nobility.

What does all of this have to do with Henry Montor joining the Stock Exchange? Nothing, really. Mr. Montor was the head of the Bonds for Israel drive in recent years. And all over the country there were guys like me who jumped at the slightest nod of the head from Mr. Montor. It's human nature, I guess. When you are ready to die for a fellow you become kind of sad when he goes and joins the New York Stock Exchange on you. We made lists, dug up new prospects, worried, laid aside all our work to help, and now this press release—Mr. Montor has joined the Stock Exchange, formed an investment firm, and he is ready to do business.

Well, why not? What did I expect Mr. Montor to do, enter a convent? Certainly not, and the course he has followed is not only legal but in keeping with the form and the habits of our society. The only thing I question, however, is the propriety of using the lists of names for press releases and for the solicitation of business which Mr. Montor acquired in the process of working for a worthy, nonprofit cause. Mr. Montor may or may not have earned this personal advantage, but it is really not too far off the beam in keeping with our present commercial society. What is interesting is that Mr. Montor's associate in his stock exchange business is Leon Keyserling. Leon Keyserling? The New Deal fellow? Now, folks, you can see how we Democrats suburbanized ourselves out of the Presidency.

With fellows like Montor and Keyserling in a stock exchange firm, you could at least sit back and wait for their market letters—pure literature. But what do we see? The first press release from Henry Montor and Associate (Keyserling) follows:

> If investment is good for America, it is good for the many millions in the middle income bracket, a great many of whom are still in the dark about the security market.

If that were all "the many millions" were in the dark about, life would be very sweet indeed. It is not so much that Montor and Keyserling remind me of Wronker and Blechman, but at least with fellows like that you would have expected nothing less than poetry.

They continue:

> We believe that more popular methods and techniques can substantially increase the number of investors.

They must have found a pamphlet I wrote thirty years ago, a forty-dollar ghost-writing job for Kennedy and Company, entitled, *Noah Was Prepared for a Rainy Day—Are You?*

I am afraid that I shall continue to split my business among my three favorite brokers in Wall Street, Ralph E. Samuel & Company, Thomson & McKinnon, and Bache & Company. But for the real big stuff I'll use the bankers, Lehman Brothers. The four firms account for a total of eleven subscriptions to *The Carolina Israelite*.

It's the spirit that counts

I DO not want to lose any speaking assignments and so I promise that this will never happen again, but I have to tell you of a terrible tragedy on one of my speaking engagements last year in a South Carolina city.

It was a small literary group, and I had been asked to review a book. I was introduced, and they provided me with a table and a chair. I carry a zipper brief case for my papers, etc. Since I was reviewing a book, I wanted to take out a copy of the volume, and keep it in front of me as I spoke. Everything was quiet. I sat there, and took my brief case and zipped open the zipper, when lo and behold a pint bottle of whiskey pops out. I had forgotten all about it.

Earlier in the week I had developed a very dry throat and someone suggested that I try whiskey, and I had forgotten all about it. The bottle actually bounced on that mahogany table, and you have no idea the noise it made in that schoolroom. I made a dive for it just as it was ready to fall on the concrete floor and luckily I caught it.

The audience meanwhile was in hysterics. Men and women were rolling in the aisles laughing and some of the women were running out toward the ladies' room. Meanwhile I had sort of collected myself, put the book out, and the bottle back in the zipper case, and I sat there, trying to be as nonchalant as possible. I went on with my lecture telling the folks about Professor Harry Overstreet and *The Mature Mind*, but it was no go. Every few minutes someone would burst out laughing; then everybody would laugh; and I had to laugh, too.

As I was getting into my car to leave, I heard folks laughing down the street, and through the night. Oddly enough, this meeting has resulted in more lasting friendships than any other in which I have participated. The folks write me from time to time and they are nearly all regular subscribers.

From the angle of "interfaith," the meeting was a tremendous success.

Princess Ileana and
Archduke Otto were here

ANOTHER casualty of the cold war is our sense of humor. In a way it is like the stock market crash of 1929. Men who had never seen a stock certificate suddenly acquired communal barroom status. For them (the panhandler, the failure, and the barfly), the stock market crash was the most wonderful event in their drab and uninteresting lives. "J. P. Morgan lost all his dough—we were all wiped out, me included." Oh, how they stood, two and three deep at every bar and nursing a five-cent glass of beer, and talking about the crash.

The same thing is happening in the cold war. Princess Ileana of Roumania is among the high-priced folks in the lecture-bureau business. She was here in Charlotte a few weeks ago addressing one of the important civic clubs. A year or so ago, the Archduke Otto von Hapsburg took up the cudgels for Jeffersonian democracy. Princess Ileana's subject was—don't laugh—"How Roumania Lost Her Freedom."

That Roumania today is a lackey of Soviet Russia there is no doubt. There is no serious doubt that the country is today part of a system which is a danger to the free world. No one attached to the principles of our American society will debate this premise. No one will question the fact that the Roumanian people today cannot speak, write, congregate, move about, or think, without fear of concentration camps or worse.

But that they were approximately in the same fix under Princess Ileana and her family is equally true. Roumania was an impoverished feudal barony still hanging on in the twentieth century. Under the Hohenzollerns (Ileana's grandfather and father), the Roumanians did not possess *habeas corpus,* trial by jury, or freedom of speech, and they never saw a ballot.

In 1920 there were 175 royal palaces for the royal family and its retainers, and there were less than 175 schools for the seven million inhabitants.

Even the Czar of Russia was disgusted with Roumania. After one of the royal family scandals (there was a public charge once that Ileana's brother, Carol, had assaulted his mother, Queen Marie), the Czar of Russia said, "Roumania is not a state, it's a profession."

What makes Mr. and Mrs. Jones run?

WE know what made Sammy run. The aggression which manifests itself occasionally among those who feel themselves insecure or inferior because of some physical or mental deformity, or due to a racial or religious minority status. There may be other reasons, of course, but at least we have a good clue with respect to Sammy.

But what makes Mr. and Mrs. Jones run? What is causing the terrible tension in our day-to-day living? Why is everybody running?

What has happened to leisure?

In 1899 Theodore Roosevelt made a speech in which he urged his fellow Americans to live "the strenuous life." He had no idea to what extent the people would follow his advice. Everybody is running. No one stops for a single moment. In Roosevelt's time there were no washing machines, refrigerators, television, movies, automobiles, telephones, refuse disposal units, pay toilets; and you had to give the door a little shove instead of being admitted by an electric eye. Yet in the absence of all these push-button wonders, there was leisure. Plenty of it. My secretary tells me of her childhood in Winston-Salem and recalls that her mother, taking care of all the household duties without a single push button or baby sitter, used to sit in a rocker for two hours every after-noon. Can you imagine a housewife today sitting in a rocker for two hours every afternoon? There is no time. The only one whose life has been made easier is the sneak. In the old days the sneak would have to trudge a few lonely roads, maybe get bitten by a few dogs before he could look through your keyhole. Today he sits in a comfortable cellar with a playback machine having himself a ball. Soon he'll be able to get our thought waves on tape recorder or microfilm.

What has happened to leisure? The wonderful progress of science and technology has brought no improvement to the hearts of men.

Everybody is running. The tension mounts, formulas are not working out despite all the question-and-answer columns by the peace-of-mind experts.

With all these things going for us, what has happened to leisure?

My mother kept the sewing machine in the kitchen near the stove. The stove did not start at the turn of a dial. It took kindling and coal, and sometimes when the coalman did not show up she had to go down four flights to get enough to start the supper fire. She cooked, washed, cleaned, sewed, got everybody off to work and to school, was all ready for them when they returned, emptied the drip pan under the icebox, and every afternoon she sat looking out of the window for a couple of hours. This was the great leisure for the im-migrant women. When you came home from school the tenement windows were all occupied by women looking out. They used to sit with their arms folded looking out: throwing a penny to the Italian organ grinder, waving a greet-ing to a friend, and just looking out—at America.

There is no leisure today. Everybody is running. And when he finally does join the golf club where he can have some leisure, he spends all his time worrying who else is trying to get in the club. No leisure. He is afraid, terribly afraid, that one day he'll wake up and it will no longer be "exclusive." This gives him ulcers, but no leisure.

The intense aspiration toward material welfare has led

to the most unexpected results. As our technology increases we become more and more impatient because the pace is too slow. We never stop to wonder whether man's victory over nature keeps pace with man's victory over himself. We are paying no attention to the balance between the miracle of science and the miracle of kindness.

It is apparent that tension increases with prosperity. It is when things are going very well that you begin to worry more. You worry, of course, because now you have more to lose and you fear everything: illness, taxes, Reds, Pinks, Assyrians, Wallachians, Senegalese—but mostly you fear death. No one yet found a hypochondriac among the peasants (or, as Einstein so wisely commented, among the peddlers or plumbers).

I remember the story told in *As I Remember Him: The Biography of R. S.* by Hans Zinsser. He was director of a mental hospital—not a public institution but one maintained for wealthy mental cases. Among his patients, hopeless cases, were a former attorney, a shipping magnate, and a Greek who in former years had made a fortune in exporting figs, dates, and other products of the Mediterranean and the Middle East. These three patients were always together discussing, in their lucid moments, the great deals and transactions they executed in the outer world. Money was no object in the treatment of these patients; the idea was to make them as comfortable as possible. So Dr. R. S. set them up in an office, with desks, dummy telephones, typewriters, and various printed legal and contract forms. His three patients went to "work" every morning. They spent their whole day buying, selling, drawing up contracts, closing deals, and sending shipments of fruits to all the corners of the world, on paper, which Dr. R. S. destroyed every night.

The three dynamos started fresh every morning. Dr. R. S. tells that when he himself would stop off at their "office" they became impatient—they were busy with their contracts, conferences, and shipments, and wanted him to leave as quickly as possible. And so they went on for some years,

Dr. R. S. assures us, with no chance of recovery, but they were very happy.

One year Dr. R. S. went to a small resort hotel on the French Riviera for a vacation. He sat on the veranda one evening and in a corner were three men, also guests at the resort, who seemed to be engrossed in animated conversation. Dr. R. S. could not help overhearing their heated discussion. One of the men was a lawyer complaining about a contract that had been broken; another man was a shipper who complained why he needed a rest—he had just lost a ship and was embroiled in bitter litigation with the insurance and salvage people; there was a big dispute over the value of the cargo. And as luck would have it, the third man was a fruit exporter who gave his own hard-luck tale about a frost that had just wiped out his entire crop for the year.

As Dr. R. S. listened to these three men he said to himself, "Why, these fellows are doing exactly the same things as my three nuts. Only my three nuts never lose a ship, every contract stands up, and all the shipments arrive in time. And they are getting much more joy out of it."

How to be healthy

THE scientists in Israel have come across something very interesting. It concerns the health of the Yemenite Jews who were transplanted en masse a few years ago ("Magic Carpet"), and who for centuries had lived in hovels in a country with the lowest standard of living in the world.

The Yemenite Jews, it appears, have all the diseases of poverty—tuberculosis, trachoma, etc.—but none of the degenerative diseases which take such heavy toll in the United States—high blood pressure, heart disease, ulcers, diabetes, and the various ailments of the veins.

Diet, of course, is the key to the whole situation, although the fact that these people had been comparatively free from the pressures of modern civilization may also have had something to do with it.

The statistics of the insurance companies are not quite clear. When they speak of the tremendous increase in the life expectancy, many people are under the impression that the average life span has been increased. There is the impression that in the days of Benjamin Franklin you lived to be thirty-five on the average, and now you live to be seventy on the average. This is just not so. The life span has not increased at all. The increase in life expectancy of nearly thirty-five years in two centuries is based primarily on the fact that infant mortality has been cut down to a minimum by science and medicine, and that brings the average up, way up.

But if you were one of Washington's soldiers and escaped death in battle and later if you were lucky enough to escape or recover from pneumonia or strep throat, you had as good a chance of living to age seventy-five as you have in 1958. Of course, the antibiotics and other wonder drugs, as well as the great advances in surgery, have prolonged many lives, although the increased pressure and emotional stress of modern living have probably cancelled out a percentage.

The late H. G. Wells was right. The life span of seventy or eighty, that is, if everything goes well, is much too short. There remains too much power and creativity in the brain even if many of the other physical functions are impaired. It would have been well for the world to have had Albert Einstein and Thomas Mann for, let us say, another twenty-five years.

But it is all diet. When the Nazis took Denmark they requisitioned everything the Danes produced. The Danes, as you know, are famous dairy farmers and the Nazis took all their butter, animal fats, cheese, and allied products for their own armies. During that period the Danes were forced to lead an austere life and lived mostly on black bread and fish. What they have found out since is that during that austere period the incidence of degenerative diseases went way down —the Danes lived longer—but when the Danes got their butter, cheese, and animal fats back, the health chart went back to "normal" with a tremendous increase in stomach, heart, blood, and vein diseases.

It is all a matter of diet, and I should hang my head in shame, being as fat as I am, and with no fewer than eleven thousand stories yet to write.

Cato's cure for a hangover

Cato the Elder, who lived about 200 B.C., had a green thumb and wrote a farmer's manual. Twenty-two hundred years ago, Cato wrote about curing hams in substantially the same way it is done today. He made a great study of seed selection, and knew as much about it as we know today. He also wrote a manual on the proper manuring of the land. He said that the best way to test the soil for productivity is to take a section of the soil and pour water through it and taste the water. If it puckers the mouth, the soil is sour. Stay away from it. He says do that before buying a farm. Cato was a pretty good man with the wine bottle and also left us a cure for a hangover. He said that the morning after, eat five or six raw cabbage leaves and you'll feel as good as new.

I rarely take a drink after dinner, so I never suffer a hangover. I wish some of my readers would try Cato's remedy some time and let me know. I have a hunch Mr. Cato knew what he was talking about.

I'll take care of the tip

He's doing you a great big favor—he'll "take care of the tip." When you pick up the check you either treat or you don't treat. Now when the fellow whom you are treating says, "I'll take care of the tip," what is he really doing? First of all, you'll notice, he always says, "Go ahead. I'll take care of the tip." "Go ahead," of course, means for you to go to the cashier.

So for twenty cents (he never tips enough), what is he doing? He's taking the edge off your own pleasure in treating, and for the great big twenty cents he is also taking himself completely off the hook, spiritually, mentally, psychologically, to say nothing of—financially. What does he mean, "I'll take care of the tip"? You pay $1.68 and he pays twenty cents—this you call "taking-care-of"?

The next time you pay the check and the fellow says, "I'll take care of the tip," do one of two things: either smile sweetly and say, "No, let's split the whole thing down the middle," or pick up a sugar bowl and knock him on the hay-ed.

Where is *The Carolina Israelite?*

NATURALLY, it distresses me to receive so many communications: "WHERE IS IT?" But the folks should understand that this is not one of those great monthly pocket-size magazines. These million-dollar publications are paste-up jobs which I could do on a half pint of whiskey with one hand tied behind my back. Every issue of these profitable magazines is the same, month after month, year in and year out.

The standard contents: first, an article on the latest cure for cancer; then a psychiatrist gives ten reasons why it is better for men not to have "outside" sex relations. This is usually followed by a ten-page art spread of naked women.

Then, of course, the monthly sermonette by Dr. Norman Vincent Peale; plus the usual dog story—"How Our Puppy's Bark Reduced the Mortgage," then a few reprints from *Guideposts* and *American Legion Magazine,* followed by the monthly "interfaith article"—"How Catholic, Protestant, and Jew Found Faith in Las Vegas."

And then the one that never misses, the new diet—"How I Lost Forty Pounds While Eating Like a Horse," and the windup on the inside back cover, a poem or historical sketch superimposed over an outline of the Statue of Liberty so heavy that you cannot read the text—which is your first break.

So, will you now stop worrying when *The Carolina Israelite* is a mere twenty-five days late once in a while?

And what to drink?

WHEN you give your food order in any restaurant in the South and stop talking for a fleeting second, the waitress begins to tap her foot and, with pencil poised, asks, "And what to drink?" There are two reasons for this: (a) the waitress does not think you have enough brains to order what you want and when you want it, (b) the management does not think you have enough brains to order what you want and when you want it. And if you are "trying to be smart, eh," and say, "I'll let you know later," the waitress looks at you with pity, contempt, and frustration, but mostly frustration.

Nothing makes the little people of this world madder than to hit smack up against a guy who refuses to send Telegram Number 2 to his mother on Mother's Day, so to speak. Here and there society does run up against a crackpot who refuses to order Number 2; and insists upon writing his own telegram.

When a waitress asks me, "And what to drink?" I always smile, broadly. I smile because I am thinking what would have happened to a waiter in old Mouquin's, or Rector's, or Bustonaby's, or Little Hungary, or Jack's, or Golden Eagle, or Keen's Chop House, or Lorber's, if he had asked a gentleman diner, "And what to drink?"

The waiter would have been found at the bottom of the Hudson River sealed in cement, and that's why I always smile when the waitress asks me, "And what to drink?" I do not wish to make a scene, so I'll meekly say, "All right, make it coffee." But they can't stop me from thinking of—cement.

Are the no-dessert fellows sincere?

You are having lunch with a couple of friends. In due course the menu is passed around and your two so-called friends say in unison, "None for me." This leaves you right out on a limb. Even the waitress looks at you with contempt as you eye the strawberry shortcake on the menu. It takes a brave man to order it.

I've tried it both ways. If you grab the menu first and give your order, and the other two guys follow this move with that "none-for-me" business, you feel like a criminal.

You may have known a guy for twenty years, but he'll make a big point of this "none for me," as if he were making an announcement of great importance. Often there is a hint of sadism as he says, "I never eat dessert." It is the pride with which he makes this declaration that is the clue to the possibility that this fellow may be a faker. I always suspect that the guy can't wait till he gets home to that pineapple upside-down cake in the refrigerator.

How to boost temple membership

ALL the "odd fish"—"Jewnatarians," nonconformists, and dissenters who live here or pass through here—visit me. In addition, the few men in the community who have no families and thus do not participate in the social life of the Jewish community spend time with me, either in my office or in a café. There were two of these bachelors whom I asked to join the temple, and, of course, they laughed at me. Up North, they told me, they went to the temple maybe once a year and they can do the same thing here. They have no children to send to Sunday School, and they have no particular desire to join in the various social activities of temple life. These were good arguments.

One day I had them together and I told them why they should join the temple. I said to them, "You live in a rooming house. Suppose you should die; look at all the trouble you'll be giving Mrs. Honeycutt. The first thing she'll do is call the police. Then they will go through all your belongings to see whom they can call up. Your body will lie up in the room until the police take it away to the undertaker. Why put people to so much trouble? Think of Mrs. Honeycutt, the landlady. Think of all the chagrin and anguish you will cause her, to say nothing of the inconvenience to the other guests. Now if you join the temple, you can go home tonight like a gentleman, stick out your chest and say, 'Mrs. Honeycutt, if anything should happen to me, please call the rabbi.' You have become a man of substance."

The two bachelors didn't even wait for the following Friday; they signed immediately in a very shaky handwriting. It's a funny thing, when people see the tail feathers of the angels, you can do almost anything with them.

Is it later than you think?

THE businessmen and tycoons have a framed device on the panelled walls of their private offices—IT IS LATER THAN YOU THINK.

The question arises, "Later than what?" unless it presupposes the idea that time will stop with your death. This is all

nonsense. Time never runs out—there will always be something very big going on, the outcome of which you will not
see. The best thing to do is to start out each day with one
idea in mind—that you will live forever. And keep going.
Start a major alteration on your house at the age of seventy,
and at seventy-five enter upon a whole new course of study
or learning a new language. Just keep going as though it will
never end. And when it does come, you'll hardly notice it.
It will be like Mr. Sean O'Casey says: ". . . soon it will be
time to kiss the world goodbye. An old man now who, in the
nature of things, might be called out of the house any minute.
Little left now but a minute to take another drink at the
door . . . to drink to Life, to all it had been, to what it was, to
what it would be. Hurrah!"

A man called—left no message

NOTHING is more disconcerting than a note on your
desk when you return from lunch, "A man called—left no
message." Of course, if it is, "A woman called—left no message," it is a different story. But when it is a man, it is an-
noying.

Who? What does he want? It is even worse when the
message is, "A man came to see you but would not leave his
name." That's bad! In the old days the fellows who ran the
stuss houses or bookie joints would always ask the secretary,
"Was it one or two?" If one there was nothing to worry about
—yet. The cops usually come in pairs. This is true of both
the revenue officers and city detectives. In some of the
brothels of New York the owner of the joint always wore his
hat and coat. When the cops came to raid the place, the
owner was always shoved out with the other customers.

How do you feel?

THIS is another silly conversation. "How do you feel?" What do you mean by that? Usually the question is asked of a man in action—a man on the go, walking along the street, or sitting at his desk working, and someone comes along and asks, "How do you feel?" What do you expect him to say? Usually he says, "Fine," but you've put a bug in his ear—maybe now he's not sure. Maybe, if you're a good friend of his, you have seen something in his face, or his walk, or his eyes that he missed that morning. It sets him to worrying a little. First thing you know, he looks in a mirror to see if everything is all right while you trip merrily on your way asking someone else, "How do you feel?"

The question, "How do you feel?" certainly is pertinent under certain conditions. Like, for instance, when you first visit a close friend in the hospital, and after he has come out of the ether, it would be fair to ask, "How do you feel?" But if the guy is walking on both legs, looking for a place to eat, going to a movie, or working up a storm at his desk, it is silly to ask him that silly question.

When George Bernard Shaw was in his eighties, someone asked him that, and he told him off. Said Shaw, "At my age, you either feel all right or you are dead."

Percentage-wise

THERE is one advantage in not reading trade papers and business surveys. You reduce to a minimum the number of times you have to cringe at the most important phrase in the business book of discipline. The phrase is any combination of words ending in the suffix "-wise." Ugh. "Quota-wise." "Percentage-wise." "Market-wise." "Catalog-page-wise." "Jobber-wise." "Profit-wise." "Price-wise." "The pin-for-forty-years-of-faithful-service-wise."

Think, therefore, of my amazement when a motion-picture review in a recent issue of the magazine *Commonweal* started out with the words, "Plot-wise . . ." on the same day the radio weatherman began his report with "Temperature-wise."

Pfui-wise, I say.

How to go on the wagon

I AM proud of myself. I have taken the bottle out of the desk drawer and now I keep it in the kitchen. Now I have to get out of my chair and walk down the hall for the stuff. I am confident this development will be a step in the right direction.

We have lost something

IN the days before television, brass plumbing, 3-D movies, and *Time, Life,* and *Fortune,* there were hosts of people who were held in respect and affection all over the world. The names of Enrico Caruso, Paderewski, Charlie Chaplin, Schumann-Heink, Nellie Melba, John McCormack, Fritz Kreisler were spoken by silver miners of Peru, by the priests of Tibet, by the gamblers of Monte Carlo, by men and women from Hong Kong to Brooklyn, the Gobi Desert to New Orleans. Today there are none. Absolutely none.

With the exceptions of several political figures like Churchill and Eisenhower (which is not the same thing at all), there's not a single personality who somehow unites the world in a common affection. As we go higher and higher in technology and science, we are going lower and lower in the romanticism of the human spirit. I wouldn't trade you one Lillian Russell for the whole thing—lock, stock, and barrel. We have definitely lost something.

Shed a tear for the smoking car

No matter how fast jet planes fly, no matter how many satellites circle the globe, nothing will ever equal the fascination that the railroad train has had for whole generations of American men and boys. There's something about the Iron Horse that has held the imagination of mankind more than any other industrial development or invention.

While the airplane has been "used" in a few murder stories, there is an entire American literature on the railroad train, and at every level of our culture. Untold millions of men and boys have walked down to the railroad tracks just to watch the train go by, and other millions who didn't go down to the tracks were doing something about it too; the men were pulling out their watches, "Old Number Thirty-eight is two minutes late today," and a farmer in the field, "That whistle sounds like snow." (They knew a great deal about atmospheric conditions from the way the whistle carried.) And the boys were listening—and maybe thinking too.

And the poetry of those wheels. You could sing with them, and recite poetry to them and even hold a political debate. As sure as anything those wheels would answer you back.

And how about the songs from "I've Been Working on the Railroad" to "Chattanooga Choo Choo," and a thousand others in between? And even in sorrow the railroad took it all in stride like a gentleman, always leaving a memory:

> He was going down-grade
> Makin ninety mile an hour

When his whistle broke into a scream.
He was found in the wreck
With his hand on the throttle,
An a-scalded to death with the steam.
                    —*Wreck of the Old 97*

The toys, and the miniature trains; the fascination of the switch engine for young and old even in this age of rockets and spaceships.

But most of all, the fellowship. The fellowship of the smoking car, where you learned about crops and farm machinery and politics and religion; about a new kind of razor and a private remedy for every ailment known to man.

No one *talks* on a plane. They mumble. I have traveled thousands of miles on planes and all I have ever heard is, "Mister, is the cigar lit?" Of course not! But once in a while I go into a little speech about how I am a "chewing man," and how it's rarely lit even when I am supposed to be smoking. But they are not amused. No one is "amused" about anything in this space-jet-rocket-age.

And soon we may have to say farewell to the smoking car and the fellowship. Some of the railroads would gladly give up all their passenger traffic now if the franchise would permit; but let us hope that we may at least continue to enjoy the thrill of watching that red caboose disappear in the distance, and perhaps even wave to the brakeman, the salute to the hundreds of millions who have made that same gesture through four or five generations of American history.

America owes it to Christianity

THE early church frowned on the study of astronomy and so the pioneer scientists, to avoid giving unnecessary offense, named the heavenly bodies Jupiter, Venus, Mars, Saturn, Neptune, etc., after the gods on Mt. Olympus.

And when it finally became evident that man would concern himself more and more with outer space, the thundering agnostics of the nineteenth century slapped their thighs in glee and shouted, "There are no saints in heaven."

But now America has an opportunity to strike a decisive blow for the Judaeo-Christian civilization. We should avoid such names as Thor, Jupiter, and Atlas for our satellites and future space platforms; and there is no *depth* at all to such trite names as Pathfinder, Explorer, etc.

To associate our scientific progress with the Olympian tradition is not only an anachronism, but involves the serious risk of a possible revival of universal paganism.

We should name our own satellites in proper order; Saul to begin with, or maybe Elijah, he who sat on the mountaintop and was fed by the ravens. And when there is no longer any danger of a "dud" let us go down the line with King David, Deborah, Paul, Peter, Augustine, Thomas Aquinas, and one which would do special honor to my own city of Charlotte, John Calvin.

About the Author

Harry Golden, born on New York's Lower East Side in 1902, obtained his formal education in the New York City schools and at C.C.N.Y. He has since been hotel clerk, teacher, reporter, promotion man on daily newspapers, editor, and publisher. It is as publisher—and writer—of *The Carolina Israelite* that he is best known, but he has a wide and well-merited reputation, as well, as a speaker and as the writer of many pamphlets for many organizations. A man of broad reading and extensive acquaintanceship, Mr. Golden dips regularly into his retentive memory to produce some of the most original and effective journalism in contemporary America. In 1952, he received the B'rith Abraham Award for his contribution to Jewish journalism and in 1957 the Man of the Year Award of the YMCA of the Johnson C. Smith University of North Carolina. Mr. Golden, who lives and publishes his paper in Charlotte, North Carolina, is married and has three sons.

[*See next page*]

"Harry Golden is, as someone said of Joan of Arc, one of those things that couldn't happen and did. He edits a provincial newspaper that is read by pundits all over the country. They read Golden because they find in him an American who enjoys America hugely. This gusto moves intelligent men to laughter and applause; and they set a high value on the man who supplies it."

—GERALD W. JOHNSON, *New York Herald Tribune Book Review*

"ONLY IN AMERICA is packed full of wit and wisdom and beautiful wry humor."

—REX BARLEY, *Los Angeles Mirror-News*

"It is about time in this frantic and troubled era that Americans who have a happy gift for humor and a strain of common sense should know Harry Golden. It is impossible to read this book without enjoying it and admiring the wisdom, warm heart and broad knowledge of the author."

—HARRISON SMITH, *Saturday Review Syndicate*

PRAISE FROM THE FOUR CORNERS OF AMERICA

• •

"Harry Golden's America runs hilariously from the old New York East Side to a South that seems so new it is only half unpacked. It is the best present prescription for what today ails the American mind and manner."

—JONATHAN DANIELS, *Raleigh News and Observer*

"Harry Golden's kind of journalism makes him, he says, as happy as a mouse in a cooky jar. His book makes the feeling contagious."

—LESLIE HANSCOM, *New York World-Telegram & Sun*

"If you enjoy nonconformists who lean on logic for their independent ideas, you'd appreciate Harry Golden. For those who knew the East Side of New York a generation ago and those familiar with the South, Mr. Golden will bring many memories of things long forgotten. To the rest of his audience he opens up another side of life that truly could be only in America."

—ROBERT C. BERGENHEIM, *Christian Science Monitor*

[Over]